PLAYING TOUGH

[ROGER I. ABRAMS]

PLAYING TOUGH

THE WORLD OF SPORTS AND POLITICS

Northeastern University Press · Boston

Northeastern University Press
An imprint of University Press of New England
www.upne.com
© 2013 Northeastern University
All rights reserved
Manufactured in the United States of America
Designed by Mindy Basinger Hill
Typeset in Minion Pro

For permission to reproduce any of the material in this book,
contact Permissions, University Press of New England, One Court
Street, Suite 250, Lebanon NH 03766; or visit www.upne.com

Library of Congress Cataloging-in-Publication Data
Abrams, Roger I., 1945–
Playing tough : the world of sports and politics /
Roger I. Abrams.
p.   cm.
Includes bibliographical references and index.
ISBN 978–1–55553–753–1 (cloth : alk. paper) —
ISBN 978–1–55553–815–6 (ebook)
1. Sports—Political aspects. 2. Sports and state.
3. Sports and society. I. Title.
GV706.35.A37 2013
306.4'83
2012042100

5   4   3   2   1

Staying within the spirit of the game and playing tough and aggressive are welcome, and those ideas should be taught and encouraged. . . . Sports can be a great model for life off the field . . . Of course, there's talent and potential, and then there's the so-called politics of the environment.

Brandi Chastain

Sometimes, playing tough with push back tactics analogous to boxing is unavoidable.

Rick Brandon and Marty Seldman,
Survival of the Savvy: High Integrity Politic Tactics
for Career and Company Success

"PLAYING TOUGH" IN POLITICS AND SPORT

It was a tough world, and being a man meant *playing tough*. Nixon was the most political man imaginable."

Michael A. Genovese

When I asked him about staying focused and *playing tough*, he told me that if you're going to play tough, you have to keep control.

Saul L. Miller, interview with hockey goalie Billy Smith

The predominant fear was that *playing tough* with Germany would lead to another slaughter. Far better to let Hitler have what he wanted and enjoy some peace.

Guy Walters

It is very difficult for parties to credibly commit
to *playing tough*, however, given the consequences
for both parties for doing so.

Francisco Cabrillo, Seán Fitzpatrick

Staying within the spirit of the game and
playing tough and aggressive are welcome,
and those ideas should be taught and encouraged.
But you also have to learn that what happens
on the field stays on the field.

Brandi Chastain

I'm hanging in here.
I'm getting back up.
I'm *playing tough* today.

Stephen R. Covey

[CONTENTS]

Well, in our society, we have things that you might use your intelligence on, like politics, but people really can't get involved in them in a very serious way— so what they do is they put their minds into other things, such as sports. [I]t occupies the population, and keeps them from trying to get involved with things that really matter. —*Noam Chomsky*

Sports serve society by providing vivid examples of excellence. —*George F. Will*

Sports do not build character. They reveal it. —*Heywood Broun*

[PREFACE AND ACKNOWLEDGMENTS]

To some, sports are a frivolous diversion. To others, they are the most important component of their lives. To most people, sports are an important part of a full life, along with family, friends, and a job. Sports inspire us and outrage us; they entertain, and, if we are fortunate, they can cause us to be very happy, if not content. Their potential for joy should be a matter of celebration and not censure.

The same is true of politics, an essential part of our lives even if we chose not to participate in the franchise and ignore the news as much as humanly possible. In modern society, it is useless to try to avoid running into government, whether driving on the city streets or seeking official approval for your marriage. Politics, and the governments it produces, determines how individuals interact with each other. It can make your life more miserable than a losing baseball team.

This book is about the historical relationship between sports and politics, about how each activity has affected the other since the beginning of recorded time. Politics has used sports (and vice versa), sometimes in obvious ways: your favorite sports team likely plays in a stadium or arena built with public funds, and your favorite politician proves he or she is just a "regular guy" by appearing at sporting events and wearing the appropriate team paraphernalia. Occasionally, major sporting events, like the Olympics, offer overt political messages. Just think about the Nazi Olympics of 1936 or the U.S.-led boycott of the Moscow Olympic Games in 1980.

Writing about the symbiotic relationship between sports and politics has allowed me to return to my roots in political science and revisit some of the sacred texts in the field. It has also offered me the opportunity to learn (and share) more stories about sports. I have avoided retelling at length stories I have related in earlier books, such as the remarkable achievements of Title IX in women's sports, an obvious example of the nexus between politics and sports. Instead, I have ventured into boxing, soccer, rugby, and Olympic sports, while telling an interesting tale I uncovered from the nineteenth-century days of purely "amateur" baseball and its connection to corrupt urban politics.

In this book, I cover a broad swath of the political "experiences": city bosses and their machines, the establishment of secure political power, the use of sports policies to achieve international legitimacy and advantage, and the use of governmental violence against other political powers and against citizens. Sports will play an essential role in each of the stories. Muhammad Ali is a perfect example. The "Greatest of All Time" became a symbol of resistance and black pride. His courage inside and outside the ring inspired many and infuriated others. At times, sports will be the side story: establishing no-show jobs for avowedly amateur baseball players was not William "Boss" Tweed's core perfidy in running New York City in the mid-nineteenth century, but it did offer an example of how he carried out his rule. Hitler used the 1936 Olympics to establish international legitimacy for his brutal dictatorship. The boxing matches in 1936 and 1938 between Max Schmeling and Joe Louis previewed a world at war. Nelson Mandela used sports in the mid-1990s to secure his revolutionary regime in South Africa. The United States would attempt to co-opt the Olympics for overtly political purposes, to protest the Soviet invasion of Afghanistan in 1980.

Foreign policy, the extension of politics on the world stage, frequently has involved sports. At times, a sporting conflict has evolved into violent warfare, as in the "Futbol War" in Central America in 1969. Finally, we will see sports turn the tables and seek public subsidies for private businesses, a generally successful ploy by franchise owners that continues to transfer millions of public dollars into private hands each year.

This is my sixth book on the business of sports, and for each of these works I have had the assistance of numerous research assistants. For this book, I would like to thank Michael Birch, Ted Bertrand, and Peter Fisher. My dear friend and colleague from Rutgers Law School, Associate Dean Marie Melito, has once again worked her magic on the manuscript. Most importantly, my partner for life, Frances Elise Abrams, edited chapters of the book to make sure readers will enjoy them. To her I am grateful not only for her skill in editing but for a lifetime of loving partnership.

PLAYING TOUGH

Richard M. Nixon, the thirty-seventh president of the United States, credited his football coach at Whittier College with inspiring his political career. His coach, however, remembered only that the third-string player "liked the battle and the smell of sweat." As president, Nixon supplied trick plays to his local team, the Washington Redskins, which proved disastrous on the field. *AP Images*

Already long ago, from when we sold our vote to no man, the People
have abdicated our duties; for the People who once upon a time handed out
military command, high civil office, legions—everything, now restrains itself
and anxiously hopes for just two things: bread and circuses.

—*Juvenal*, Satire

There is a certain tendency in the civilization of our time to
underestimate or overlook the need of the virile, masterful qualities of the
heart and mind. . . . There is no better way of counteracting this tendency
than by encouraging bodily exercise and especially sports which develop
such qualities as courage, resolution, and endurance.

—*Theodore Roosevelt*, Professionalism in Sports

[INTRODUCTION]
SPORTS AND POLITICS

Roman playwright Juvenal bemoaned his society's descent to the level of "bread
and circuses," but all communities need bread to survive, and "circuses," at
least in the form of sporting events, appear to be almost as essential. Sports
and society have been linked since ancient times, and politics, in terms of
some fundamental means of community organization, has been ever present
as well. Teddy Roosevelt, the paradigmatic American politician, appreciated
how fitness of body and mind energized the body politic. Over his entire political career, as was the case with many politicians, he was a "circus" of spirited
oratory, masculine role-playing, and earnest cheerleading. As long as sports
did not become too dangerous—he warned the presidents of the Ivy League
colleges that he would intervene unless they made football safer—Roosevelt
was "for it!" as he might say with a grin and a raised fist.

PRESIDENTIAL SPORTS

At times, it has been difficult to distinguish fact from fiction when it comes
to sports and politics. There are some events we are almost certain actually

occurred. Establishing a tradition that would last for more than a century, on April 14, 1910, President William Howard Taft, Roosevelt's successor, threw out the first ball on Opening Day at National Park in the nation's capital in a game between the Washington Senators and the Philadelphia Athletics. The former Yale first baseman was accompanied to the game by his wife, his vice president, and most of his cabinet. As the *Boston Globe* reported, Taft hurled the ball "with a vigorous heave straight into the waiting hands" of Washington's starting pitcher, Walter "Big Train" Johnson, who was so inspired that he pitched a one-hitter. (It would have been a no-hitter had Senators outfielder Doc Gessler not tripped over a spectator while chasing a fly ball off the bat of John "Home Run" Baker. Fans of that day were allowed to stand in the outfield.) On the other hand, it is said that President Taft originated the seventh-inning stretch when, during the same contest, he arose in the seventh inning to stretch his abundant torso. Out of respect for the nation's chief executive, the spectators stood as well. Could this have been the origin of the custom? It seems more apocryphal than factual.

Many presidents have played golf, including almost every incumbent since Teddy Roosevelt, although few performed extremely well at the frustrating pastime. Despite his bad back, John F. Kennedy was likely the best duffer in the presidential parade; Dwight D. Eisenhower was a close second. Bill Clinton played by his own rules, often taking extra shots without adequate notation on his scorecard. Lyndon Johnson was the worst of the presidential golfers. Barack Obama, the current incumbent of the White House, tried without much success to use the golf course as a venue to seek political rapprochement with Republican nemeses. Obama also plays a mean game of basketball, according to those who have felt his sharp elbows on the court.

Presidents and other politicians have used sports to soften the public's image of their leadership. When New York City mayor Rudy Giuliani wore his New York Yankees cap, he hoped to be seen as just one of "the guys" rather than as a tenacious politico. Obama does the same with his Chicago White Sox paraphernalia. George W. Bush wore a Texas Rangers cap, but, after all, he had been a part owner of the club.

Some presidents adopted obscure outdoor sports to avoid the claustrophobic grip of the Oval Office. Herbert Hoover devised a medicine ball tossing game and enlisted aides who would participate daily in his pastime. George H. W. Bush installed horseshoe pits in the White House lawn. His son, George W. Bush, was an avid dirt bike rider. Teddy Roosevelt was up for any strenuous activity, including boxing in the White House. Bill Clinton jogged around Washington, stopping at McDonald's for a welcomed break of french fries. Fishing was a popular activity for a number of chief executives, aided by Secret Service agents who stocked the ponds to the gills. Whatever their choice of athletics, presidents appeared to the public to pursue their sport with a passion.

Many athletes have aspired to political office, although few successful politicians ever excelled at sports after leaving politics. Gerald Ford, the nation's only unelected president, had been an All-American football star at the University of Michigan and was offered contracts to play professionally. Professional athletes Bill Bradley, Jim Bunning, Jack Kemp, Steve Largent, Jim Ryun, J. C. Watts, Dave Bing, Kevin Johnson, and many others have successfully made the move to the political ring, and some even tried out presidential runs.

Richard M. Nixon always wanted to be a regular guy and sought acclaim for what he considered his vast knowledge of sports. Instead he was a misfit president, a third-string tackle at small Whittier College, and a perpetual intermeddler whose advice to pro football coaches couldn't be ignored because it came from the White House. During his acceptance speech for the Republican presidential nomination in 1968, Nixon thanked his "remarkable" college football coach for inspiring him. (His college coach remembered that "Dick liked the battle and the smell of sweat.") In office, Nixon supplied trick plays to his local team, the Washington Redskins, which proved disastrous on the field. He telephoned Don Shula of the Miami Dolphins at 1:30 in the morning with a suggested pass play—send receiver Paul Warfield on a down-and-out—that fell incomplete. He wrote over thirty letters to baseball players during his time in office. Nixon also offered to arbitrate the 1972 labor dispute in Major League Baseball, an offer that was politely declined by the owners and the players union. (Clinton made the same offer in 1994, and the parties accepted, only to leave the White House as far apart as they had been when they entered.)

In 1969, Nixon decided to attend the college football game between the University of Texas and the University of Arkansas. He announced that the winner of that contest would be the national champion, ignoring the fact that the Penn State squad was also undefeated. In the Oval Office after winning his second term while deeply mired in the Watergate scandals, Nixon told his aides that his primary legislative objective would be lifting the NFL television blackout policy that kept fans from seeing local playoff games. On his infamous Oval Office recordings, Nixon said: "If you can get playoff games, believe me, it would be the greatest achievement we've ever done."

Faced with increasing protests about the Vietnam War, Nixon retreated into the world of sports, announcing to the press that he was watching football games and not the protests. Nixon said shortly before he left office: "A man is not finished when he is defeated. He is finished when he quits." On August 9, 1974, Nixon quit the presidency.

SPORTS AS A POLITICAL PLATFORM

While sports offered politicians the veneer of the common man, they also offered premier athletes a platform from which to express their political views. Although most athletes have remained apolitical, there are numerous examples of those who were able to raise fundamental issues of fairness and politics because of their athletic success. Muhammad Ali, whose singular boxing career we will examine in detail in Chapter 5, refused induction into the armed forces in 1967 because of his religious principles and, as a result, became a political and secular symbol of courage to some and infamy to others. Track stars Tommie Smith and John Carlos raised their clenched right fists in political protest on the Olympic podium in Mexico City in 1968. In 1996, after converting to Islam, Mahmoud Abdul-Rauf, a guard with the Denver Nuggets, refused to stand during the national anthem. After a one-game suspension, the league worked out a compromise under which Abdul-Rauf would stand but could close his eyes and look downward, praying during the anthem. Beginning in 2004, Toronto first baseman Carlos Delgado decided he would no longer stand for "God Bless America" during the seventh-inning stretch of Major League Baseball games as a protest against America's wars in the Mideast. At the urging of their club owner Robert Sarver, the Phoenix Suns voted unanimously to wear "Los Suns" uniforms in 2010 to protest Arizona's new draconian anti-immigrant laws.

Similarly, sports may cause voters to express their political dissent. Four days after Britain was eliminated from the 1970 Fédération Internationale de Football Association (FIFA) World Cup by West Germany, Britain's Labor Party unexpectedly lost the national election, tossing Harold Wilson out of office as prime minister. That may have been only fair, because Wilson had won the office in 1966 after England unexpectedly won the World Cup.

Some athletes are considered so unique to national pride and self-respect that politics must intercede to keep them from being lured away by world rivals with much greater financial resources. After the 1962 World Cup, European soccer clubs such as Real Madrid, Juventus, and Manchester United tried to sign Brazilian superstar soccer player Pele, but the Brazilian Congress declared Pele an "official national treasure." His sale or trade to a foreign club was forbidden by law.

We remain uncertain, however, about some events that purported to unite sports and politics. Did Fidel Castro have a baseball tryout with either the New York Yankees or the Washington Senators before he took to the Cuban hills to lead a revolution? It is difficult to find adequate proof for the story. Although Castro spent decades berating "the Yankees," the object of his ire was the American government and not the American League club from the Bronx. Castro certainly had the right stuff to play the American national game; he had pitched for the University of Havana in the 1940s and was said to have had a terrifying curve ball. (As might be imagined for a Communist leader, Fidel was a left-hander.) The Pittsburgh Pirates scouted Castro, but they were not impressed.

Did another Communist revolutionary, Mao Zedong, actually swim nine miles down the Yangtze River on July 16, 1966, as reported by the China News Agency? It would have been a prodigious effort for any seventy-five-year-old man, a world record for sure. The world press had spread rumors that Mao had experienced a heart attack, thus explaining the political importance of demonstrating his fitness. Curiously, the official picture of the historic event only showed Mao's head bobbing above the water, a primitive version of "photo-shopping," which was not unusual in Communist dictatorships, where fallen leaders were quickly erased from earlier photographs.

The story of the third Communist sports and political leader is the least believable of the trio. Kim Jong-il, the recently deceased dictator of North Korea, was said to have quickly mastered the golf course, a matter of great interest in golf-crazy East Asia. On his first visit to the fairways and greens, the Dear Leader is said to have shot thirty-eight strokes under par, including at least five (and perhaps eleven) holes-in-one. He also bowled a perfect 300 game.

At times, fact and fiction have blended into mythology. The story of the professional Ukrainian soccer players who were ordered to play a match against the conquering Nazi army in 1942 is a frightening example. The great Kiev Dynamo team played a team of the invaders, but, contrary to the orders of the ss, it triumphed. Despite incarceration without rations, Dynamo won the rematch as well. It then won a third and a fourth time. Finally, although warned they would be executed if they won the next contest, they prevailed in the match. German sharpshooters picked off some players on the pitch, and later all remaining Ukrainian players were rounded up, tortured, and sent to concentration camps.

Whether these events are fact, fiction, or some hybrid, the connection between sports and politics has always rung true, and there is value in examining the nexus. Nations have always used sports as a "soft" weapon in international relations. Sports offer the opportunity for nations to compete in contests for supremacy, normally without death as the penalty for winning or losing. Every nation, every region, is known by the quality of its sports teams. Even a small city like San Pedro de Macoris in the Dominican Republic is famous, but not for its fine university or its commercial activity. Rather, the city has become renowned because more than seventy-five of its young men have played Major League baseball. Similarly, the astounding victory by the young amateur U.S. Olympic ice hockey team over the professional Soviet squad at the 1980 Winter Games in Lake Placid, New York, gave American citizens a boost of confidence at a time of economic doldrums and uncertain leadership. (Few recalled, however, that the same Soviet team had trounced the neophyte Americans 10–3 only a few weeks earlier.)

The 1956 Olympic Games in Melbourne offered the opportunity for Hungary to seek a form of revenge against the Soviet Union only a month after Soviet tanks had crushed their revolution by invading Budapest. The Hungarians were the defending world and Olympic water polo champions. The match became water mayhem rather than aquatic athletics. Hungary triumphed 4–0 in what would later be called the "Blood in the Water" match. Ervin Zádor, the Hungarian player who emerged from the pool with blood pouring from his face, explained: "We felt we were playing not just for ourselves but for our whole country." The match had to be stopped by the referee when the crowd rushed to the edge of the pool shouting abuse and spitting at the Russians. The Hungarians were recognized as having the greatest national water polo team in history, but it took more than thirty additional years for Communist rule to end in their home country.

Sports are certainly important in people's lives, but politics is a human "game" where much more is at stake. Winners take power; losers should take care. There are rules in the game of politics, sometimes set by the structures of government and sometimes established on an ad hoc basis to justify arbitrary rule over others. Once in power, political leaders have often turned to sports as a useful means to foster their political legitimacy or at least maintain societal quiescence, but they have won at the political games that really counted.

PLAY

Humans have always lived together in communities and found their identity as part of groups. Within those groups, they met their essential needs for food, shelter, and reproduction. While these groups enjoyed different levels of complexity and sophistication, they shared common characteristics that flowed from the common humanity of their members.

Early in human existence, along with meeting their fundamental needs, humans developed a sense of play, much of it purposeful. Play is universal, found in every group of humans and in many other sentient beings. Some of the play is repeated into games, often without written rules and sometimes resembling more of a brawl than an athletic contest. These events are as much a part of human behavior as sleep or meals. These games help refine the physical tools needed to survive in hostile environments. They also provide the joy of competition. We now call these games sports, although they are more than the mere "diversion" referred to in the French word *divertissement*, the origin of the term "sport." Those who prevailed in competition gained what the Greeks referred to as the ideal of "beautiful goodness," becoming as close to the gods as if they had climbed the slopes of Mount Olympus.

The innocence suggested by the word "play" may be deceptive. Sporting games were sometimes played as a competition between tribes or towns. They offered each social unit a centripetal identity and allowed the release of customary inhibitions as a means of social control. Those origins hold true today. More people gather on a regular basis to witness sporting events than for any other reason. They identify with their sporting clubs because the teams purport to represent them, even if the athletes come from somewhere else. Sports offer all a sense of play, place, and common activity within the public space.

The changing norms of civilization alter how we view sports. Play and leisure sports have not always been promoted by society's influentials as a social good. New England clergymen periodically denounced sports as the work of the devil, without useful ends. Such "wickedness," they proclaimed, undermined the work ethic and the moderation essential for a devout populace. The Massachusetts Bay Colony prohibited shuffleboard and bowling. In 1774, the First Continental Congress added its censure of leisure pastimes and sports: "We will . . . discountenance and discourage every species of extravagance and dissipation, especially all horse-racing, and all kinds of gaming, cock fighting, exhibitions of shows, plays, and other expensive diversions and amusements."

By comparison, General George Washington appreciated the value of sports. In 1777, while encamped at Valley Forge, Washington urged his officers to promote vigorous exercise: "Improve all the leisure time your Brigade may have from other duties in maneuvering and teaching the men the use of their legs, which is of infinitely more importance than learning the manual exercise. Cause the Officers to attend regularly and perform their part of these duties with the men. . . . Games of Exercise for amusement may not only be permitted, but encouraged." Washington himself engaged in throwing and catching a ball for hours on end. He even played cricket at Valley Forge, while other bat-and-ball games were played by his men.

The nineteenth-century Victorians believed that sports undermined character. Sports were played by members of the working class only during those few hours a week when they were not actually working. Teddy Roosevelt changed that attitude in America. He was a one-man, always-in-motion machine seeking to inspire young men "with vim" and "the competitive spirit."

> There is a certain tendency in the civilization of our time to underestimate or overlook the need of the virile and masterful qualities of the heart and mind which have built up and alone can maintain and defend this very civilization, and which generally go hand in hand with good health and the capacity to get the utmost possible use out of the body. There is no better way of counteracting this tendency than by encouraging bodily exercise, and especially the sports which develop such qualities as courage, resolution, and endurance.

T. R. would lead foreign ambassadors on excursions by foot through Washington's Rock Creek Park, climbing precipices and fording streams. His exuberance was infectious, and Americans followed his lead, or at least they tried to keep up.

Sports have not always represented the best in human morals or decency. Cheating, for example, has always been a part of sports, certainly since the time of the ancient Greeks. At the third modern Olympic Games, in 1904 in St. Louis, American Fred Lorz almost stole victory in the marathon. Just before he was to be awarded the gold medal by Alice Roosevelt, the president's daughter, it was discovered that, after Lorz had become exhausted following nine miles of running, his manager gave him a ride in his car for the next eleven miles. From there, he ran on to the finish line.

Despite their risks and shortfalls, sports have become the most important communal activity in the lives of many, perhaps most, people. They have fostered social cohesion and a sense of belonging. They promote regional and national unity. They have also become a significant commercial venture, a multi-billion-dollar business, played by many and enjoyed by many more.

POLITICS

Humans who joined together into tribes discovered early on that they needed a system for making decisions that affected more than a single individual. Ad hoc governance was unpredictable, and it lacked finality. How would it be decided when it was time to migrate with the changing seasons? Who would be empowered to determine disputes over the ownership of property? What would be the basic values and attributes of a group, and how would they be protected? Tribes formulated rudimentary political structures as a more efficient means to determine direction in lieu of ad hoc decision making. These political structures matured in complexity as societal challenges multiplied and the size of the tribal unit increased.

For the most part, ancient human societies adopted political structures where power was based on age and lineage. Kings and their sons (and sometimes their daughters) ruled. At the same time, conformity to societal norms was critical. As societies evolved into civilizations, political complexity escalated. Stratified societies needed mechanisms for vertical mobility to sift the most talented people from the masses. The Greeks used a form of democracy, although participation in the polity was severely constricted.

As tribal groupings evolved into nation-states, sports, play, and politics further intertwined. During the time of the Roman Republic, mobility into positions of power came from the vote of citizens during periodic elections. Candidates for Roman consul and other positions of power in the early republic sought to win the favor of the voting masses through sports. Candidates and officeholders alike would sponsor sporting contests to entertain the citizenry. These entertainments, held in the arena, would be paid for by candidates, and voters would come to enjoy the sporting circus.

Sports offered the Romans an opportunity for contact between elected officials (and those seeking elected office) and the citizenry. Aspirants for public office in the Roman Republic could demonstrate both their ability to organize festivities and their generosity toward the people they would lead. To put on good games was a sign of respect for the citizenry. It would win trust, affection, and, ultimately, votes. Rich private individuals also organized these games, often simply to reinforce the prestige of their family or clan. The political fortunes of a politician would likely depend on the perceived success of these performances. Julius Caesar, for example, put on wondrous shows in 65 BC, thereby building support for his political career to follow. Later, Roman emperors would present public sporting entertainment to maintain their power. The 50,000 spectators who attended performances at the Coliseum came to witness professional gladiators who fought at times to the death against each other but also against wild animals and defenseless slaves, all to the delight of the masses.

Not much has changed in two millennia, except that there are fewer deaths on the pitch today. Italy's most powerful modern politician has been Silvio Berlusconi. Although already a prosperous businessman who owned Italian media outlets, real estate, and advertising and insurance concerns—by 2009, his net worth was estimated by *Forbes* magazine at $9 billion—Berlusconi only became a viable political figure after he purchased one of Italy's fabled soccer clubs, A. C. Milan, in 1986 and returned it to its earlier days of glory. His shows were as wondrous as Caesar's. Berlusconi flew his players into the crowded San Siro stadium on helicopters with Wagnerian trumpets blaring on the loudspeakers. He treated his players as princes of the realm.

As president of his own soccer club, Berlusconi raised his visibility and his political prospects as a populist, although in fact he was a conservative business magnate. He campaigned for political office using his soccer club's successes as evidence of what he would accomplish as prime minister. Berlusconi became the most powerful politician in the Italian state, serving as prime minister from 1994 to 1995, 2001 to 2006, and 2008 to 2011.

Berlusconi's performance as a politician and as prime minister was a combination of consummate showmanship and moral ambiguity. He repeatedly returned to his base of support, the millions of devoted fans of A. C. Milan. He built his own political party and named it after a soccer chant: "Forza Italia"—"Go Italy." He campaigned for office as a soccer magnate. Italians would rally to his theme that under his leadership the country could be run as efficiently as a victorious soccer club.

Berlusconi demonstrated the unity of sports and politics. Although obviously a man of influence in the halls of business, he was only able to leverage his wealth into political power from the soccer pitch. His platform drew a direct line of descent from the ancient Romans, based on the successes in the sport he sponsored. In the performance of his official duties, he continued the theatrics he had used as the premier oligarch of Italian soccer, a man without any apparent limits or restraints. He united in one person the glory (and, at times, the perfidy) of sports and politics.

Of course, Berlusconi was not the only sports businessman who has sought political office, although he was among the most successful. George W. Bush became managing partner of the Texas Rangers baseball club in 1989. It gave him the visibility he needed to win the governorship of Texas in 1994 and then the presidency of the United States in 2000. Of course, Bush came from a successful political lineage—his father and grandfather both served in Congress, the former later becoming president—and so his sports prominence might simply have been a way station to politics. (It also made him wealthy. He converted his investment of $600,000—mostly borrowed money—into a bounty of almost $15 million.)

Bill Bradley, an All-Star in the NBA, and Jack Kemp, a star quarterback in the American Football League, both ran successfully for Congress but unsuccessfully for president. College and NFL Hall of Fame football player Byron "Whizzer" White did not pursue elective politics, but he served in the third branch of government, the Supreme Court, for more than three decades. No one was surprised when Edison Arantes do Nascimento, generally known by his nickname "Pele," perhaps the greatest soccer player of all time, announced in the 1990s that he intended to run for president of Brazil. It was one goal, however, that he could not score.

Boxing has produced at least two important politicians. Vitali Klitschko, the reigning World Boxing Council heavyweight champion, may prove to be a successful athlete-politician. He leads a political party, the Ukrainian Democratic Alliance for Reform (UDAR, which means "the punch" in both Ukrainian and

Russian), in opposition to the Ukrainian government. He currently serves as a deputy of the Kiev City Council, a staunch opponent of official corruption. While the national support for UDAR hovers below 5 percent, that is sufficient to make Klitschko a potential player in future parliamentary elections. Ukrainian politics is subject to perpetual turmoil, the kind where a great boxer may score an upset. Manny Pacquiao, a world boxing champion in several weight classes, was elected to the Philippine Congress. He has indicated that he may run for president. Both Klitschko and Pacquiao are national heroes because of their athletic accomplishments, which may prove to be valuable preparation for their political ascendancy.

THE CORRUPTION OF SPORTS AND POLITICS

Politics is not necessarily conducted under the rules of fair play, and neither are all sports. Political corruption is often deep-seated, even in the most advanced societies. Bribery greases the wheels of government, and violence turns them at rapid speed. Politics does not necessarily require a meritocracy, and, even though sports claim to reward merit, they are infused with exploitation, decadence, provincialism, and injustice. Everything politics touches can likewise be corrupted by a full dose of realpolitik.

Stalin imprisoned the celebrated footballer and founder of Spartak Moscow, Nikolai Starostin, during the Great Purges of the late 1930s. Stalin's courts had found Starostin guilty of "lauding bourgeois sport and attempting to drag bourgeois motives into Soviet sport." His prison term in Siberia, however, was comparatively lenient, because his guards valued his football acumen and accomplishments. After Stalin's death, Starostin returned to a position of influence in Moscow as president of Spartak, where he served for almost four additional decades. Lavrentiy Beria, Stalin's head of the NKVD (later the KGB), headed his own soccer club, Dynamo Moscow, and used the power of his secret police to coerce the best players from other Soviet clubs to transfer to his club and don the traditional kit colors of blue and white. If they refused, they would be interrogated, convicted, and shipped off to Siberia. Beria strengthened his defense by warning the coach that machine guns would be aimed at the players' backs were they to retreat toward their goal.

Simon Kuper, in *Soccer Against the Enemy*, tells stories that demonstrate the paranoia that can afflict a political regime when it comes to soccer. The East

German secret police, the hated Stasi, maintained surveillance on ordinary citizens who did not support its favored soccer team, Dynamo Berlin. The club was run by Erich Mielke, the chief of the secret police. Helmut Klopfleisch was one such victim. An electrician who loved soccer, he spoke fondly of clubs on the other side of the Berlin Wall, in particular of the West Berlin Hertha BSC club. Ultimately, after being hounded for years, Klopfleisch was deported to the West because of his soccer allegiance, likely a most favorable outcome for the East German.

Authoritarian regimes may have good reasons to fear sports. Sports stadiums can serve as forums for the passionate exercise of free speech that could deliver a political message that would never be allowed in the public square. It is the one place where revolutions can brew hidden under chants and curses. At the same time, however, stadium crowds can play out the worst form of sectarian rivalry and violence, for example between the Catholic Celtics and the Protestant Rangers fans in Scottish soccer. Soccer contests mirror political hostilities. Sports might just be politics by another means.

Football Club Barcelona, the standard-bearer of the Catalan region of Spain, had always represented a challenge to Generalissimo Francisco Franco's rule. Matches between the general's favorite club, Real Madrid, and FC Barca were political, as well as sporting, dramas. The Barcelona eleven always served as a source of regional pride and resistance, and remain so today, long after Franco's demise. It is a national team for a region that is not a nation, a symbol of its identity, almost sacred in nature.

The Argentine junta understood how important a victory in the 1978 World Cup, which they would host, would be to their military rule and to public perceptions of their country on the world scene. Soccer had been an essential part of the Argentine culture for a century. One general stated: "If it were necessary to make some correction in the image of us which exists abroad, the World Cup will be just the occasion to show the Argentine's real way of life." That would certainly be the case. The generals also hired a New York City public relations firm to portray the brutal junta in its most benign light.

The world's premier sporting event had been awarded to Argentina long before the bloody coup in which the generals had taken power, and they needed success on the pitch to unite the country under their rule. One important match stood in the way, the semifinal playoff tie against Peru. Argentina needed to prevail by four or more goals. It won 6–0. The generals had bribed the Peruvian government with tons of free grain and millions in loans, and made payments directly to the Peruvian players. They bought the World Cup and, with a tickertape celebration and unbridled public joy, they were able to extend their rule for five more years until civilian rule was restored after Argentina's disastrous defeat in the Falklands War in 1982.

Even the Olympics have not remained immune from corruption. The great ice skating scandal of the 2002 Salt Lake City Winter Games is a prime example. The French judge in the pairs competition, Marie-Reine Le Gougne, agreed, when pressured by the head of the French skating federation, to trade her vote in exchange for the Russian judge's vote for the French team in ice dancing. After the misconduct was disclosed, the disadvantaged Canadian pair of David Pelletier and Jamie Sale were also awarded a gold medal.

WOMEN, SPORTS, AND POLITICS

For the most part, women have been excluded from both politics and sports. Until the passage of Title IX, American girls and women were subject to institutional gender discrimination in secondary schools and colleges. The 1972 statute has had its greatest impact in the sports arena. It took more than a statute, however, to raise the public's awareness of the systematic discrimination women faced.

The premier female athlete of the twentieth century was Billie Jean King, a tennis player. Although notable for her twelve Grand Slam titles and for creating the Women's Tennis Association, the Women's Sports Foundation, and World Team Tennis, her greatest impact came across the net from Bobby Riggs in a bizarre and widely televised vaudeville act. Riggs, a senior tennis professional who described himself as a "hustler," challenged King to demonstrate that a woman could play competitively against a man. Watched on television by fifty million people worldwide, King's straight-set triumph focused the public's attention on women as athletes. Although King was not an elected official, her articulate, confident, and assertive public leadership on issues of women's and gay and lesbian rights offered a role model to others and influenced the development of public policy.

The Olympic movement belatedly offered a venue for women to demonstrate athletic excellence. The ancient Olympics were all-male affairs, often filled with homoerotic overtones that were unavoidable when all the athletes were naked. The modern Olympics began in 1896 with an all-male program. Baron Pierre de Coubertin, their founder, explained that the inclusion of women would be "impractical, uninteresting, unaesthetic, and incorrect." However, women gradually gained recognition for separate-sex events in tennis, archery, and swimming. By the time of the Amsterdam Olympics in 1928, five women's events had been added to the program.

Avery Brundage in 1936 was president of the United States Olympic Committee and would later become president of the International Olympic Committee (IOC). He represented the views of many male international sports officials when he explained that women should only compete in some events within the pantheon of sports: "I am fed up to the ears with women as track and field competitors . . . her charms sink to something less than zero. As swimmers and divers, girls are [as] beautiful and adroit as they are ineffective and unpleasing on the track."

In the 1920s, Dr. Arabella Kenealy raised serious concerns about the effect of athletics on women's bodies. Strengthening muscles would affect internal organs, in particular the reproductive system. At the same time, "the modern craze for feminism, athletics, sports and politics is destroying the emotional element in women, so that they are ceasing to be interested in love-stories, romantic passion or human ideals." Kenealy also believed women had smaller brains than men but, apparently, did not include herself in the small-brain category.

Despite their enormous advances in the second half of the twentieth century, woman athletes remain marginalized. Augusta National, the site of the Masters golf tournament, did not admit its first two women as members until 2012. Muirfield, the famous Scottish golf course, does not even allow women to enter the clubhouse. They are prohibited from playing the course unless accompanied by a gentleman.

With the exception of ice skating and gymnastics, women's Olympic events do not garner the highest level of public appreciation. The Soviet bloc recognized, however, that a gold medal won by a woman counted as much in the table of Olympic medals as one won by a man. East Germans, among others, used performance-enhancing drugs to enhance the medal prospects of their woman athletes. In 1968, the East German women performed poorly, but in the 1972 Olympics they medaled in every track-and-field event and won all but two swimming gold medals. Their performance demonstrated the power of chemistry. Girls as young as eleven, who were told they were taking vitamins, were given steroids, the "blue beans" that accelerated muscle buildup and reduced recovery times but also produced horrendous side effects. The state-sponsored doping regime lasted for decades and caused irreparable damage to an estimated eight hundred woman athletes.

USING SPORTS AS A TOOL OF COLONIALISM

Nations have always extended their economic and political power beyond their borders. For centuries, the Roman Empire covered most of Europe, the Near East, and Northern Africa. The Russian Empire transcended the Asian continent. Spanish and Portuguese explorers conquered foreign lands in search of gold and then divided up their new possessions into colonies they ruled for centuries. No empire, however, surpassed the British expanse in the nineteenth century. "The sun never set" on the British Empire, because it transcended the world, and the sun was always shining on one or more of its colonies. With a population approaching half a billion people, the British Empire represented imperial greatness, as well as political and economic exploitation.

Conquering less developed and poorly armed native forces was only the beginning of Britain's colonial experience. For the British to maintain royal control over their far-flung empire, they needed a strategy of effective social and political control consistent with their underlying assumption of white racial supremacy. Sports would play a critical role in that strategy, in particular in the selective use of the home-grown British sport of cricket. It was hoped that carefully orchestrated cricket matches between the colonialists and the natives would solidify the British Empire. Allowing cricket to serve as a symbol of imperial cohesion and British customs and values would bestow a benefit on an influential class of natives who could be co-opted to help govern the colonies.

In 1926, when the empire was at its fullest extent, a British newspaper could exclaim: "Profound is the chain of empire through the agency of sport. The playing fields have done more to cement the bonds of Imperialism than many a diplomatic conference." The British used their sports, in particular soccer and cricket, to teach natives of their colonies about English values, which colonial rulers saw as purely positive embodiments of daily life. Subjugated people also saw the darker side of those values and of sports. The British followed a strict policy of segregation within their colonies. Their nationals lived in "reserved areas" away from the native population and frequented British-only clubs. The policy was openly and doggedly racist.

Although late to join in the race for colonial possessions, the United States mimicked the European imperial powers. It even adopted its own version of the British strategy of using sports to exact obedience and cohesion in its colonial population. American baseball would serve this imperial purpose, in particular in the Philippines, conquered from Spain in the Spanish-American War. For the most part, however, the United States followed the strategic vision of military theorist Alfred Thayer Mahan: do not bear the burden of colonialism, just extend economic capitalism and the military reach to protect it. Economic activity was the only real game in town.

PING-PONG DIPLOMACY

At times, sports have played a fortuitous role in fostering positive international relations. The most famous of those instances involved a game of table tennis that opened up relations between the United States and the People's Republic of China. America and China had experienced more than two decades of estrangement, highlighted by a war on the Korean Peninsula. To protect its revolution, the Communists kept the West at bay. For American politicians, the Red Menace had reached its epitome on the Asian mainland.

An American table tennis team was in Nagoya, Japan, in 1971 for the Thirty-First World Table Tennis Championship. On April 6, members of the team received an invitation from the Chinese team to visit China. On April 10, 1971, the team, accompanied by journalists, became the first American sports delegation to set foot in Beijing since 1949. Although there are different theories as to why the invitation was tendered, most believe it was the product of a chance encounter between American player Glenn Cowan and Chinese player Zhuang Zedong.

Of course, a change in the relationship between two enemies requires more than a brief encounter between two athletes. China and the United States both sought a change in the status quo. Inviting the table tennis team was simply the excuse to open the door a crack. The Nixon administration quickly followed through the door, and by 1972 the staunch anti-Communist Richard Nixon had traveled to China.

While "ping-pong diplomacy" may have been among the most famous examples of the role of sports, there have been others. India and Pakistan are longtime enemies who share a common devotion to cricket. Matches between the two have served as the venue for discussions between their political leaders. Although lasting rapprochement remains elusive, sports serves as the glue that may possibly bridge the gulf.

CONCLUSION

There are times when the nexus between sports and politics arises in an instant, like the striking of a match. Baseball manager Ozzie Guillen learned about the combustible nature of South Florida politics shortly after he took the helm of the Miami Marlins in 2012. Guillen had long ago established a reputation as an opinionated, if not always judicious, speaker on issues involving baseball and anything else. As the successful manager of the Chicago White Sox, he had spouted his views on a variety of controversial issues, but he was brushed back by the intensity of the South Florida Cuban community's reaction to his interview in *Time* magazine in which he expressed his respect for Fidel Castro. Guillen had stepped on a landmine.

The exile community in South Florida erupted in anger, calling for Guillen's ouster as manager, accompanied by a boycott of the franchise's games. The club quickly distanced itself from the views of its new manager, stating: "There is nothing to respect about Fidel Castro. He is a brutal dictator who caused unthinkable pain for more than fifty years. We live in a community filled with victims of his dictatorship and the people in Cuba continue to suffer today." It suspended Guillen for five games, donating his salary to charity. Guillen appeared before the media to express his contrition and personal embarrassment. His public statements sounded like the Russian opponents of Stalin in the 1930s confessing their sins in order to avoid the bloody purge.

The Guillen affair reminded sports entrepreneurs that they depend on the goodwill of their patrons even in an era of massive television contracts and commercial success. Guillen's misstep set back the Marlins' carefully orchestrated plan to rebrand the franchise for South Florida's growing Latino community. The team had built a new stadium and signed high-priced free agents. It hired as the face of the franchise the most famous Latino manager in Major League history, and he caused the business plan to explode with a few poorly chosen phrases. After the 2012 season, the Marlins fired Guillen.

We can easily criticize the Cuban community's continuing obsession with Castro long after he has lost day-to-day control of his dictatorship. One might hope that after so long a period of exile that hatred would dissolve. The reaction to Guillen's slip may have been overblown, but it certainly reflected the reality of the relationship between sports and politics. You must watch what you say, because your job may depend on it.

Sports serve politics well in many capacities. Because sports command public attention, they offer a way to inculcate values such as discipline, hard work, and obedience. At the same time, they offer entertainment to divert the populace from other activities. They serve as a rallying point for societal hegemony.

On occasion, sports present a jarring dissonance from established societal themes. When Curt Flood, a black baseball player, refused to accept a transfer from St. Louis to Philadelphia, he wrote a letter to Commissioner Bowie Kuhn: "After 12 years in the major leagues I do not feel that I am a piece of property to be bought and sold irrespective of my wishes. I believe that any system that produces that result violates my basic rights as a citizen and a human being."

Flood's letter resonated with his times. The American ethos of silent obedience, especially among persons of color, was under challenge, and Flood's letter spoke to the public debate. Although he would ultimately lose his legal challenge before the United States Supreme Court, his courage was noteworthy. He was the symbol of a new American resistance that would have to be accommodated.

Some sports seem deaf to political reality. The National Football League reinforced what it thought was the prevailing ethos by forcing players to play football on the Sunday after President Kennedy was assassinated. (The NFL later learned its lesson, canceling all games scheduled for the Sunday after the September 11, 2001, tragedy.) It is not surprising that the football club in the nation's capital is called the Redskins, at the very least an insensitive reference to the country's earliest inhabitants. After the massacre of eleven Israeli athletes at the 1972 Munich Olympic Games, a British marathoner was asked how the slaughter affected him. He responded: "It postpones my race for a day." Avery Brundage, the head of the International Olympic Committee, insisted that "the Games must go on."

In fact, sporting events can catalyze change, engage individuals in group activities, and, ultimately, may provide salvation for societies otherwise divided by race, economics, and heritage. Sports can offer a space where merit and fair play control. To see them as a simple diversion is to ignore reality. Sports is much more than a game.

William Magear Tweed ran New York City's Tammany Hall in the 1860s when amateur baseball flourished in the metropolitan area. His Mutuals baseball club prospered in no small measure because Tweed placed all the ballplayers on the city's payroll with no-show jobs. Freed from the responsibility of earning a living, the ballplayers could concentrate on perfecting their skills in playing America's new team sport. *Library of Congress*

Of course, we can't pay you. That would be against Base Ball
Association policy and, as New York's Commissioner of Public Works,
I would never break the rules. —*William M. Tweed*

The appearance of law must be upheld,
especially when it's being broken. —*William M. Tweed*

[1]

EARLY BASEBALL
AND THE URBAN
POLITICAL MACHINE

The nineteenth century in America was a time of explosive population growth, remarkable technological change, and a disastrous civil war. At the same time, in this period of upheaval the men and women of this country created a uniquely American culture. European immigration and domestic migration dramatically increased the population density of urban centers. The Industrial Revolution added a manufacturing sector to an essentially agrarian economy, and American-made goods became available to the world. Completing the business left unfinished at the founding of the nation, the Civil War solidified a union of states at a significant cost. More than 2 percent of the population, 620,000 lives, were lost on the nation's battlefields.

Amidst all this change, uproar, carnage, and social transformation, the country created a culture that, for the first time, was distinctively American. That dominant culture—its music, arts, social habits, cuisine, and folklore—also included activities that filled newly found leisure time. For the first time, nineteenth-century Americans enjoyed hours each week that could be devoted to play and entertainment, a pleasure not possible when work filled every day but Sunday from sunrise until sunset. One activity of this new indulgence was a uniquely American sport, one filled with "vim, vigor [and] vitality," as Albert Spalding later wrote in *America's National Game*. It was baseball, born shortly before midcentury and soon played nationwide. It was baseball that would capture the attention of the nation and reflect the dynamism of America.

The nineteenth century also gave birth to new forms of political governance, and these were directly related to meeting the needs of the surging urban population. The American political system, as ordained in the constitutions of the United States and each of the states, contemplated periodic democratic elections in which citizens freely selected their leaders. The legitimacy of governmental power under this political compact rested on "the consent of the governed," as Thomas Jefferson wrote in the Declaration of Independence in the eighteenth century. Public officials, elected for limited terms of office, would periodically seek a reaffirmation of their governance power by the electorate, which would then hold them accountable for their actions. This original and elementary version of American politics, of course, was never quite accurate, although it remained a compelling myth. It was just as reliable as the fable constructed later that in 1839 a nineteen-year-old Abner Doubleday had invented the national game of baseball on Mr. Phinney's dirt field in bucolic Cooperstown, New York.

Democracy was the privilege of only a few in America. In fact, about ten percent of Americans, white male landowners, were entitled to vote in the early decades of the nation. More than fifteen percent of the inhabitants were slaves, half were women, and the remaining males were landless. None could vote. In some states, there were religious and literacy tests that barred many others from voting. In some states, "heretics," Jews, Quakers, and Catholics did not enjoy the privilege of political participation. Thus, in fact, the "consent of the governed" meant the consent of those few white Christian men who held a property stake in the country and thus could be counted on to exercise democracy in the best interests of the nation.

America's game—baseball—was equally enveloped in fable. Abner Doubleday, later to become a Civil War general who commanded Union troops at Fort Sumter, was attending the United States Military Academy at West Point in 1839, the year when he was said to have conceived of the "national game." In fact, Doubleday's family had moved away from Cooperstown the prior year. Abner Graves, a mining engineer, was the sole source of the Doubleday myth. That was more than sufficient in 1908 for organized baseball to elevate Doubleday to the status of creator. (Graves shortly thereafter murdered his wife and was committed to an asylum for the insane.)

We can come much closer to the truth about both American politics and

American baseball in the nineteenth century and, in the process, reveal how they were intertwined from the very beginning. We have always had a variety of political systems in America, and have not yet achieved universal suffrage. Despite the outcome of the Civil War, we remain an amalgam of heterogeneous republics—a union of states—with local, regional, and national officials elected in various ways. At times, our core principle of consent has operated close to the idealized norm. At other times, government has been distorted by wealth, prejudices, avarice, misdealing, and partisanship. Within a decade of the election of George Washington, political parties gained control of the American electoral process. As a new and overwhelming set of problems beset our major cities in the mid-nineteenth century, a new variant of the party structure, the political machine, grew to dominate the administration of government. It would offer a perversion of democracy under which an urban gang would maintain control for decades and loot the public treasury in the process.

Baseball, that most American of games, rather than emerging full-blown from the head of one man, was also the product of evolution. Bat-and-ball amusements had ancient roots, and assorted variants were played throughout the colonies. The version that would form lasting roots attracted public attention because it was a game people could play at various skill levels. It was a communal experience. While Americans previously had watched horse racing, boxing, or boating, baseball was the country's first sport in which a broad cross section of adults could actually participate, seeking exercise, honor, glory, and fun. Although we are able to identify those who were involved in formulating the rules that led to the modern game, baseball very much remained a work in progress until late in the nineteenth century, much like the nation for which it would serve as the national pastime.

AMERICAN GOVERNANCE

The American political myth clashed with the political realities in a nation that was outgrowing its rural and agricultural roots. For the most part, in early America government had played a minor role in people's affairs. American governance was a crazy quilt of influence centers—some elected, others hereditary, still others the product of commercial success.

From the earliest colonial days, inhabitants participated in voluntary associations, what the *Federalist* papers decried as "factions." Some of these groups were based on religious or commercial interests, while others were purely fraternal. As Eastern and Midwestern cities burgeoned through immigration from foreign lands, in particular from Ireland and Germany in the mid-nineteenth century, voluntary associations multiplied, providing immigrants with an essential anchor against the disturbing winds of urban complexity and chaos. Persons thrown into new, unforeseeable, and often friendless circumstances joined with others to create a communal sense of belonging to help weather the gales of American daily life.

By the middle of the nineteenth century, urban areas had swelled in size and economic importance. New York City's population, for example, expanded eightfold, from 123,706 in 1820 to 942,292 in 1870. The existing structures of government, built to meet the needs of much smaller municipalities, could not solve the social problems created by this dramatic expansion of population. Instead of restructuring government and creating the administrative structures needed to address these changed social conditions, informal, but effective, urban political organizations, such as Tammany Hall in New York, filled the political vacuum.

The new urbanites founded their own social clubs and associations, seeking a collective identity in their often forlorn and destitute enclaves. These clubs, based on class, ethnic, religious, or business groupings, became the rock on which the new urban political machines built their political bases. In fact, some machines created clubs as a means of social control, reducing the prospects for social disorder and urban unrest. These clubs, devoted to social and political goals, also engaged in popular recreation such as baseball. Thus, from the beginning, politics and sports intertwined.

IN THE BEGINNING

It might be said that Alexander Cartwright, William Wheaton, Daniel L. "Doc" Adams, and their Knickerbockers club committee invented baseball in the 1840s. Although different versions of bat-and-ball games had been played in eastern cities for decades, the New York game that the Knickerbockers formulated had genuine staying power. We would recognize the game they played as akin to baseball as we know it today.

A group of young men from New York City formed the Knickerbockers in 1845 to provide an opportunity for athletic exercise to "those whose sedentary habits required recreation." Voluntary private associations, such as the Knickerbockers, were the city's focal point for physical recreation, and exercise was seen as the antidote to the miasmas of the unhealthy, immoral, and dangerous urban environment. It was also fun, and it was not work. Even before the creation of their formal organization and the development of their famous baseball rules, this fraternal group of young clerks, storekeepers, and artisans—at one point having as many as two hundred members—played various bat-and-ball games on the fields at Twenty-Seventh Street and Fourth Avenue in Manhattan. Members of this communal and sporting fraternity claimed for themselves a reputation as "gentlemen," and they paid dues to the organization in exchange for the social and athletic opportunities it offered.

Cartwright was the twenty-five-year-old son of a shipping proprietor. He worked variously as a bookseller, bank clerk, and sometimes as a surveyor in New York City, and had served as a volunteer fireman in Knickerbocker Engine Company No. 12, the name he and his colleagues appropriated for their new club. Over six feet tall, Cartwright was an imposing figure for his time. The members of the Knickerbockers club played the game Cartwright and his colleagues had devised—a clever variation of rounders and town ball, both well-established pastimes at that time in East Coast cities. They first played their new game in October and November 1845. This more "manly" game of baseball fit perfectly the fast-growing urban environment where there was inadequate time and space for full games of cricket, and the town ball practice of "soaking" runners by hitting them with the ball seemed too primitive.

Although the Knickerbockers considered themselves well-born gentlemen, they were actually white-collar workers and skilled craftsmen. They were certainly not aristocrats, but they did have leisure time after work that could be filled with athletic and social diversions. Club members subscribed to principles of sportsmanship, fraternity, and proper conduct. Under their baseball rules, they imposed fines on a player using profanity, arguing with an umpire's decision, or refusing to obey the directives of the team captain. In these earliest days of the game, baseball seemed primarily a good excuse to throw a dinner party, a gala postgame repast, after a pleasant and friendly athletic exercise.

Manhattan was running out of available playing space, and so the young men ferried across the river to the "Elysian Fields" on the heights above the Hudson in Hoboken, New Jersey. It was there, on June 19, 1846, that they first played the new game against a rival team made up of former members of the Knickerbocker club (called the "New York Nine"). The Knickerbockers laid out a field with three "bases" and a circular home plate. They borrowed the field's diamond shape from the bat-and-ball games commonly played in Philadelphia, but extended the distance between the bases to about ninety feet. The flat bases were canvas bags filled with sand or sawdust, replacing the rocks or posts that had earlier been employed. Their game would normally be played by nine men on a side, with a "short roving infielder," the shortstop, stationed between the second and third bases. This new "regulation" game was an adult pastime designed to exhibit skill, agility, and eye–hand coordination. Cartwright's team lost that first match against the New York Nine 23–1, but he did not play. The assembled teams had asked him to serve as the game's single umpire. After all, they were playing under the rules he had helped devise.

In short order, daily and weekly newspapers extolled the virtues of the new Knickerbocker game. Henry Chadwick, the game's premier chronicler, explained in his 1860 book *Beadle's Dime Base-Ball Player* that the sport required "the possession of muscular strength, great agility, quickness of eye, readiness of hand, and many other faculties of mind and body that mark a man of nerve." Moreover, playing baseball, especially for one's community, would soon become a matter of enormous personal and local pride. Chadwick and others sought to purify the game even further, urging the elimination of the rule that allowed the defense to record an out by catching a hit ball on one bounce. He wrote in 1860 in the *New York Clipper* that by improving the rules his goal was to make the game "more perfect."

The value of playing Cartwright's game was equal shares of good recreation and good spirits. After their physical exercise, the Knickerbockers would dine at McCarty's Hotel, adjacent to the Elysian Fields. In short order, early baseball would become an important and approved social pastime, recognized by the influential Muscular Christianity movement as a means to supplant the blood sports normally hosted by the local saloon, such as cockfighting, ratting, and bear-baiting, although these "entertainments" would continue through the remainder of the century.

Reverend Henry Ward Beecher, Congregationalist minister of the Plymouth Church in Brooklyn, extolled the value of the new game. Baseball, he told his flock, could help develop a healthy spiritual life and exemplify the "virtues of physical exercise, discipline and teamwork." As a moral and well-regulated recreation not bound by dour Calvinism or steeped in savage violence, baseball would fit nicely into "wholesome" America, uplifting the working class and offering groups solidarity and pride, especially important in an urban culture where so many immigrants needed to be Americanized.

In the years to come, although the Knickerbockers would not join the rush to competitive rivalry, commercialization, and professionalism, it would make other innovations, for example introducing brightly colored uniforms similar to those worn by their progenitors, the volunteer fire departments. Club members would remain constant in their devotion to their traditional social values and the purpose of their enterprise. Members came and went—Cartwright himself was soon to head west, ending up in Hawaii—but the "ancient and honorable" Knickerbockers had made their mark on the evolving American cultural scene. Even at its inception, proponents of baseball understood that there was value in extolling tradition, even if that tradition was only a few years old.

Within the first decade of the sport, numerous other social and athletic clubs formed in New York, including the Gotham, Empire, Star, and Eagle fraternities. They adopted the Knickerbockers' "regulation" baseball rules. Uniform standards of play created a common metric that allowed for competition and permitted the growing number of athletic clubs to play challenge matches. With the spread of the game and the commonality of the rules, within a decade the game evolved from a purely athletic exercise to a competition. It was no longer sufficient for those who played to enjoy the fresh air of northern New Jersey and the social repast of a fine dinner. Now the game would be played for pride, accomplishment, and victory.

Baseball clubs were formed by men who shared common work experiences, such as policemen (Manhattans), saloonkeepers (Phantoms), dairymen (Pocahontas), schoolteachers (Metropolitans), and men in the food trades (Baltics, Jeffersons, and Atlantics). The important Eckford club of Brooklyn was made up of shipwrights and mechanics from the Williamsburg and Greenpoint areas of the New York dry docks, and they named their club for Henry Eckford, an early Brooklyn shipbuilder. Masonic orders, workers' benevolent associations, and party ward organizations played the game. Volunteer firemen, always the symbol of great civic pride, took up baseball, drawn by the same principles of teamwork that had always characterized their activities in fighting urban fires. As we shall see, one of the clubs that traced its origin to volunteer firemen, the Mutuals, would play a particularly important role in the development of the game and in its connection to political power.

The amateur clubs of the 1850s had been manned almost exclusively by local athletes. Players developed pride in, and allegiance to, their clubs and to their neighborhoods, cities, and towns. They paid dues in order to enjoy club status—the Niagaras of Buffalo, for example, had 350 members, each paying annual dues of five dollars—and the dues covered club expenses. Each of these fraternal clubs was governed by a constitution under which they elected officers annually. Members met regularly in their "club rooms," often at a hotel or a saloon. Membership in the clubs offered a sense of belonging, with baseball just one of their social activities. They would meet to practice on days between formally scheduled challenge matches against rival clubs. The baseball fraternity judged these early clubs not only by the quality of their play on the field but also by the sumptuousness and hospitality of their postgame meal and festivities. Toasts and speeches rounded out match days.

The Knickerbocker rules were not formally printed until they appeared in *Porter's Spirit of the Times* on December 6, 1856, and then in the *New York Clipper* a week later. Word of the new game, however, had already spread across the country. Chadwick wrote that the game had become "epidemic just now." The *New York Ledger* implored young men to "run out, merchants, lawyers, clergymen, bookkeepers, editors, authors, clerks and everybody else who can, and have half a day of it in the fields every week during the ball season."

The Knickerbockers certainly did not appreciate that they had done anything special, and they did not actively promote the adoption of their rules. For many years after their first historic (but losing) match in 1846, they were content to play their game as an intramural exercise within the club as a means to enhance the athletic well-being of the participants. The other clubs that had adopted their rules, however, were ready to take on all comers, but always paid their verbal respects to the "ancient and honorable" progenitor club's role in the development of the game.

By the mid-1850s, the game had become a ubiquitous feature of New York male social life. In 1856, *Porter's Spirit of the Times* wrote that "every available plot of ground for ten miles around the metropolitan area" was devoted to playing the new game of "base." The "first nines" of the sporting clubs played match games that attracted much public attention in the antebellum period. Thousands attended, and the results were reported in the press. In this new phase, the game had clearly evolved. It was played not simply as physical exercise but as competitive sport. The clubs abolished the practice of postgame dinners as an old-fashioned custom that distracted from the main purpose of the exercise—to win at the game. Soon capitalism would capture the sport much as competition had, and it would convert baseball into a money-making enterprise.

Accomplishment on the baseball field soon attracted the interest of politicians who saw in the pastime an opportunity to command the public's attention while demonstrating in a convincing fashion the prominence of local achievement. Brooklyn produced dozens of baseball clubs. Forever in the shadow of Manhattan, even 150 years ago, the *Brooklyn Eagle* could crow with pride in 1862: "If we are ahead of the big city in nothing else, we can beat her in baseball." While the game had spread to the Midwest and beyond, there was no question that it was the child of the New York metropolitan region, which, by then, had established its lasting preeminence in American commerce.

Having evolved from athletic exercise into a competitive enterprise, baseball needed some formal organization. On March 10, 1858, representatives of twenty-two amateur clubs from the New York area met at Smith's Hotel on Broome Street in Manhattan to form the National Association of Base Ball Players. The clubs represented neighborhoods and ethnic groups, as well as occupations. Under the aegis of the National Association, the clubs wrote a set of rules of play with only a few codicils added to the Knickerbockers' text. Now champions could be recognized and boasting rights established based on challenge match victories, an important source of American psychological capital both then and now. The game had certainly lost its innocence. Baseball would be played with the object of winning. When these social and athletic clubs played against each other—normally as part of a series of three scheduled games—they would present their very best players for the contests, their "first nines." The winners would normally receive as a trophy a gilded ball worth more than a hundred dollars. If winning mattered to the clubs—and it did—soon players would have to be attracted to play for a club with offers of pay for their efforts.

Thus, within little more than a decade, the meaning and role of baseball had changed. Baseball games evolved from an urban recreation to competition between localities, ethnic communities, and class groups. Baseball was soon commodified as part of the new American consumerism. Those who created and defined this new essential characteristic would seek to promote it as an enterprise with commercial potential no longer tied to local resources or affection.

Although not yet as popular or widely played as cricket, baseball's growth spurt demonstrated its resonance with the nation's character. By the 1860s, the number of clubs in the National Association had surpassed three hundred, and hundreds more nationwide did not even bother to join. As the popularity of the game spread across many working-class neighborhoods, the Knickerbockers' emphasis on elitism waned, and the game's commercial prospects and political implications rose to prominence.

Baseball's amateurism paradigm lasted well into the 1860s, although there had been some "ringers" who were paid under the table even as early as the 1850s, such as pitcher Jim Creighton in 1859 and Al Reach shortly thereafter. The best players would change clubs for increased pay. (Creighton, for example, played for the Niagaras, the Stars, and finally the Excelsiors of Brooklyn in a two-season period until his untimely death at age twenty-one from an internal injury caused by a massive swing during a game.) The earlier paradigm of localism changed when the commitment to victory and achievement overcame the pride of community.

Competition had superseded fraternity as the controlling American ethos, and baseball changed along with it. In order to win, players were recruited and compensated by local businesses, donations from the general community, and ultimately from admission fees. The purposes and practices of the game changed fundamentally. Some recognized that this was not a totally positive development. As the *Brooklyn Eagle* wrote, this resulted in "the breaking up of all local feeling in regards to baseball."

However, the recruitment of better ballplayers and, ultimately, their open professionalism improved the quality of play. Baseball clubs became small businesses. As a result, baseball captured the public's attention as an attractive urban entertainment. In 1858, tens of thousands of baseball enthusiasts descended on the new Fashion Race Course in Queens for a three-game all-star series pitting the best baseball players from Manhattan against their counterparts from Brooklyn. The horse racetrack had erected a wooden fence around the field and charged admission, the first time that had ever occurred in the still ostensibly amateur game. The proceeds from the series went to a firemen's fund for widows and orphans, a decision that reflected the history of many baseball clubs as outgrowths of volunteer fire brigades.

By 1862, entrepreneurs began to construct more permanent stadiums, as baseball continued to evolve as part of the growing commercialized consumer culture. William H. Cammeyer converted his ice-skating pond in Brooklyn into an enclosed baseball field, the Union Grounds, and collected a ten-cent admission fee from each spectator who came to watch the best clubs play baseball. Cammeyer's Grounds, located on the corner of Lee Avenue and Rutledge Street, served as the home field for the Brooklyn Eckfords and later for the New

York Mutuals, who would share in the proceeds. Other entrepreneurs followed Cammeyer's lead in New York and around the country.

Once again, the object of the popular game had changed. While competition would remain within the game's bloodlines, now baseball had become an openly commercial entertainment. Charging admission provided a source of income for the clubs, which until recently had only thought of their sporting activity as a healthy recreation. This commercial aspect made certain the eventual transformation of the amateur pastime into a business of professional clubs. The growing popularity of the sport also ensured that it would attract the interest of urban politicians.

THE MUTUALS OF NEW YORK

The Mutuals became one of New York City's best amateur clubs. In 1857, the preeminent New York Democratic politician, William Magear Tweed, participated in organizing the social and athletic club, formed by volunteer firemen who were members of the city's Mutual Hook and Ladder Company Number One. Although Tweed never served as president of the Mutual club, as has sometimes been reported, he was involved in the organization from its creation. Tweed was a member of the club's board of trustees along with a parade of Democratic politicians. Throughout the twenty-year history of the organization, the Mutuals always had city aldermen, state legislators, and judges on its board of directors. The longtime president of the Mutuals was City Coroner John Wildey, Jr., a ballplayer himself, who played first base for the Mutuals in its early days. Other influential Tammany officials played important management roles with the ballclub. For example, Alexander Davidson, chief clerk in the New York City Office of the Streets Commissioner, was the secretary of the Mutuals. The Mutuals were widely known as "Tammany's club."

Every season, the Mutuals would challenge, and normally triumph over, other premier clubs in the region. As members of the National Association, the Mutuals had pledged to maintain its amateur status, but, like many of its competitors, it would not. As competition between baseball clubs grew, it became apparent that the Mutuals' "first nine" needed more time to practice and play their game. Club management wanted to attract better players for the squad. Coroner Wildey and Boss Tweed did exactly what they had done with thousands of their loyal followers. They placed the "amateur" baseball players on the city payroll without requiring them to perform any work for the city in exchange. By accepting those positions, the Mutuals' "first nine" players became secret professionals, in clear violation of association rules. Their only obligation was to play championship baseball. The Mutuals would be the first, but not the only, club to demonstrate the symbiotic relationship between baseball and politics.

Sportswriters—a new profession that grew as baseball became a more popular attraction—generally referred to the Mutuals as an adjunct of Tammany's operations. The *New York Clipper* reported in 1865 that "politicians are commencing to curry favor with the fraternity of ballplayers, as a class of our 'fellow citizens' worthy of attention of our 'influential men.'" The *Clipper* was talking about the Mutuals, and the report was accurate. Tweed and the Tammany men saw the Mutuals as part of its outreach to the public. The politicians would attend games, mixing with the crowds, who would play a critical role in the urban machine's political dominance.

On the field, the Mutuals played the game with distinctive intensity. Voluntary firemen were not known for their meekness; neither were members of urban political machines or the baseball clubs they sponsored. Arriving at a structure on fire—a significant problem in a city built mostly of wood—fire companies would brawl with rivals who had also arrived on the scene. Similarly, the baseball Mutuals would maintain their ruffianism on the ball field and were considered "notorious" by many. As the *New York Times* noted, when the Mutuals played away from New York City, they brought with them "their fame and universal success," which often involved rough play: "New York alderman and other 'sports'" were in attendance to "back them." During a Mutuals match against a club from Irvington, New Jersey, a city just west of Newark, a riot broke out. Hugh Campbell, an Irvington outfielder, claimed he was "sucker-punched." No one doubted his report. The same thing happened in a Mutuals game against Troy in 1871, when Mutuals manager John Wildey ended up bloodied. The Mutuals would play the game with a zest characteristic of an urban mob, the antithesis of the gentlemanly manners of the Knickerbocker club. Certainly, the Knickerbockers would disdain such thuggery.

The Mutuals were also involved in the first reported fixing scandal of the new game, not a surprise for a club run by the urban political mob. Three members of the club took a bribe to throw a game against their archrival, the Eckfords, on September 28, 1865. After the participants admitted their perfidy, they were banned from baseball, if only for a little while. However, compared with the astounding crimes committed by their sponsors, the Tweed Ring, the Mutuals' transgressions were trivial.

Despite their hooliganism—or perhaps because of it—the Mutuals were a widely popular club, and thousands came to watch them play. The press referred to them variously as a "celebrated," "well-known," "noted," "renowned," and "crack" ballclub, and their matches were always reported as the "most exciting" of the season, attended by the most spectators. Reporting on the Opening Day intramural game in 1867, for example, the *New York Times* wrote on April 17: "It is to such clubs as the Mutuals that our national game is indebted for its wide-spread popularity, for besides having one of the best practice grounds in the country, they generally turn out such a jolly crowd on their opening day as to make the game very attractive to witness. It is no wonder then, that the crowd at the Fields on Monday could be counted by the thousands, and that they applauded and laughed and enjoyed themselves as people do who attend a lively theatrical performance." Immediately below the story about the Mutuals practice session there appeared the newspaper's listing for "City Politics." The "newly elected officers of the Tammany Society," the *Times* reported, included: "Sachem . . . William M. Tweed."

By 1867, even though amateurism remained the required norm, some of the best Mutuals players were sharing in the gate receipts for their games. By 1868, many had been placed on a straight salary for their work on the field, and by 1869 the entire team was openly paid as professionals. That year, the New York City Council voted to end the charade and appropriated $1,500 to fund the Mutuals.

BOSS TWEED AND TAMMANY HALL

From the founding of the nation until well into the nineteenth century, government offices were filled by men from the middle and upper classes. As officeholders, they saw their role as temporary service rather than a career. They were modern-day recreations of Cincinnatus, the model of Roman virtue, who served as consul to protect his city from its enemies in the fifth century BC, before returning to the countryside when the threat was repulsed. American politicians were similarly motivated by selfless civic virtue.

By the middle of the nineteenth century, however, the new circumstances facing American cities caused urban politics to change. Millions were without adequate food, shelter, health, and sanitation services. The teeming cities were a jumble of immigrant groupings, formal political parties, civic organizations, social clubs, and street gangs. Those who would now aspire to political power could do so only by stitching together enough of these groups into a coalition that could control the elective process and thereby address some of their overwhelming problems. The most successful politicians took one step further, forming organized urban political "machines" that could systematically (if illegally) manage the electoral process. Politics in American cities had become a business run by full-time professionals.

Although there were many cities that were run by political machines, the most effective organization by far was in New York. New York City was a Democratic Party stronghold, but the party was as disorderly as the electorate. The Society of St. Tammany, named for Indian leader Tamanend, would bring order out of this political chaos. It operated out of a hall built in 1830 on East Fourteenth Street in Manhattan. Although it had originated as a social and political club with an anti-aristocratic orientation, by the 1840s Tammany had adapted to the new urban circumstances to become the avowed champion of the poor and immigrant masses. At the same time, it became a champion at greed and corruption. Tammany's most notorious leader was William "Boss" Tweed. Over a five-year period from 1866 until 1871, Tweed and his cohorts—the "Elegant" Oakey Hall, Peter "Brains" Sweeny, and Richard "Slippery Dick" Connolly, known collectively as the Tweed Ring—stole upward of $200 million from the city and its residents. They set a standard for Hall civic corruption that has never been surpassed.

Like many other urban politicians of the time, Tweed had formed the initial base of his support from the membership of volunteer fire departments. In 1848, Tweed and State Representative John J. Reilly ran the Americus Engine Company Number 6 ("The Big Six"). Tweed gave The Big Six its symbol, a snarling red tiger, the emblem later attached to his political vehicle, Tammany Hall. The seventy-five firemen of the Big Six could be called on by Tweed to do anything, at any time. Tweed and his colleagues soon recognized that chartering and funding fire brigades and social and athletic clubs provided a reliable political base. Tweed founded the Mutual Hook and Ladders Company No. 1. Later, as we have noted, he organized the members of this brigade into the amateur baseball and social club called the Mutuals.

Tweed began his political career around the time the young men of the Knickerbockers were perfecting their new version of baseball. He learned the fundamentals of his political trade through petty corruption, selling governmental favors and licenses in his ward and handing out jobs from his law offices at 95 Duane Street. Developing a chain of friends, Tweed climbed the ladder of elected jobs—alderman from the Seventh Ward, congressman for a term, Deputy Streets Commissioner, Commissioner of Public Works, state senator, and chairman of the State Finance Committee. In 1857, the year he helped form the Mutual Baseball Club, he became a member of the New York County Board of Supervisors, on which he served from 1857 to 1870, with four terms as the president of the board. At the same time, Tweed rose within the ranks of Tammany Hall, becoming chairman of the General Committee on January 1, 1863, and later that year the "Grand Sachem," the first time one man had held both positions.

Tweed, a mountain of a man, crude and blusterous, could be a suave "jolly rogue" when necessary. He could also be charitable, especially when spending someone else's money. He made friendships for political purposes and offered personal favors as the source of his power. Although not a great public speaker, he was a remarkable organizer. He enjoyed mixing with his people, including attending Mutual baseball games when he was not at Harry Hill's dance hall on Houston Street.

Early in his career, Tweed recognized that the flood of immigrants was a political godsend. His city was filled with confused strangers—fresh from the farms of the old country—who lacked the skills, direction, and capital that would be needed to prosper in their new country. By 1870, a half million of those new residents lived in tenement slums and cellars. Beggars and children roamed the streets, and Tweed made sure that Tammany was there to offer order, jobs, health services, sanitation, coal, and food to ease the ever-present chaos. Immigrants lined up to be naturalized wholesale by Tammany judges. In exchange, Tweed had found the source of his continuing political power.

Immigrant groups formed their own churches, newspapers, mutual aid societies, theaters, militia, and fire companies, and, with Tammany's direct assistance, they obtained public jobs. Ever threatened by nativist groups, the multitudes of Irish Catholics and German Protestants fit comfortably under Tammany's umbrella. Tweed orchestrated the logistics of practical urban politics with genuine enthusiasm. Tammany's boss presided over an empire of patronage—with 12,000 jobholders, all of whom owed their paycheck to Tweed and the machine. Because of their fashion for tall, sleek hats, these rank-and-file were called the Shiny Hat Brigade, and they held jobs in every branch of city government. Many of these

Tammany loyalists had no real work obligations. They were only required to pick up their pay, while performing no service of any value to the public.

On election day, of course, Tammany would call on this army of supplicants to ensure that "democracy" would work as the machine required. Loyalists would vote early and often, stuff ballot boxes, intimidate those who might vote another slate, and manipulate the counting of ballots. Tweed's troops would spring into action with gangs, renegades, and intimidators like the Bowery Boys making sure that only those chosen by Tammany prevailed at the ballot box. Thugs from the Five Points section of New York City—the Gophers, Dead Rabbits, Gorillas, the East Side Dramatic and Pleasure Club, and the Limburger Roarers—could be called on to provide the muscle. With everyone acting in his own self-interest, the system thrived, at least until an overabundance of greed attracted too much public attention.

In Democratic New York, the critical election was normally the primary, since rarely could the Republicans offer genuine competition in the general election. Statewide elections, in particular for the governorship, required the manipulation of nominating conventions, where tight organization proved vital. Tweed would claim for Tammany the position of the "regular" Democratic Party, even though it was only one faction. He would attack the splinter groups that would challenge Tammany's status.

The Democratic Party included many dissidents, mostly those who had forsaken Tammany or had been expelled for various reasons, including challenging the incumbent leadership. Fernando Wood was elected New York City mayor in 1854 as a Tammany Democrat, but then lost the 1857 election and was expelled from Tammany. He proceeded to form his own political organization of dissidents, the Mozart Hall Democrats. Under its banner—and using the full array of election tactics he had perfected at Tammany—Wood was returned to city hall in 1859. Tammany never did hold a monopoly on the use of dishonest election practices.

The Republicans maintained control of the state legislature in Albany and through various measures sought to manipulate city government. In the Charter of 1857, the legislature divided responsibilities for much local city business among various departments, whose leadership was elected independently by the voters, thus removing them from the mayor's purview. Some of the officials designated to run new "commissions" were appointed directly by Albany, a way for upstate Republicans to share in the booty—both in patronage and plunder.

City Democrats raised the hue and cry that this Republican maneuver deprived the city of home rule regarding vital services, such as police protection. This gave Tweed an emotional issue on which to run his candidates for state office. It also increased the gap between the needs of the immigrant population and the services provided by Albany's various commissions. Tammany stepped in with direct payments to the needy and jobs in those areas of government it still controlled, and lobbied the legislature to modify its plan for governance. Tweed himself ran for state senator and quickly assumed a position of prominence and influence in Albany. Ultimately, in 1870 Tammany bought the legislative votes it needed to reverse the charter, creating a strong mayoral government in the city, balanced against a powerful board of aldermen. Tweed controlled both, and, in the process of "reform," he was able to vanquish local Democratic rivals—the "Young Democracy," whose adherents had held city offices at the behest of the legislature. As a result, members of the Young Democracy, according to the *New York Times*, retreated to their clubhouse, Irving Hall, "to wail their monstrous melody to the moon."

The election of 1868 demonstrated how the Tammany machine operated at its most proficient level. While Tweed was not very concerned about the national election—General Grant was almost certain to prevail in the first election after the close of the Civil War—state and local contests were critical. Tweed needed to maintain control of significant municipal offices, the governorship, and the judiciary, which was elected in New York. His candidates won all those elections, using the horde of newly minted citizens naturalized by Tammany judges. These naturalization mills would grind out a thousand new voters a day. In 1868, over 41,000 immigrants were naturalized, sometimes at a rate of three a minute.

Tammany organized the effort to ensure that there were sufficient votes to prevail. "Repeaters" would vote, shave off their beards and vote again, and shave off their mustaches and vote a third time. With forged papers, they would vote still again. City vote totals were withheld until upstate Republican districts reported. Then winning totals in New York City were posted that were sufficient to overcome the Republican rival's lead for statewide offices. The election was won with stuffed ballot boxes, fraudulent voters, and corrupt counting. (Occasionally, even Tammany made mistakes by reporting more Democratic votes in a district than there were registered voters.) The Republican-controlled Congress appointed a committee to investigate the obvious electoral corruption, but, after hearing from dozens of witnesses, left town with the status quo unchanged.

As deputy street commissioner from 1863 to 1870, perhaps his most important political position, Tweed controlled thousands who were on call to ensure the continued dominance of Tammany. The city was growing rapidly and, as the streets paved by Tweed's men moved northward, new buildings and new transportation offered the Ring abundant opportunities for personal profit at a standard rate of tribute of 15 percent. The town was filled with speculators, especially in real estate, and they, too, needed government approval that they could purchase and count on. Tweed offered the machine's services and also purchased land himself, becoming the third-largest landowner in the city in the process.

TAMMANY AND THE MUTUALS

Tweed and his Ring appreciated the value of success, both in political plunder and on the baseball field. It came as second nature to these political gangsters to offer no-show jobs to those who would bolster the prestige of their organization. The ploy would assure recruiting and retaining the best ballplayers by providing municipal patronage jobs at an annual cost of perhaps $30,000 to the city. A dozen or so phantom jobs out of 12,000 was, frankly, insignificant. For the 1868 season, the club used the prospect of no-show jobs to recruit three players from New Jersey and three more from Brooklyn to complement the three natives of Manhattan.

On July 4, 1867, Tammany laid the cornerstone of its new clubhouse in New York on Fourteenth Street to the east of Irving Avenue. The day before, according to the *New York Times*, the Mutuals of New York, Tammany's baseball club, had played "the most interesting and exciting" game of the season against the Eckfords club of Brooklyn. The game was tied at the end of the ninth inning, 20–20, and was declared a draw. The following week, in a rain-shortened rematch of these two "first-class" clubs, the Mutuals triumphed 28–9.

Inside the Fourteenth Street edifice, Tammany officials, arrayed into committees and councils, would dispense thousands of government jobs and receive tribute in exchange for their favors. Ward clubs spread out across the city, providing needed services in local areas. Tammany provided good fellowship as well as patronage. Even the *New York Times*, later an implacable foe that would spearhead Tweed's downfall, could write that Tammany was "a wonderfully and admirably-constructed and conducted machine . . . the wheels work smoothly, the pulley run without a jar, the cogs slip into one another perfectly, while everything is kept well oiled and greased from the public funds of our wealthy citizens."

Tweed himself sought social respectability through sports, joining the American Jockey Club along with August Belmont, William R. Travers, James R. Hunter, and Leonard Jerome. He attended Mutual games, while leaving operational responsibility for the club to Coroner Wildey. Although Wildey, as player-manager, had played first base for the Mutuals in its early years, after the Civil War he devoted himself to the management of the enterprise. In addition to the city jobs Tweed and his cohorts had arranged, Tweed also paid $5,000 out of his own pocket for travel expenses when the Mutual club ventured out of the New York area, in particular on what the press referred to as its "famous" trip to New Orleans in 1869.

Tweed met his political demise when his hubris came into conflict with the ideology and business needs of the *New York Times* and *Harper's Weekly*, spearheaded by the sharp pen of cartoonist Thomas Nast. When the *Times* could add actual facts to its exhortations, Tweed was doomed politically. The trigger was a riot that broke out between Irish Protestants (the Orange) and Irish Catholics in July 1871. Sixty people were killed and more than 150 were injured. Shortly thereafter, disaffected members of the city administration leaked damaging information to the *Times*. The headline stories of official corruption ran daily. Eventually, Tweed was indicted and convicted for stealing between $25 million and $45 million. He would die in prison.

POLITICS AND SPORTS

Tweed was not the only politician or political boss to see a value in sports. Nearly all baseball clubs had some connections to city politicians. In fact, one recent study of baseball club officials and stockholders found that half of them were politicians—including 50 mayors and 102 state legislators. The *Sporting News*, in an 1895 retrospective of the early amateur days of baseball, claimed that "the Atlantics of Brooklyn, Athletics of Philadelphia, Unions of Morrisania, Nationals of Washington, all derived their support from politics." The *Brooklyn Eagle* called the Pastimes of Brooklyn "the City Hall Club" for its connection to municipal affairs in Brooklyn.

The political connections were not limited to the New York area. Another politician, John Morrisey, a congressman and state senator from Troy, New York, controlled that town's Haymakers, who purported to be simple "farm boys." They were not. Morrisey was also not a simple politician. He was a gambler of the first order, who would put significant amounts of cash on the line betting on his "first nine."

Federal government clerks formed the Potomac club in the District of Columbia in the summer of 1859. Later that year, a second club of government clerks, the prominent Nationals, received the financial support of the Treasury Department. Arthur Pue Gorman was the Nationals' club president and would later become a United States senator. He held a powerful position in Treasury during the mid-1860s and used the prospects of a government job to attract and retain the best players for his club. The two government teams played each other on the back lawn of the White House on what is now the Ellipse. In 1867, the Nationals club was the first eastern team to travel west of the Alleghenies to spread the gospel of the new game. (Of course, the players continued to draw their federal paychecks while they were "abroad.") Thousands came (at fifty cents admission) to see their local heroes take on the famed Nationals.

On August 30, 1865, President Andrew Johnson greeted the Atlantics of Brooklyn at the White House. According to the *Brooklyn Eagle*, "he took each one of the party by hand." He apologized for not seeing them play, but "[p]ublic duties denied me that privilege." The president had obviously been briefed on the outcome of the Atlantics' match against the Nationals:

THE PRESIDENT: You defeated our boys handsomely.

REV. MR. CRANE: Not so badly, sir; it was the best fielding of the year.

THE PRESIDENT: Perhaps they may have better luck next time. Gentlemen, I thank you for the honor of your visit.

The *Eagle* was obviously correct when it concluded: "Baseball is now the rage in Washington." The following year, on September 13, 1866, in Washington, D.C., President Johnson did attend a game, where the local champion Nationals faced the visiting Brooklyn Excelsiors. Over 7,000 were in attendance. It would not be the last match attended by the chief executive, even as he fought against impeachment in the Senate.

In late August 1867, Johnson entertained a visit to the White House by the New York Mutuals, Boss Tweed's club. The president used the occasion to declare baseball to be "the National Game." He then attended the August 26,

1867, game between the Mutuals and the Nationals, with his entire cabinet joining in the festivities.

Politicians enjoyed distinct advantages that could benefit baseball clubs when the game became a commercial enterprise. They had inside information from city hall that might be relevant to baseball entrepreneurs. Even if they did not make policies—which they often did—they knew where land was available to erect rudimentary stadiums and, later in the century, they knew where transportation lines were going to be authorized. Well-positioned "pols" could protect their clubs against rivals. They could control licensing fees, permits, and police protection at and around the ballparks. They could control assessments for tax purposes. The advantages, of course, were not all one way. When politics evolved from an upper-class civic obligation to a career, politicians sought job security through control of a variety of factions, clubs, and associations, many of which were sports-related or sports-based. Baseball and urban politics enjoyed a close and mutually beneficial relationship.

BASEBALL PROFESSIONALISM AND THE PROMOTION OF THE CITY

We have followed baseball's evolution from athletic exercise to a competition between clubs representing various neighborhoods, work associations, and ethnic groups. Seeking victory, baseball clubs soon sacrificed localism in exchange for better players, who often had to be recruited with payments, in violation of prevailing rules. The game became a commercial venture, with spectators paying admission to watch the best players play America's game. There was one more development that would firmly set the foundation for the game as we know it today. Baseball would become national in focus, and that development came not from New York City, the game's birthplace, but from the Midwest.

The New York version of baseball spread westward beyond the Appalachians. Americans enjoyed a new mobility as a result of the spreading railroad, and students and others who watched or played the game on the East Coast brought it home to the Midwest. That was how the "regulation game" came to Cincinnati in 1860, and within the decade the Queen City would take the lead in establishing baseball as an openly professional commercial enterprise.

Clubs across the Midwest followed the lead of the New York clubs. They sought out competition against same-city clubs and teams representing nearby municipalities. Large urban centers, such as Chicago and Cincinnati, moved to the next stage by recruiting the best players to represent them on the field of play. It was Cincinnati that first recruited the finest talent nationwide. Ultimately, in 1876 it would be a Chicago businessman and member of the city's board of trade, William Hulbert, who would devise the structure for an eight-team National League of professional baseball clubs.

Throughout the Midwest, cities challenged other cities to baseball matches. That was why Cincinnati formed its first club, in response to a challenge from nearby Dayton, Kentucky. City pride was at stake, and businesses and government would provide the needed financial and other civic support. Hundreds joined as members of the Cincinnati club, but only the "first nine" would play in intercity competition. Prevailing at this manly sport offered bragging rights, an important American currency. City officials also were quick to identify that political capital was to be made in the ceremonial roles they were given at the games, and the local baseball clubs became surrogates for community aspirations and self-worth. When local notables appeared in the crowd, the game became an endorsed activity.

The eastern clubs, experienced in playing the game, traveled widely as self-proclaimed ambassadors of baseball. They came to teach those in the hinterland who had not yet developed the skills and techniques needed to play the game at the highest level. In the 1860s, the Excelsiors of Brooklyn toured over a thousand miles throughout Upstate New York. These travels were financed by the nonplaying honorary members of the clubs, as well as by government and business entities. The players on the Nationals of Washington traveled on their government paychecks as clerks at the Treasury Department. The press reported that as a direct result of the tours there was an intense outbreak of "baseball fever."

All fans of baseball history know about the legendary Cincinnati Red Stockings. Their 1869 undefeated national tour was a significant milestone in the development of the national game. The club traveled 12,000 miles and played before a total audience of more than 200,000 spectators. The civic and political leaders of the Queen City, including the city's political boss and publisher of the *Cincinnati Enquirer*, John R. McLean, appreciated the commercial value of sponsoring a baseball team of the best professionals available in order to raise the visibility of the "western" city. They hired Harry Wright to lead their initiative, and he would perform splendidly.

Harry Wright was the English-born son of a professional cricket player who came to America to play his father's game for the St. George's Cricket Club of Staten Island, just southwest of Manhattan. Wright also enjoyed the new American game of baseball, playing for the Knickerbockers for a while before taking a paid position in 1865 in Cincinnati at the Union Cricket Club. The next year, he was recruited to lead the Cincinnati Base Ball Club. He hired his brother George, a brilliant shortstop, and a "first nine" of the finest ballplayers in the nation to join the club at substantial salaries.

The Red Stockings are often referred to as the first all-professional team, but they were not alone. A number of other established clubs entered the 1869 season with a full payroll of open professionals. Until 1869, pay for playing baseball was never openly acknowledged. With the 1869 season as a watershed, the game divided between those clubs who would maintain the old commitment to amateurism and those who saw the business potential of professional entertainment. By 1869, professionals had taken over the National Association and elected James N. Kern, a United States marshal, as president.

Money meant a commitment to top-level competition, and Cincinnati demonstrated how much success could be achieved. Harry Wright wrote that the club served as "ambassadors for the city." As one Queen City citizen said: "I don't know anything about baseball or town ball, nowadays, but it does me good to see those fellows. They've done something to add to the glory of our city. They advertised the city, advertised us, sir, and helped our business." They visited the White House, President Grant calling them a "Cinderella" team whose standard of play was high. Although the 1870 tour proved almost as successful on the field, the city fathers had tired of funding the professional team. Club members declined to authorize the $5,000 needed to maintain the professional nine and disbanded the team after the season ended. The Red Stockings tour, however, and its recruitment of the best players nationwide, had converted the game from the local to a national stage.

Urban politicians like Boss Tweed and baseball players like Harry Wright worked in tandem to grow the sport of baseball for their own particular purposes. For Tweed, the game further solidified his hold on the public spotlight. For Wright and his cohorts, the game became a source of recognition and remuneration. Their purposes meshed, and in the process they converted a pastoral pastime into a commercial enterprise that would capture American imagination and aspirations.

At first, Chancellor Adolf Hitler opposed hosting the 1936 Olympic Games, a prize he inherited from the Weimar regime. Joseph Goebbels, Hitler's reich minister for public enlightenment and propaganda, convinced Der Fuehrer that the Games offered a public relations bonanza for the Third Reich. The Nazi Olympic Games epitomized the unity of politics and sports. Sports had become simply another weapon in Hitler's growing arsenal. *AP Images*

It is true that the Olympic Games are not political in spirit or in idea, but this gathering of men and women of all countries sounds a political note in a higher sense. There is afforded here an opportunity for all, beyond all political differences and differentiations, to get to know one another and thus to promote understanding among nations. —*Joseph Goebbels*

This whole thing is not a question of politics. It is a question of humanity. —*Judge Jeremiah T. Mahoney*

[2]
THE NAZI OLYMPIC TRIUMPH

Joseph Goebbels was the voice of the Nazi regime from 1933 to 1945. As the reich minister for public enlightenment and propaganda, he orchestrated the Third Reich's public relations. Every aspect of German life and culture came under his vigilant gaze. A brutal and psychotic bureaucrat, Goebbels stood at Adolf Hitler's right hand through the rise and fall of one of the world's most savage regimes. He also presided over Nazi Germany's magnificent nonmilitary success, the 1936 Olympic Games.

The American memory of the events of the 1936 Olympics focuses on the refusal of the dictator Adolf Hitler to shake hands with the triumphant African American track-and-field star, twenty-two-year-old Jesse Owens, after he had won four gold medals at the Olympiastadion. Hitler's vision of exalting Aryan physical prowess on the world stage was dashed on the cinder track by the son of a sharecropper and the grandson of a slave. Goebbels had planned the two-week Berlin spectacle as a demonstration to the international community of the commanding strength of character and physical fitness of the German people, the foundation for the Nazis' plan for world military domination. Alas, as far as the Great Leader and his reich minister were concerned, it was the

American athletes who conquered, in particular the black track athletes, who Hitler referred to pejoratively as America's "black auxiliaries."

The only problem with this politicized recollection of the Eleventh Olympiad is that it does not reflect what actually occurred. History is written by the victors, and the Allies ultimately triumphed over the Nazi menace in the 1939–1945 world conflict. Jesse Owens did win a quartet of medals, but it was the German Olympic team that bested the Americans in the total medal count by a substantial number. Owens recalled that Hitler did congratulate him—Owens claimed to have carried a photograph of the event in his wallet for years—while President Franklin Roosevelt never sent Owens a letter of congratulations. Even if Hitler did not personally shake Owens's hand, many saw him salute the great athlete to acknowledge his achievements. Hitler certainly did not snub Owens. Owens later told author William L. Shirer: "It strikes me, he's a good sport. I like his smile." Upon his return to the United States, Owens rejected any bad feeling: "Mr. Hitler had to leave the stadium early, but after winning I hurried up to the radio booth. When I passed near the Chancellor he arose, waved his hand at me and I waved back at him. I think the writers showed bad taste in criticizing the man of the hour in Germany. There was absolutely no discrimination at all."

The German crowds had wildly cheered Owens, even upon his initial arrival in Germany long before his first event on the track. The crowds chanted "Yes-say," as his first name was pronounced in German. In the Olympic stadium, he received the greatest ovation of his career, one that frankly shocked the Nazis, in particular Goebbels, who diligently propagated the belief that blacks were primitive and subhuman.

The 1936 Berlin Olympic Games and the Bavarian Winter Olympics held earlier that year in Garmisch-Partenkirchen outside Munich were grand propaganda successes for the Nazis, the greatest peaceful triumphs of their twelve-year barbaric rule. Spectators demonstrated their adoration for their fuehrer, and the world took notice. The Nazis purposefully and successfully used sports to achieve their political goals. For ten days in February and two weeks in August, Germany was a cheerful, friendly, and happy place—a Potemkin village skillfully designed by Goebbels to deceive the world. However, the United States ambassador to Berlin, William Dodd, was not fooled. He wrote to the State Department: "It is no exaggeration to say that the Jewish population awaits with fear and trembling the termination of the Olympic period which has vouchsafed them a certain respite against molestation."

The modern Olympic Games had always contained a political subtext. All participating nations in the Olympic movement, in particular those that hosted the Olympics, used sports to achieve social and political objectives both at home and on the international stage. It was the Nazis, however, who perfected the brand, and, in the process, vanquished their athletic opponents and achieved their political goals beyond all expectations.

THE PREFACE TO THE GERMAN OLYMPIAD

The Third Reich had inherited the opportunity to host the Eleventh Olympiad from the Weimar Republic, which in 1931 had been awarded the event in recognition of Germany's new, albeit short-lived, democratic regime and its reintegration into the world community of nations after the Great War. However, as late as 1932, before he gained power, Hitler had denounced the modern Olympic movement as a "ploy of Freemasons and Jews." He would not allow Aryan purity to be sullied on a level playing field littered with athletes from degenerate races. Hitler favored German-only competitions and communal athletic demonstrations of physical fitness rather than universal festivals where subhumans could exercise their animal instincts.

Somewhat belatedly, however, Nazi autocrats came to appreciate the potential political power of sports as a tool for organizing and motivating society and preparing generations of young men for the war to come. The Nazi ethos had evolved: "Athletes and sport," a Nazi publication stated, "are the preparatory school of the political will in the service of the state." Nazi minister of sport Hans von Tschammer und Osten saw sports as a "way to weed out the weak, Jewish, and other undesirables." At the same time, the Olympic Games would provide a tool for organizing the German masses. The festival in Berlin would allow Hitler to prove to the world his peaceful intentions. Many would be fooled by the ruse.

After Hitler assumed power in January 1933—appointed chancellor in accordance with German law by the president of the republic, Paul von Hindenburg—Goebbels convinced him that the Olympics offered the new regime a world stage on which to demonstrate the efficacy of the Nazis' political and racist vision. The huddled masses around the globe would learn how the Nazis had eliminated poverty in Germany and renewed Teutonic pride and patriotism. The propaganda value of the project could not be denied.

There were also significant domestic benefits to the Olympics. The Nazis had been a radical fringe group only a few years earlier and, after dramatic successes at the polls, had captured a major political state. Their consummate political stroke, however, raised confirming doubts within Germany. Could the Nazis operate a government, especially when a majority of Germans had never voted for the National Socialists? The organization of the Olympic Games would put to rest any such misgivings and offer a rallying point for the nation. The Olympics would provide a larger and longer version of the orgies of pagan pageantry that the Nazis conducted annually at Nuremberg.

Hitler particularly found irresistible the prospect of building grandiose stadiums as concrete symbols of the growing power of Nazi hegemony. These projects would be the first steps in rebuilding Berlin as the capital of the world, and Hitler could show off the grandeur of his vision. Hitler proclaimed that sports were now a national priority: "If Germany is to stand host to the entire world, her preparations must be complete and magnificent." In the Nazi handbook *Sport and State*, published in 1934, Hitler announced the controlling principles: "In the Third Reich it is not only knowledge which counts, but also strength, and our absolute ideal for the future would be a human being of radiant mind and magnificent body, that people may again find a way to riches through money and property." The Olympics would serve well as a public works project, a national rallying point, and an international show of Germany's re-emergence as a world power.

The Reich committed a substantial sum for the Olympic spectacle, 20,000,000 reichsmarks—about $8 million—to fulfill Hitler's vision of greatness. (At the same time, the Olympics were not Hitler's primary investment. The Reich spent billions of marks on rearmament from 1933 to 1935.) Expenditures on the Olympic festival were marks well spent. The propaganda impact was a bonanza. The Nazis built facilities that long outlasted their regime.

The Olympic Games would focus the world's attention on the Nazis' success in drawing Germany out of the Great Depression through discipline, order, and strength. All who came to watch the Olympics—and more than a million would attend—received a booklet about Berlin with an introduction by Goebbels that plainly presented the leitmotif that these games were about Nazism: "National Socialism as an idea has cast a spell upon the whole world. . . . May all foreign visitors to this city, in the rhythm of her life, in the tempo of her work, and in the enthusiasm with which she devotes herself to Adolf Hitler and his idea, catch a breath of the spirit with which the new Germany is inspired."

The glory of the sports festival would match Hitler's aspirations for world influence. It would bring the fuehrer the respect and prestige he sought from those who mattered most, the world's influential classes, which had disparaged Germany in the wake of its defeat in the Great War. All would witness how the product of Aryan breeding and training would excel in the Olympic Games. This, according to the Nazis, "would contribute substantially towards further understanding among the nations of the world."

The Nazis' clenched military fist clothed in the velvet glove of Olympic semblance would frighten off potential enemies and procure like-minded friends for the regime. Uniformed Sturmabteilung (SA) and Schutzstaffel (SS) troops were everywhere at both the Winter and Summer Olympics, keeping a watchful eye on both Germans and visitors. Few who attended the sports festival would leave unimpressed by the potent militarism of the regime. On the forthcoming battlefield, Nazi gloves would come off. Meanwhile, the Olympics would divert the public's attention while Hitler furthered his preparations for war.

Through an absurdist contortion of modern fables, Minister Goebbels had tied the German *Volk* of the twentieth century to the ancient Greeks of legend, especially to the militaristic Spartans. The ultimate decay of the Greek nation, Goebbels insisted, stemmed directly from its failure to maintain and protect racial purity, a fault that the Nazis would not emulate. Publicly, Goebbels repeatedly insisted that the Berlin Olympic Games would stand "entirely above politics" when in fact it was blatant politics at its most dramatic and proficient. Although Germany's official Olympic committee was supposed to remain independent of political influence, under the precepts of the Nazi regime sports were simply another arena of politics. Bruno Malitz, a Berlin sports official, explained: "For us National Socialists, politics belongs in sports—first because politics guides everything, and second, because politics is already inherent in sports. . . . Politics belongs in sports. It is logical to expel the Jew from German sports activities. There is no such thing as a Jewish German."

The Nazi regime was publicly committed to the persecution of its internal enemies, but with the choreographed display of open and friendly welcome to the athletes of all nations, the German Olympics would offer the Nazis the moment they sought to counterbalance any negative perceptions. Olympic attendees, both athletes and visitors, would return home as ambassadors of a good feeling for the Third Reich and its "will for peace." The Germans, who attended the Olympic events in great numbers, would feel pride in the Nazi slogan: "One nation, one people, one leader."

CREATING THE OLYMPICS

At Olympia in the Kingdom of Elis, the ancient Greeks held a quadrennial athletic and cultural festival that lasted from 776 BC until almost AD 400. For more than a millennium, Hellenic male athletes gathered to participate in foot races of various lengths, boxing, wrestling, chariot racing, and other field events. Victors received wreaths of olive branches and substantial monetary awards. (None were amateurs, however; the nonpayment of athletes would be a modern Victorian affectation.) The word "athletics" derives from the Greek verb *athleuo*, meaning variously "I struggle, I contest, I suffer." The ancient games, the site of legendary exploits, offered arduous tests of manhood on fields where many participants suffered and some even died.

One person who purported to study the ancient Greek experience was Pierre Fredy, Baron de Coubertin, a French aristocrat who fashioned himself a scholar and an intellectual in the field of sports education. His version of those ancient halcyon events was a rather dubious one, albeit well intentioned. He chose to interpret the ancient games as the peaceful pursuit of human perfection by young men interested only in sports and not in personal gain or national pride. Sports, Coubertin thought, would bind nations together, and wars would end while nations participated in the games. His humanistic vision of international sports was based on a utilitarian concept of world peace. If athletes could be brought together as was done at Olympia, there would be joyous competition devoid of strife. Athletes would come to the games only to participate and compete rather than to win. Coubertin's version of ancient history was a naive, albeit inspirational, illusion.

Coubertin's skewed portrait contorted what actually happened at the ancient Greek games. Each athlete in antiquity wanted nothing less than victory and the spoils his accomplishments would produce. He would bend the rules to triumph. Victors were well compensated by their city-states, receiving cash rewards, tax exemptions, free meals for life at public expense, front-row seats at the theater, and generous pensions. The events of the Olympics were not secular festivals; they were essentially part of a religious spectacle dedicated to Zeus. (Halfway through the games, one hundred oxen were sacrificed to the god, who was thought to have watched the games from atop a nearby mountain.) The victors, announced by the trumpets of the heralds, wore the olive wreath crowns of Zeus, which denoted the athletes' semidivine and mythologized status. Odes were written in their honor, and victory statues erected to memorialize their fame.

The monetary prizes at the Greek games were substantial. Victors were welcomed home with celebrations in their honor, escorted into their cities by heralds and hundreds of chariots. They received barrels of pure olive oil. Runners-up, however, received no prizes; no "silver" or "bronze" medals were awarded. Coubertin would have been dismayed: in ancient Greece, only winning mattered.

City-states shared in the victors' pride. Any *polis* that could boast about its athletic champions could claim prominence on the Greek Peninsula. However, much like present-day professional athletes, Olympic champions would change their affiliation for the right price. Greek historian Pausanias, in his *Guide to Greece*, discussed one example, the case of Sotades: "Sotades at the ninety-ninth Festival was victorious in the long race and proclaimed a Cretan, as in fact he was. But at the next Festival he made himself an Ephesian, being bribed to do so by the Ephesian people. For this act he was banished by the Cretans." By the second century BC, these full-time professional athletes had formed guilds, like present-day unions, that would represent their interests. Athletes could even demand an appearance fee for agreeing to participate. The calendar of games expanded to include annual sporting events held in Athens, Delphi, and Corinth, as well as in Olympia, which remained the "pinnacle of contests," as the poet Pindar wrote in the fifth century BC. Staged in the blistering heat of mid-August with the naked male participants covered in oil, flies, and dust, the games were agony for the athletes. Spectators, however, shared in a competitive exultation, especially for the premier event, the four-horse chariot race.

The ancient games provided commercial opportunities for those who sold their wares at the events—concessionaires, artists, musicians, even poets and philosophers. The games always had a defining political context, with competing city-states using athletic victories as a surrogate measure of the value of their communities. The ancient festivals also offered city-states the opportunity to announce new political alliances. Thucydides described a one-hundred-year military treaty entered into by the Athenians, Argives, Mantineans, and Eleans that was proclaimed on a bronze Olympian pillar. Olympia also was the site of an arbitration tribunal used to settle some political disputes among Greek states. It often failed, and, as a result, war was a constant condition over the ancient Olympic millennium.

The games of the ancient Olympics and the other athletic festivals held annually in Peloponnesia fostered the preparation of each city-state for war. Athletes who trained to sprint on soft sand, throwing the discus and enduring the strain of competition, were ready for the stresses of real military battles. There is the legend that in 510 BC wrestler Milo of Croton wore his Olympic dress into battle against Sybaris, including his victory wreathes from six triumphs at Olympia. His mere appearance caused panic among his foes and ultimate victory for his home city-state.

None of this actual history of the Greek games, however, would affect Coubertin's vision. He vowed to create his own version of the venerable competition. They would be "true sport, proudly, joyfully and loyally." Coubertin had been inspired by the annual "Olympian Games" held in Shropshire, England. Dr. William Brookes had organized this athletic pageant, filled with ritual and ceremony, starting in 1859. These actual events, combined with the baron's readings about medieval chivalry, appealed to his elitist sentiments. He would devise a modern international sports festival that would be inspired by the spirit of what he called "Olympism," although it owed more to the sporting culture of the British public school system, in particular that practiced at the Rugby School in Warwickshire, than it did to the ancient Greeks.

In the early 1890s, the world was enjoying a hiatus in more than a century of almost constant warfare. Coubertin's goal was to use this interregnum to create a substitute both for calamitous conflict and sectarian strife. By the 1890s, the French defeat in the Franco-Prussian War of 1870 had receded in the public mind, and the Asian conflicts in China and between the Russians and the Japanese were a few years in the future. The baron organized an international congress on sports held at the Sorbonne in Paris in 1894, and he vowed to bring the ancient games back to life. The revived festival would be based on his motto: "The important thing at the Olympic Games is not to win, but to take part; for the essential thing in life is not to conquer, but to struggle well." Sports would be a substitute for narrow nationalism and traditional faith. As Coubertin wrote in his *Memoires Olympicques*: "For me, sport is a religion with church, dogma, ritual."

There were political problems from the start. France refused to participate in the Sorbonne meetings if the Germans were invited to attend, the first threatened boycott of the Olympics thus occurring even before the games had begun. Coubertin knew that the German *turnverein* gymnastic movement was the most advanced in the world and that without the Germans his plan would fail. Coubertin skillfully invited Baron von Rieffenstein, a German living in London, to attend in an "unofficial" capacity, and the French relented. The weeklong Sorbonne congress unanimously approved a plan for a modern sports festival imbued with the "spirit of Olympism," just as prescribed by Coubertin. The baron announced that the Olympics would be independent of politics and nationalism. State involvement with the Olympic Games, the baron warned, would bring with it "a fatal germ of impotence and mediocrity." He handpicked the members of the first International Olympic Committee. They would not represent their nations of origin, but rather the IOC members would represent the international Olympic movement as "ambassadors *from* the committee *to* their respective countries," elevating the status of the IOC above that of the countries that would dispatch athletes to the Olympics. The IOC would answer only to itself.

The IOC announced that the first modern Olympic Games would be held in 1896 in Athens, the athletic festival's ancestral homeland, an honor the Greeks had not sought and did not particularly appreciate. From the beginning, the IOC and Coubertin faced problems with their blueprint. The longtime prime minister of Greece, Charilaos Trikoupis, strongly objected to the plan. Athens simply did not have the financial resources needed to host such an event. (Trikoupis had earlier announced to the Greek parliament: "Regretfully, we are bankrupt.") Coubertin countered with an international public relations campaign accompanied by a private fund-raising effort and an end run around Trikoupis to the Greek royal family.

Prime Minister Trikoupis would become the first political casualty of the modern Olympic Games. Although he was finally convinced that Athens should host the Olympics, the country's creditors forced Trikoupis out of office in 1895. He died on March 30, 1896, one week before Coubertin's games began, as scheduled, in Athens.

Collecting a variety of events that would be held over a week, Coubertin's first modern Olympics included races of various lengths, cycling, fencing, gymnastics, rifle and pistol shooting, swimming (in the open sea), tennis, weightlifting, and wrestling. He invented the modern marathon, first run at a distance of forty kilometers. No marathon was run in ancient times, although Coubertin adopted the legend of Pheidippides, the Greek messenger, as his inspiration. Sent from the battlefield of Marathon to Athens to announce the defeat of the Persians in 490 BC, Pheidippides ran the entire distance without stopping and burst into the Athenian assembly, exclaiming "Νενικήκαμεν" (Nenikékamen: "We have won") before collapsing and dying.

Athletes from fourteen countries attended the Athens Olympic Games. Participants would receive no prize money and, under the prevailing rules of Victorian propriety, they would not have to compete in the nude as the ancient Greeks did. Politics was to be set to one side, but, of course, no one actually thought that could or would happen. After all, the athletes of the world could not compete as individuals; they were required to participate in the Athens events as members of national teams. Even at the first Olympics, American tourists were obnoxious. Observers complained about the "absurd shouts" of the spectators who had traveled from America for the contests.

General Douglas MacArthur later referred to the Olympic Games as "war without weapons." It was certainly war, but countries carried "political" weapons in an effort to slay their political opponents. The athletes would be the "soldiers." As MacArthur, president of the United States Olympic Committee in 1927–1928, later explained: "We have not come so far just to lose gracefully, but rather to win and win decisively."

The earliest modern Olympic Games included some rather unusual events. The 1900 Olympics, held in Paris as part of an international exposition, included live pigeon shooting, the only time in Olympic history that animals were killed on purpose. Leon de Lunden of Belgium won the gold medal, killing twenty-one birds. The Olympics also included Basque pelota (a form of jai-alai), ballooning, croquet, tug-of-war, and underwater swimming. Few attended the games, and the public seemed apathetic, if not totally uninterested.

In 1904, St. Louis was hosting a world's fair celebrating the centennial of the Louisiana Purchase. The Olympics joined the many attractions—including the introduction of ice cream cones, hamburgers, hot dogs, peanut butter, iced tea, and cotton candy—as simply another sideshow. The 1908 London Olympics offered the first official boycott. Irish athletes refused to attend based on Great Britain's refusal to grant independence to their homeland. The Olympics staggered through its first four unsatisfying "festivals."

By the Fifth Olympiad, in Stockholm in 1912, however, the baron's idea had finally caught the public's attention. The Stockholm Olympic Games were noteworthy both for the quality of their organization and the exchange between King Gustav and American athlete Jim Thorpe. When King Gustav told Thorpe he was the "greatest athlete in the world," Thorpe reportedly responded simply: "Thanks, King." By the time of the Stockholm Olympics, Coubertin's games had grown from the 311 athletes participating in Athens to 2,500 athletes representing twenty-eight countries.

Baron de Coubertin's invention proved to have staying power, in part because of his personal commitment to the cause. Every four years, an increasing number of national teams participated in friendly athletic competition. Peaceful internationalism, however, never replaced narrow nationalism or religious fervor. There were always disputes about the judges and complaints about the conditions, but the modern Olympics stumbled forward. The harsh reality of the World War I slaughter interrupted the Olympic Games scheduled for Berlin in 1916, and the defeated nations (Germany, Austria, Bulgaria, Turkey, and Hungary) were not invited to the 1920 or 1924 Olympics, which were held as scheduled in Antwerp and Paris.

The 1924 Paris event was the last that Coubertin would attend, as his festival moved on under new leadership. After his death in 1938, Coubertin was buried in Lausanne, Switzerland. In accordance with his last will, the International Olympic Committee removed his heart and placed it in a monument in a sacred grove in Olympia, Greece.

CONVERTING DEMOCRACY INTO DICTATORSHIP

Germany in 1933 was suffering from an economic catastrophe, civil unrest, and political upheaval. The Weimar Republic, the unstable democratic system that had ruled Germany from the end of the Great War, still commanded majority support from German citizens, but a growing minority found the platform of the National Socialist Party an attractive alternative to moderate liberalism. The leader of the Nazis, a small, mustachioed Austrian named Adolf Hitler, catalyzed utter disgust among many, but fervent adoration among his growing band of followers. Hitler and his cronies understood the importance of militancy, street violence, and public demonstrations of power. Nazi brownshirt irregulars, the party's private army, had grown in size to hundreds of thousands of men willing to be used to intimidate political and social enemies. In the presidential election of 1932, Hitler polled 37 percent of the vote in the race against Field Marshal Paul von Hindenburg and captured 230 seats in the Reichstag election. The Nazis were the largest party in Germany's parliament.

In January 1933, in an effort to still the political unrest consuming the Weimar Republic, President Hindenberg used his power as the elected leader of the republic to appoint Hitler as chancellor. With a swiftness that surprised many, Hitler used his position to nullify the power of his political opponents and institute extraordinary changes in German society. Apparently, no one believed what Hitler had written the prior decade in *Mein Kampf:* "We are enemies of democracy because we recognize that an individual genius represents at all times the best in his people and that he should be the leader. Numbers can never direct the destiny of a people. Only genius can do this. We are the deadly enemies of internationalism because nature teaches us that the purity of race and the authority of the leader alone are able to lead a nation to victory."

Hitler seized power over the German state, arresting thousands, then tens of thousands, and finally millions. He burned down the parliament building, blamed it on the Communists, and imprisoned them. There was no question in Hitler's mind who was at fault for Germany's circumstances: "[The Jew's] ultimate goal is the denaturalization, the promiscuous bastardization of other peoples, the lowering of the racial level of the highest peoples as well as the domination of his racial mishmash through the extirpation of the volkish intelligentsia and its replacement by the members of his own people."

In the March 1933 election, the Nazi Party received 44 percent of the votes, winning 288 seats in the German parliament. With the support of their conservative nationalist allies, who held fifty-two seats, the Nazis controlled a majority of the legislature. The Nazi majority was even more substantial in fact because none of the eighty-one Communist deputies were allowed to take their seats. On March 23, 1933, the parliament enacted the Enabling Act, which gave dictatorial authority to Hitler and his cabinet.

Imposing a police state based on fear and intimidation, Hitler's regime eliminated all opposition, opened concentration camps, and enacted laws that stripped Jews and other undesirables of their economic and social rights and citizenship. One of Hitler's initial acts was to ban Jews from membership in sporting organizations, a modest, but cruel, first step toward segregation, imprisonment, and eventual extermination. German democracy had created this monster, who would carry out his programs without internal or external constraints or opposition.

THE FAILED BOYCOTT

To many in the international community, participating in the Berlin Olympic Games was unthinkable. Hitler's political program was an anathema that could not be ignored or countenanced. The International Olympic Committee, however, was unwilling to wrest the Olympic Games away from a Nazified Germany. Blinded by their self-delusion that Olympism rose above nationalism and politics, the leaders of the global sports movement resisted all efforts to disassociate themselves from the Nazi evil. The Americans, led by Avery Brundage, the forty-six-year-old head of the United States Olympic Committee, thought that politics and sports could be disconnected. He was also intrigued by Hitler and his regime, and found few problems with the way the regime was treating the Jews of Germany. Brundage reported, regarding any claim of discrimination: "That question was answered by assurances from German political and sports leaders that there would be no racial, religious or political interference of any kind. I know of no reason for questioning these guarantees. In any case, Germany has nothing whatsoever to do with the management of the games. The Germans provide the facilities and make preliminary arrangements, but that is all."

Brundage was openly sympathetic to the Nazis' authoritarianism. He joked that, after all, his men's club in Chicago also excluded Jews. In that regard, his thoughts mirrored those of Count Henri Baillet-Latour, the head of the International Olympic Committee: "I am not personally fond of Jews and of the Jewish influence." It was not surprising that the leaderships of both the American and International Olympic committees were willing to take Nazi pronouncements of their benign intentions at face value even though they were blatant deceptions. In fact, General Charles Sherill of the United States Olympic Committee warned that any American boycott of the Berlin Olympics would result in a "wave of anti-Semitism" against American Jews. Apparently, under this reasoning, attending the Berlin Olympics would help the Jewish community. Under Olympic rules, it would be left to national Olympic committees of each nation to decide whether they would boycott the venomous German regime, but their leaders seemed from the start to give Berlin a chance to prove the Nazi claims of fairness and amiability.

Avery Brundage epitomized the Olympic movement post-Coubertin. A midwesterner—born in Detroit and raised in Chicago—Brundage was a self-made man who had become wealthy in the construction business. Sports were his hobby, and he aspired earnestly to become a great leader on the international sports scene. He was a staunch devotee of amateurism, attacking "forces of greed and commercialism." He warned against "evasion and chicanery" by prominent athletes: "It will be a sad and sorry day for this great land of ours when we reach the stage where we cannot even play without thinking of the ever-present dollar. . . . If we give way . . . our civilization is headed for the same decline that overtook the Greek Empire."

At first, Brundage expressed some misgivings about the prospect of holding the Olympics in the capital of Nazism. In April 1933, he wrote to the editor of the *Jewish Times* that it was his personal and unofficial opinion that the Olympics "will not be held in any country where there will be interference with fundamental Olympic theory of equality of all races." Nazi athletic officials responded to Brundage that, of course, there would be no discrimination in Germany. That assurance apparently satisfied Brundage, who promised he would visit Germany himself to make sure that the claims of anti-Semitism were groundless. Brundage vowed not to allow German or American Jews to stand in his way. As Red Smith wrote: "Although Avery was frequently wrong-headed, he could also be arrogant and condescending."

Brundage was inspired by Hitler's presence as a bulwark against the evils of communism, which he equated with World Jewry. As president of the Amateur Athletic Union (AAU) in 1928 and then as president of the United States Olympic Committee in 1929, Brundage was the most important American proponent of international amateur athletics. His work on behalf of the Nazi Olympics earned him a position on the International Olympic Committee. It was the elevation to a global platform that he had sought for years. In 1952, he achieved his career aspiration when he was elected the president of the IOC, a position he held for twenty years. Brundage ran the elite international sports organization as if it were a state of its own—perhaps better said as a state of "his" own. He was the overbearing master of athletic politics.

Despite Brundage's pronouncements in support of Hitler and his Olympic Games, the question of an American team boycott remained a live issue. An intense internal battle raged over fundamental American values, a conflict that tells us much about American politics and sports. Brundage, as the great admirer of Hitler, vehemently opposed any boycott, dismissing those who saw the event as a stage for German propaganda: "The Olympic Games belong to the athletes and not to the politicians," Brundage insisted. The athletes should not be concerned about "political issues." In fact, anyone who wanted to boycott, Brundage opined, was seeking to use sports as a political weapon. (Apparently, it never dawned on him that this was precisely the objective of Hitler and Goebbels.)

Brundage simply ignored the writings of leading Nazis, like Kurt Munch, who wrote in *Knowledge About Germany*: "Non-political, so called neutral sports-men, are unthinkable in Hitler's state." When it became apparent that politics was intertwined with the Berlin Olympics, Brundage retreated to isolationism; sport, he said, "cannot, with good grace or propriety, interfere in the internal, political, religious or racial affairs of any country or group." Finally, Brundage stated that every country has had its little problems: "Regardless in what country the Olympic games are held, there will be some group, some religion or some race which can register a protest because of the actions of the Government of the country, past or present. . . . The Olympics are an international event and must be kept free from outside interference or entanglements—racial, religious or political—if we are to achieve the main objective of spreading democracy and the high standards of amateur sport throughout the world."

As opposition to participation in the Berlin Olympic Games mobilized, Brundage even adopted the verbiage of Nazi propaganda. Opposition to the Berlin Olympics, he said, was simply "a sinister Jewish plot." Those who partici-pated in this effort were "alien agitators and their American stooges." His "study tour" of Germany in 1934 had confirmed the conclusions he had already reached: "America could learn much from Germany," he reported. "She is efficient and hard working and has spirit." He stated that the German Jewish athletes with whom he had talked were perfectly satisfied with their circumstances. In any case, any Jews the Nazis punished likely were Communists, and the amateur sports association of the United States "cannot, with good grace or propriety, in-terfere in the internal political, religious or racial affairs of any country or group."

Brundage embodied his views in a booklet released by the United States Olympic Committee, *Fair Play for American Athletes*. "Why," he asked, "shall the American athlete be made to be a martyr to a cause not his own?" Once again, he blamed the effort to boycott the Olympics on the Communists and warned the U.S. government not to interfere. Roosevelt obediently remained mute on the issue. German Jews, Brundage said, were simply of no concern to American athletes. In fact, he correctly assessed the views of most of the athletes themselves, who were totally focused on their sport and the opportu-nity the Berlin Olympics offered to excel on the international stage. Had they been asked—and they were not—they would have voted overwhelmingly to participate. Those who opposed participation were simply un-American forces spreading "malicious propaganda."

There were a few prominent American athletes who refused to participate in the Berlin Olympic Games, in particular Jewish athletes such as Milton Green, Herman Neugass, and Norman Cahners. At the time, Green held the world record in the 45-yard hurdles. Neugass, a sprinter at Tulane University, had held the world record in the 100-yard dash. Cahners ran track for Harvard University. Charlotte "Eppie" Epstein, coach of the women's Olympic swimming team, refused to participate in the Berlin Olympics. However, for the most part the athletes on the U.S. team were apolitical, including the important contingent of black athletes, unconcerned that Hitler intended to use the visiting athletes as pawns in his international political chess game.

Despite the prevailing anti-Semitism in the highest echelons of American sports officialdom, Americans were not blind to what was happening in Germany, and there was a growing cohort who wanted no part of Hitler's murderous regime. Religious leaders responded to Brundage by saying that opposition to American participation in the Berlin Olympics was not "a purely Jewish issue. It is an American issue."

After Brundage moved up to lead the United States Olympic Committee, former New York judge Jeremiah T. Mahoney replaced him as president of the Amateur Athletic Union, the track organization that would certify participants on the U.S. Olympic team. Mahoney understood that the Nazis operated a poisonous regime that sought to pillage the Olympic movement for political purposes: "Until the Nazi regime has ended, the American people will have no reason to believe that the true spirit of sportsmanship, to which the Olympic Games are devoted, can find expression in Germany." He saw Nazi promises of nondiscrimination for what they were—expedient lies—at the same time Brundage called all opposition to American participation as "treason for political reasons."

A few international figures in the sports establishment stood up to the Nazi menace. Ernest Le Jahncke, an American who was a member of the International Olympic Committee, wrote to IOC president Baillet-Latour. His letter, which was published by the *New York Times*, concluded: "Place your great talents and influence in the service of the spirit of fair play and chivalry—instead of the service of brutality, force and power. Take your rightful place in the history of the Olympics alongside of de Courbetin instead of Hitler." As a result, Baillet-Latour had Le Jahncke expelled from the IOC.

Brundage could not believe that Americans actually cared about the Jews of Germany, but the strength of the boycott movement evidenced the growing anti-Fascist sentiment in the United States. Mahoney said that America could not remain blind to the evil actions of the Nazi regime, while Brundage focused only on how the Nazis treated their Jewish athletes and whether they would welcome Jews competing from other countries. On these criteria, Brundage argued, the world should believe Nazi promises. Brundage said that no Jew had ever represented Germany in the past, suggesting that it should not be evidence of discrimination to find no Jews on Germany's team for the 1936 Olympics. In any case, concern about the general state of the Jewish community in Germany, according to Brundage, was far beyond the jurisdiction of the Olympic movement.

The controversy over the boycott of the Berlin Olympics came to a head in December 1935 when the executive committee of the Amateur Athletic Union narrowly voted against Judge Mahoney's resolution to boycott. The full conference confirmed the vote by a similar slight margin. Ultimately, the United States sent its traditionally large team to the 1936 Olympic Games. American athletes would play in Hitler's Olympics.

Similarly, the International Olympic Committee, led by President Henri Baillet-Latour, dismissed all objections to the Berlin Olympics as "political." The international Olympics movement, he said, would remain purely nonpolitical. In any case, the Nazis had repeatedly promised the IOC that the Olympics would be open to all persons without discrimination. To defeat the threatened boycott of their Olympics, the Nazis had used effective politicking combined with blatant fabrication. The leaders of the sports world naïvely fell for the Nazi duplicity, much as British prime minister Chamberlain would fall for Hitler's entreaties a few years later in Munich.

The Nazis needed one more endorsement for their Olympics to bolster their status. Baron Pierre de Coubertin, the architect of the modern Olympic movement, would serve as the ultimate vouchsafe. He had fallen on bad times, needing both recognition and money. The Nazis promised the former and supplied the latter. They promised to support Coubertin for the Nobel Peace Prize and bribed him with a half-million dollars. Although Coubertin was never nominated for the Nobel, he did receive Germany's cash. Although too ill to travel to Berlin, he sent a recorded message of support for the Berlin Olympics, lauding their organization as the product of "Hitlerian strength and discipline" serving "the Olympic ideal." The baron's remarks, his last public pronouncements, were played at the opening ceremonies.

The Western boycott movement ultimately failed as a result of a variety of influences: the naïve belief of many in the sports establishment in the separation of politics and sports, trust in the disingenuous Nazi promises, the ardent affection of some leaders for the Nazis' goals and aspirations, the personal ambition of leaders of sporting organizations, and an almost universal aversion in many countries to political confrontation of any kind. Olympic leadership enjoyed its sinecure. There was no reason why leaders of the world's sports oligarchy would be any more perceptive about the dangers of Nazism than the world's political establishment, which would value Hitler's promises until he invaded Poland. As a result, the Olympics would give Hitler exactly what he wanted and needed—recognition as a viable participant in the world's political system and legitimacy among the next generation of Germans, whom the National Socialists needed to capture for their political movement and, ultimately, to fight their wars.

THE WINTER GAMES

The Nazis' first challenge in mounting the Olympics in the Fatherland was to rebut the perception of the world's media and many world leaders that Germany oppressed and stigmatized its minorities. This would be difficult because almost from the first days of the regime in 1933, the government had systematically persecuted homosexuals, Roma, Jehovah's Witnesses, Catholics, Communists, Socialists, and other political enemies. Its primary target was Germany's 600,000 Jews.

The Nazis stripped Jews of all civil, economic, political, and social rights. By the time of the 1936 Olympic Games, the planned segregation and, ultimately, incarceration of the Jews was well under way. Although only 600,000 of the population regarded themselves as Jewish, the Nazis expanded that number to over three million as a result of the Nuremberg Laws of 1935, under which a person was defined as Jewish if one of their grandparents was Jewish. To practice some occupations, people were required to prove they had no Jewish forebears back to 1800. The Nuremberg Laws formally deprived Jews of all rights as citizens and barred Jews from marrying non-Jews. As the *New York Times* reported in November 1936 in answer to the question of how these laws affected Jews in their daily lives:

> The answer must be: In every aspect of their daily existence and in every function, political, social, economic and private, which goes to make up the life of

man. No non-Aryan . . . can be a civil servant, a judge, a teacher, a professor; he may not be admitted as a lawyer or as a doctor, nor become a journalist or publisher; nor be employed in a public orchestra or theater or film studio; or be apprenticed to an Aryan firm. All municipal employment is closed to him, and so are all semi-official organizations, such as gas and electric companies, insurance companies, banks and railways; all forms of public welfare work; all forms of agriculture . . . ; all domestic service in Aryan households; all employment in Aryan firms, factories or shops.

For the most part, the Nazis successfully abated their public anti-Jewish policies during a brief period before the Winter Olympics, at least to an extent sufficient to fool the world. Held at the Bavarian mountain resort towns of Garmisch and Partenkirchen outside Munich—"Ga-Pa," as the region was called—the Winter Olympics would provide the dress rehearsal for the summer spectacle planned for Berlin. The Nazis were able to temper (although not without difficulty) the rabid anti-Semitism of the populace and control the public vitriol, if only for a fortnight.

The regime carried through with its cosmetic changes. It ordered the removal of all anti-Jewish signs. It removed *Der Stürmer*, the most extreme rabid anti-Semitic newspaper, from the newsstands. Garbage was removed from the streets, and buildings were painted. Jews visiting the Olympic Games were to be "treated as politely as Aryan guests." (These official orders made plain, however, that "the fundamental attitude of the German people toward Judaism remains unchanged.")

The Nazi plan of deception was a particular challenge in the Bavarian region of the Reich known for its virulent anti-Semitism. IOC President Baillet-Latour confronted Hitler directly to fulfill his promise to remove the racist signage, and Hitler agreed to have them "purged." At the same time in 1936, however, the towns of Garmisch and Partenkirchen had publicly pledged to make their towns "Jew-free." Throughout the Winter Olympics, the streets of both towns were filled with men in army uniforms, and the ss served as the official Olympic security force.

Despite the best efforts of the Nazi regime, however, the world's press had long recognized that the policies of Nazi Germany were despicable and that Hitler's rule was brutal and absolute. The focus of reporting on the Olympic festivities, however, was firmly on sports rather than on the oppression of

German citizens. Strangely, many outsiders found the government's success at ameliorating its virulent campaign against Jews to be propitious. If the Nazis could turn their hate on and off, then, perhaps, its political promises could be believed because the regime had the political power to carry out ameliorative policies. Of course, the Nazis also had the arrogance to change their minds, as the world would soon learn.

The "Ga-Pa" Olympics were a triumph of sports. Hitler and his entourage of Goering, Goebbels, and various other notable Nazis attended the events and bathed in the adoration of the crowds. The high point of the festival was the performances of Sonja Henie, the Norwegian figure skater. Hitler saw Henie as symbolizing Aryan womanhood. He would have been shocked to learn about her later affair with American black boxing champion Joe Louis.

The athletes who participated in the Winter Olympics remained apolitical, just as the Nazis wanted. Hitler even allowed a token Jew, Rudi Ball, to play on the German hockey team. Ball had returned from exile at the Nazis' request in exchange for a promise to allow him and his parents to depart Germany after the Olympics. It was one promise the Nazis actually kept.

As the Winter Olympics ended and the medals were awarded, Hitler could feel pleased with the effort. Germany had declared it was central to the world of both sports and politics. No one could contest that claim. Hitler had demonstrated that he was a world leader and that Germany was a hospitable and friendly place for visitors. He had diminished anxiety about his political intentions while diverting the attention of the world's press. Of course, Hitler's program of persecution continued unabated even as the skiers and bobsledders sped down the mountains of Bavaria.

THE CONTEXT

During the hiatus between the 1936 Winter and Summer Olympic Games, Hitler proceeded with his plan to remilitarize the Rhineland in violation of the Versailles Treaty, which had ended the Great War. Hitler used the positive Olympic experience as part of his contorted argument in support of remilitarization. He explained that the French, who rightfully were most concerned about the military move, had been "able to see that the German people had undergone an internal transformation in their thinking" when the French sent their team to compete at the Winter Olympics. Hitler explained that his

March 1936 Rhineland military action was somehow one of "reconciliation," a remarkable and twisted ruse. Neither France nor Britain would raise arms against Hitler's action as he hid behind the façade of the Olympic festival. Everyone at Ga-Pa had been filled with such gemütlichkeit that no one was ready to call Hitler's bluff.

The Western powers accepted Hitler's audacious military action in reoccupying the Rhineland. Hitler knew the troop movement could lead to war, and he was not yet ready to launch the frontal attack that would occur in three years. The commitment of just one French division could have easily repulsed the German advance into the Rhineland. Yet, the memory of the Great War was still fresh in the minds of politicians in Paris and London, and appeasement seemed the more prudent course. Few of the world's leaders had great affection for Germany, but fewer still wanted a resumption of hostilities. Hitler's gamble had paid off. On March 29, 1936, in a national plebiscite, 98.79 percent of the German electorate voted approval of Hitler's action.

An unexpected, but welcomed, sports victory also intervened between the Winter and Summer Olympics. A Nazi favorite—although not a member of the party—heavyweight boxer Max Schmeling, knocked out American Joe Louis on June 19, 1936, in New York's Yankee Stadium. Goebbels played the victory as a triumph for the regime and for Aryan superiority. (Two years later, as we shall see, Louis would return the favor, knocking out Schmeling in the first round. This time Goebbels was silent as to its racial implications.) Hitler was at the height of his international popularity as some countries of the world hoped, without any basis in fact, that the festivities of the Olympics fulfilled the fuehrer's genuine aspirations. The games, however, were just part of Germany's political maneuvering.

While the world's athletes prepared to come to Berlin to contest for Olympic medals, nations looked on in anguish at the events in Spain, where a civil war offered portents of the world conflict to come. In July 1936, as Jesse Owens triumphed at the Summer Olympics, the Associated Press proclaimed that all of Europe feared the Spanish conflict could grow into a "war of dictatorship against liberal socialism." Even the desire to insulate his Olympic Games from reality could not keep the reichfuehrer from aligning with Generalissimo Francisco Franco's Nationalist forces and participating in the slaughter. With the world's athletes prepared to travel to Germany, Hitler's Berlin Olympics would go on as scheduled.

THE TORCH RELAY

Each edition of the modern Olympics invented new "traditions" that had no ancient antecedents. The inaugural Olympics in Athens commenced with the release of pigeons. Baron de Coubertin devised the five interlocking Olympic rings in 1912, and they were first used at the Antwerp Olympics of 1920, where a new Olympic Oath was introduced. The Dutch invented the use of the Olympic flame for the Amsterdam Olympics of 1928. In 1932, Los Angeles built an Olympic village for the athletes, who previously had to live in cheap hotels or stay with friends. The Nazis would add to the list in a way that plainly signaled their intentions of conquest.

Part of the Nazis' political mythology included the fabricated ties between ancient Hellenic civilization and the modern Aryans. Nazi pseudohistorians traced the origin of the Germanic tribes to the hills of the Greek states, preferring to place their origin in warlike Sparta rather than democratic Athens. In convincing Hitler that Olympism was a propaganda bonanza, Goebbels emphasized that it would allow the Nazis to demonstrate their movement's roots in ancient Greece. Goebbels then co-opted a central Olympic symbol—the flame—as the centerpiece of a torch relay that would symbolize the "spiritual bond" between Greece and Germany. Three thousand runners would carry the fire from Olympia to Berlin along a route that included all the countries Hitler would conquer in the coming years. Lining the Olympic roadway, Nazi sympathizers signaled their allegiance to the Reich with shouts of "Heil Hitler" accompanied by raised arm salutes. Finally, in the Olympic Stadium, the final runner passed the torch of antiquity to the modern inheritors of the tradition, representatives of the Nazi regime. The torch relay was another Nazi triumph. Hitler could claim, as the Olympics were about to begin: "The sportive, knightly battle awakens the best human characteristics. It doesn't separate, but unites the combatants in understanding and respect. It also helps to connect the countries in the spirit of peace. That's why the Olympic Flame should never die."

THE SUMMER SPECTACLE

The Associated Press reported on August 5, 1936: "Der Fuehrer joined in terrific applause accorded the American ace [Jessie Owens] whose performances now have thrilled upwards of 300,000 spectators three straight days." On this world stage, the values of the Nazi regime would be applauded as well, even as the regime tightened the noose around its internal enemies and prepared its military for action against its foreign foes. *Der Agriff*, the Nazi newspaper, had cautioned its readers: "We must be more charming than the Parisians, more easygoing than the Viennese, more vivacious than the Romans, more cosmopolitan than London and more practical than New York." Berlin was ablaze with flags and bunting, with the German flag displayed in abundance. Under Hitler's laws, Jews were prohibited from displaying the German flag, but nothing prevented them from flying the Olympic banner, and they did so gladly in defiance of Hitler's yoke.

Most remember the 1936 Olympics because of the remarkable gold medal performances of Jesse Owens, likely the greatest track star of all time. Born James Cleveland Owens in Oakville, Alabama, the youngest of ten children, Owens grew up in Cleveland, where his elementary school teacher nicknamed him "Jesse." (Responding to her question as to his name, he said "J. C. Owens," which became simply "Jesse.") A brilliant high school athlete, Owens set world records even before matriculating at Ohio State University. There he demonstrated his world-class form. As Grantland Rice later wrote: "Jesse was as smooth as the west wind." He would run effortlessly at record speed.

In the course of one hour at the Big Ten Conference championship meet in Ann Arbor in 1935, Owens, the "Buckeye Bullet," set world records for the broad jump, the 220-yard dash, and the 220-yard low hurdles. He also equaled the world mark for the 100-yard dash, despite his usual poor start. His mild manner and deferential demeanor made it difficult for others not to like him. Avoiding politics—a survival strategy followed by most blacks in the 1930s—Owens had not participated in the debate about a boycott of the Nazi Olympics. He did not seek to be a leader of any cause, except one—personal excellence in track and field. His tone was one of conciliation rather than confrontation. He was an easy choice for the United States Olympic team.

Owens almost did not achieve his four gold medals in Berlin. The year before the Olympics, he was not even the fastest man in the world at his premier event, the 100-yard dash. That honor went to Eulace Peacock, a track-and-field athlete from Union, New Jersey, who had bested Owens in seven of the ten races in which they both competed prior to the Olympics. Peacock also outjumped Owens in the broad jump. Peacock, however, suffered a bad right hamstring injury in April 1936 and lost to Owens at the Olympic trials on Randall's Island in New York City.

Owens was not scheduled to run as part of the United States 4×100-meter relay team. The day before the race, Lawson Robertson, the track coach at the University of Pennsylvania, replaced Marty Glickman and Sam Stoller with Owens and Ralph Metcalf. Glickman and Stoller were the only two Jews on the U.S. track team, and United States Olympic Committee Chairman Avery Brundage, concerned about offending Hitler, had ordered their replacement. Jesse Owens spoke up for his two teammates, but Dean Cromwell, who was the track coach at the University of Southern California, snapped back: "You'll do as you're told." Glickman responded that there would be a "lot of criticism" back in America for removing the only two Jews. Cromwell responded: "We'll take our chances."

In the Olympic stadium in Berlin, Owens needed more good fortune to prevail. He was one foul away from elimination in the broad jump (now called the long jump) when, it is said, Carl "Luz" Long, a member of the German team, suggested to him that he stay on the safe side by marking a takeoff point several inches before the takeoff board. Long had already set an Olympic record in the preliminaries, and he was Owens' chief adversary in the competition. Following Long's advice, Owens easily qualified and went on to win the gold medal, while Long took the silver. Owens later commented: "It took a lot of courage for him to befriend me in front of Hitler. . . . You can melt down all the medals and cups I have, and they wouldn't be a plating on the twenty-four karat friendship that I felt for Luz Long at that moment." Long would be killed in 1943 in the Battle of San Pietro in Italy.

Later, reflecting on the Olympics, Hitler commented: "The Americans should have been ashamed of themselves for allowing their medals to be won by Negroes." It is true that athletes of color performed with distinction in Berlin, but their performance bred American national pride and not shame. While the Olympics belonged to Owens, there were eighteen African Americans on the U.S. team, triple the number who had competed for the United States in the 1932 Los Angeles Olympics. African American athletes won fourteen medals, nearly one-fourth of the fifty-six medals awarded the U.S. team in all events. They dominated the popular track-and-field events. (In addition, thirteen Jews won medals at the Nazi Olympics, including six Hungarians. There is no evidence that the fuehrer knew about this participation by people his regime had officially labeled as "vermin.") Arthur Daley, writing a year-end summary in the *New York Times*, commented: "What in the world ever happened to those white Aryans?" Others were not as kind regarding American black athletes. America's premier sportswriter, Grantland Rice, referred to the African American track stars as "our Ethiopian phalanx."

The track-and-field events in Berlin offered the crowd a collection of exciting races, from the 100-meter sprint to the marathon. The U.S. swimming and diving team performed well, sharing medals with the Japanese men and Dutch swimmer Hendrika Masterbroek, who won three gold and one silver medal.

As the events in Berlin unfolded, it was apparent that Hitler was the real star of his own Olympics, and he took full advantage of the event to wage war through the peaceful means of the Olympic festival. The German team was composed mainly of members of the Wehrmacht, the German military. (Even the pigeons released during the opening ceremonies had belonged to the German military.) The Olympic festival also included cultural presentations throughout the city of Berlin that demonstrated German renown in science, music, and the arts. The ancient Olympic Games had included contests in poetry, music, and eloquence. For the Nazi Olympics, however, Hitler did not want any competition that might risk Germany's preeminence. Hitler's well-known fanaticism was nowhere to be found, only German proficiency in organization. The Americans who had traveled to Berlin thoroughly enjoyed the festivities, and they were said to have been bemused by Hitler's moustache. The Olympics were Germany at its best, presenting a rosy and cultured picture to the world.

The German team competed with excellence before their fuehrer. Overall, the German team amassed eighty-nine medals, thirty-three of them gold, far outpacing every other country's total. Some performances were truly remarkable. Arthur Daley wrote for the *New York Times* that "the mere presence of Herr Hitler was enough to give any Reich athlete inspiration wings to do things he had never even dreamed of doing before." Lieutenant Konrad Freiherr von Wangenheim, an equestrian, completed the cross-country run, then broke his collarbone in a fall on the steeplechase course, part of a three-day event. He remounted his horse Kurfurst and finished the thirty-two obstacles remaining on the course that day. During the following day's show jumping, his horse fell on him. He returned to the saddle and completed the course. The German team won the gold medal. Eight years later, on the Eastern Front, Wangenheim was captured and hanged by the Soviets.

HITLER'S GREAT SPECTACLE

Goebbels had been correct in his political analysis from the beginning. The 1936 Olympics offered the Third Reich an unprecedented opportunity to positively affect world public opinion on the eve of Hitler's military adventures. It would also give the Nazis the tool to further mobilize German youth in support of their extremist regime. The success of the 1936 Olympics combined with Hitler's remarkable success in reoccupying the Rhineland without a shot being fired left the German populace enchanted by their fuehrer. They were bewitched by his bombastic bluster, his combativeness, and his prophet-like presence. The Olympics secured the prestige of the three-year-old Third Reich, and the biggest star of the Olympic Games was Adolf Hitler.

Author Thomas Wolfe wrote about the greatness the regime had shown: "The games were overshadowed competitions to which other nations had sent their chosen teams. They become, day after day, an orderly and overwhelming demonstration in which the whole of Germany had been schooled and disciplined. It was as if the games had been chosen as a symbol of the new collective might, a means of showing to the world in concrete terms what this new power had come to be."

The International Olympic Committee was also duly impressed with the Nazi Olympics. They demonstrated German efficiency in organizing such large-scale events. The sports facilities were awe-inspiring. The IOC immediately awarded Germany the 1940 Winter Olympic Games, an event that never occurred because of the intervention of World War II. In 1937, Hitler told Albert Speer, his architect, that after the 1940 Tokyo Summer Olympics, all future Olympic Games would be held in Germany, likely centered in a 400,000-person stadium he would build in Nuremberg. Albert Speer wrote: "Hitler was exulting over the harmonious atmosphere that prevailed. . . . International animosity toward Nazi Germany was plainly a thing of the past."

The successes of the Nazi Olympics were a glorious affirmation of Nazi dominance in Germany and foretold its successful domination of the world—at least for a few years. The Nazis used the Olympics as if it was a propaganda film, carefully staging and inventing events to perpetuate the fundamental dogma of the regime. The Nazis' official photographer, Leni Riefenstahl, recorded (and at times re-created) every glorious moment of the Olympic Games for her film *Olympia*, which would open in April 1938 as Hitler began his final march toward war. An instrument of propaganda itself, the film offered a lasting portrayal of the Olympics, with different versions tailored for distribution. Within Germany, the film was heavy on Hitler's godly visage, further solidifying the fuehrer's hold on his populace. Internationally, the film was recut to emphasize the Nazis' subterfuge about peaceful aspirations. The *New York Times* saw in the Olympic Games Hitler's devotion to peace, a "new viewpoint from which to regard the Third Reich." In its 1936 end-of-the-year review, the *Times* proclaimed: "The Olympic Games surpassed everything, including all previous Olympics."

The world's press had already documented the Third Reich's descent into tyranny and oppression, and the Nazis were especially pleased with the positive effect the Olympics had on these perceptions. Frederick Birchall wrote for the *New York Times*: "Foreigners who know Germany only from what they have seen during this pleasant fortnight can carry home only one impression. It is that this is a nation happy and prosperous beyond belief; that Hitler is one of the greatest political leaders in the world today, and that Germans themselves are a much maligned, hospitable, wholly peaceful people who deserve the best the world can give them."

Visitors to the Olympics were impressed with the way the Germans adored their leader. A British hurdler, Violet Webb, wrote about the mass hysteria: "As he went into the stadium you would have thought God had come down from heaven." Hitler had pirated the Olympic Games away from the International Olympic Committee, much as he had seized Germany away from the majority of its population and its civilized past. In his diary, Goebbels wrote: "When I am alone with him, he speaks to me like a father. I love him so much." Less than a decade later, Goebbels, Hitler, and their families would die together in the chancellor's bunker in Berlin as Russian troops stormed the city that the Nazis predicted would rule the world for a millennium.

The Nazi Olympic Games epitomized the unity of politics and sports. Sports had become another weapon in Hitler's growing arsenal. For those who paid attention, however, the Nazi Olympics foretold the tragedy that would soon descend on the world. Uniformed military was everywhere. Driven to exultation, the German people had turned into willing fodder for Hitler's military adventures less than twenty years after two million of their countrymen had died in the Great War. All was epitomized by the ultimate moment of the opening ceremony, when 20,000 pigeons were released in the air accompanied by a military artillery barrage. The frightened birds circled back over the stadium and dropped their guano over all the athletes and the tens of thousands of spectators in attendance.

Joe Louis, the black son of an American sharecropper and the grandson of a slave, and Max Schmeling, the "Black Uhlan of the Rhine" and the embodiment of the new Germany of Adolf Hitler, met twice in the ring at Yankee Stadium in bouts that symbolized the world's political divide. Schmeling knocked out Louis in the twelfth round of their 1936 fight, but Louis avenged that defeat in 1938, giving hope to democracies that they could ultimately prevail against the growing totalitarian menace. *AP Images*

One hundred years from now some historian may theorize, in a footnote
at least, that the decline of Nazi prestige began with a left hook delivered
by a former unskilled automotive worker who had never studied the
policies of Neville Chamberlain and had no opinion whatever in regard
to the situation in Czechoslovakia. —*Heywood Broun*

Joe, we're depending on those muscles for America.
—*Franklin Delano Roosevelt*

[3]
THE WAR OF THE WORLD
JOE LOUIS V. MAX SCHMELING

Joe Louis and Max Schmeling were polar opposites in the public's mind. Louis, the "Brown Bomber," was the black son of an American sharecropper and grandson of a slave. Schmeling, the "Black Uhlan of the Rhine," was the embodiment of the new Germany of Adolf Hitler. Their two battles in the boxing ring at Yankee Stadium in 1936 and 1938 reflected the world's political rivalry of the 1930s: America as the fortress of democracy; Nazi Germany as the perfection of social politics under the authoritarian leadership of a self-anointed "genius," as Hitler called himself in *Mein Kampf.* The boxing ring would become the venue for a geopolitical battle set in the starkest terms between these men and the ideologies they represented. Both would fight for their countries as well as for themselves.

The boxing matches also raised the matter of race, the issue that had divided and confounded Americans for more than three centuries. Americans were preoccupied with skin color, and Joe Louis brought this obsession to the forefront. Louis was among the most written-about figures in the twentieth century, along with Franklin Delano Roosevelt and Charles Lindbergh. The press stories rarely, if ever, failed to mention his race. Black Americans saw Louis as a Moses sent by the Almighty to lead his people to freedom. To others, Louis represented the conundrum of American life: was it more important that he was an American or that he was black?

Both commerce and politics have always benefited from clever marketing, as did the Louis-Schmeling fights. When the product market offers choices, it is best to attempt to differentiate your goods from that offered by your commercial rival: "My product is wonderful; his is bad." Louis and Schmeling were marketed to the public as good versus bad proponents of opposing political systems, although neither claimed to be anything more than an athlete. Louis appreciated the ambiguity of being a popular black man in a dominant white culture. Schmeling was a chameleon who changed political color as Germany underwent an extreme transformation in the 1930s, but by the middle of the decade he had accepted Nazi rule in his homeland and bathed in its adulation. The Louis-Schmeling fights riveted the public's attention in the countries they represented and throughout a world about to go to war.

Polarity has always existed in politics. Marshaling support for a political cause provokes hyperbole and extremism. Athenian politicians regularly castigated their opponents for taking bribes, an accusation that was often true. It is not by chance that leaders of the Athenian democracy were called "demagogues." Thomas Jefferson, the beloved Founder who drafted most of the Declaration of Independence, urged his supporters to launch vicious attacks on the Federalists. Jefferson instructed James Madison to lash out at Alexander Hamilton: "For god's sake, my dear Sir, take up your pen, select the most striking heresies, and cut him to [pieces] in the face of the public."

American politics has not turned any more polite in the last two centuries. Abraham Lincoln's enemies in the 1864 election portrayed him as a "despot." In turn, Lincoln's Republicans attacked George McClellan, the Democratic nominee in 1864, as a "coward." Throughout the cold war, Americans castigated the Soviet system as "godless," the worst epithet that could be hurled by members of a society where faith in the Lord is a fundamental currency of life. In 2012, presidential candidate Newt Gingrich denounced President Obama's "secular socialist machine that represents as great a threat to America as Nazi Germany."

The same principle of contrariety seems to apply in sports. That is especially the case when world politics offers the backdrop. The "Miracle on Ice" at the 1980 Winter Olympics provided the perfect bipolarity: a collection of American amateur and collegiate hockey players playing (and besting) the world's premier professional squad, the Soviet national hockey team. Even better than combat on an ice rink, boxing between fighters from potential (or actual) enemies offers ritualized warfare engaged in by proxies in a controlled setting. When you combine the almost irresistible impulse to divide the world into good versus bad with the blood sport of boxing, you have created an event for the ages.

A CONTEXT OF MALEVOLENCE

Outside the boxing ring, the geopolitical world of the 1930s was in chaos. Adolf Hitler was appointed chancellor of Germany in 1933, and by 1936 his program of racial purification and rearmament was proceeding at full speed. As the supreme and unquestioned leader of Germany, he attacked the economic depression and the social condition of the nation he had captured without conditions or limitations, much as he would later attack the European states that stood in the way of his global aspirations. Certainly, by virtue of their outward adoration of Hitler, it appeared that most Germans loved their fuehrer and what he promised. Hitler would adopt a boxer, Max Schmeling, as the standard-bearer for his perilous ambitions on the world stage. Although it remains unclear whether Schmeling was actually a political devotee, he was perceived by the world as Hitler's protagonist. Schmeling's actions indicated he was willing to play by the rules set by the National Socialist Party.

At the same time, while Franklin Roosevelt's administration worked to pull the United States out of its own economic crisis through democratic means, a quiet black boxer from the Midwest named Joe Louis came to symbolize the aspirations of the United States. Louis was an awkward choice in a country where persons of color were regarded at best as marginal participants in society and at worst as subhuman. In the 1930s, more than 50 percent of black men were unemployed, and cities where they lived were hurting as manufacturing jobs disappeared and the American spirit dwindled. If anything, the Depression caused America's prevailing views on race to harden.

The views of American racists were not totally dissimilar from those of the Nazis. While official and abiding discrimination against blacks was the code in the South, where blacks were officially separated from white society, throughout the United States blacks were considered second-class citizens. Life was hard for all Americans and worse for persons of color. Most American sports fans would have selected someone with white skin to represent them in the sporting world, but Louis proved he clearly was the best boxer in the country. Americans had to choose whether to stand up for their country or their blatant racism. Eventually, they chose to cheer for Joe Louis. His success in the boxing ring would force even the most malevolent of white Americans to make an exception to their universal disparagement of black Americans. If there were any doubters, Louis's display of patriotic fervor during World War II would seal the case.

The *New York Times* pronounced Joe Louis a "fistic marvel," and he would live up to his billing. Born in a two-room shack in the Buckalew Mountains of Alabama, the seventh son of a cotton picker, Louis was raised in Detroit, where, in his late teens, he began boxing in the amateur Golden Gloves competition. Working on the line at the Briggs auto factory and then at Ford's River Rouge plant, Louis found that he did not have enough time left in a week for boxing. He left the auto plant and never returned.

Two years and twenty-four professional victories later, Louis was ready for the first of two bouts against the pride of Nazi Germany, Max Schmeling. Their two encounters were powerful examples of the confluence of boxing and politics. From the ring set up near second base at Yankee Stadium in 1936 and 1938, Joe Louis and Max Schmeling would command the world's stage as representatives of political systems that would soon contest for world military and political domination.

BOXING

Boxing was a primitive and brutal sport where two men pounded each other with their gloved fists until one became unconscious. The misnamed "sweet science" has been witnessed for thousands of years. In the days when humans first gathered into clans and tribes, fighting sports served as a preparation for the hunt and as training for tribal combat. Ancient Samarians and Egyptians staged public bouts. Perfected in ancient Greece and Rome, the sport combined strength and agility. Its simple rules appealed to basic human instincts. Survival and conquest in the face of an aggressor seeking to impose his will on his opponent were always popular parables. As an event in the ancient Olympics, Hellenic boxers wore tightly wrapped leather thongs on their hands, sometimes adding metal studs to their fist bindings. There were no weight classifications, no time-limit rounds or bells. Many bouts were one-sided and very bloody, an aspect of the sport that was always popular.

Boxing was the most celebrated sport in England in the late eighteenth and early nineteenth centuries. Such "fist battles" were wildly popular, even though they were generally illegal. George Borrow, an English author, wrote in his classic memoir *Lavengro* in 1851: "I have known the time when a pugilistic encounter between two noted champions was almost considered in the light of a national affair; when tens of thousands of individuals, high and low, meditated and brooded upon it, the first thing in the morning, and the last thing at night, until the great event was decided."

Rules were not standardized until 1838, and, even after the regulation of the sport, deaths in the ring were common. Perhaps it was the danger to participants that attracted patrons from all walks of life. Bare-knuckle fighter Simon Byrne, the "Emerald Gem," was involved in two fatal matches, one as the perpetrator, the other as the victim. In 1830, he fought Sandy McKay, who collapsed after forty-seven rounds and died the next day. Three years later, Byrne died as a result of injuries inflicted in the ring by James Burke, the English champion, during the longest recorded prize fight, ninety-nine rounds, which lasted over three hours. Byrne died a few days later.

Interestingly, boxing was virtually unknown in colonial America, although it prospered in England. There are reports of early nineteenth-century bare-knuckle fights in southern states that pitted black slaves against one another. Sometimes, slave boxers would be forced to wear iron collars in the ring. Southern slave owners would train their chattel to fight, hosting challenge matches and gambling on the outcomes. Sometimes these fights were to the death. By midcentury, the brutal sport had spread nationwide, even while it remained illegal, regularly condemned by civic and religious leaders. As part of a scorned underground culture, bare-knuckle bouts became a favored urban pastime.

After the Civil War, there were few interracial matches in America. John L. Sullivan, the "Boston Strong Boy" heavyweight bare-knuckle champion from 1882 to 1892 and the most important American athlete of the nineteenth century, refused to fight any black contenders, including Peter Jackson, known as the "Black Prince," who held the Australian and British Empire championships and was the appropriate challenger for the belt. Sullivan explained simply that he would never fight "a member of the colored race." Sullivan's views represented those of white European immigrants who relished their superiority over "the colored race" and would not risk jeopardizing that status in the ring.

Boxing became mainstream American entertainment as a result of the efforts of Richard Kyle Fox, an immigrant from Ireland in 1874, whose sordid *National Police Gazette* became the leading journal of the sport, read almost exclusively by men awaiting haircuts in barbershops. Fox promoted fights, defined the weight classes, offered championship belts, and reduced the sport's well-earned reputation for dishonesty. Although he was hardly a model of culture, civility, or racial harmony, Fox and his scandalous newspaper elevated the low-life sport of boxing to a national stature rivaled only by baseball. Political and social leaders would attend the fights that Fox promoted. Fox arranged a bout between John L. Sullivan and Paddy Ryan in 1882 that was billed as a match for "the championship of the world," the first time that designation had ever been used. Sullivan prevailed. With the British codification of the Marquis of Queensberry rules in 1892, which were endorsed by both Fox and Sullivan, boxing's transformation into a modern sport was complete.

Theodore Roosevelt had harsh words for boxing in 1890: "A prize-fight is simply brutal and degrading. The people who attend it and make a hero of the prize fighter, are . . . to a very great extent, men who hover on the borderlines of criminality. . . . They form as ignoble a body as do the kindred frequenters of rat-pit and cock-pit. The prize fighter and his fellow professional athletes of the same ilk are, together with their patrons in every rank of life, the very worst foes with whom the cause of general athletic development has to contend."

By the time T. R. had succeeded to the presidency, however, he would change his mind. In fact, he personally sparred with professional pugilists in the White House. The retired heavyweight champion John L. Sullivan paid President Roosevelt a visit, the fifth time the Boston Strong Boy had come to the White House, having previously met with presidents Arthur, Cleveland, Benjamin Harrison, and McKinley.

Other less enlightened politicians saw political and military value in boxing. In *Mein Kampf*, Adolf Hitler extolled the virtues of the activity: "There is no sport that so cultivates a spirit of aggressiveness, that demands lightning-quick decisiveness, that develops the body to such steely smoothness." Hitler characterized democratic politicians and others in the "cultivated classes" as physically weak specimens, more concerned with "etiquette" than with power. He urged all Germans to "harden the body and train it to endure an adverse environment." Had Germans learned to box instead of pursuing "intellectual training," Hitler wrote, they would have prevailed in the Great War. Hitler would make boxing a matter of mandatory training, and, of course, he barred Jews from participating in any aspect of the sport. The Nazis disapproved of the commercialization of boxing—except when it came to Herr Schmeling—but welcomed all other aspects of the brutal sport. The Nazis promoted amateur boxing as part of their all-encompassing social and political revolution. All high school boys were expected to participate.

In America, members of disadvantaged groups saw participation in boxing as an avenue for advancement. Blacks and Jews used boxing as a passageway out of economic marginalization. By the 1920s, Jews dominated the American boxing business as promoters and managers, and as pugilists, such as Benny Leonard, Barney Ross, and Abe Attell. (It is unclear whether heavyweight champion Max Baer was Jewish, although he wore a Star of David on his trunks, which made him a popular boxer in the center of American prizefighting, New York City.)

Boxing was a fabulous modern entertainment, combining athletic prowess with show business. It went from an outlaw sport to a gala public festival, attracting a nation's elite who attended boxing matches attired in the finest evening wear. During the 1920s, boxing was a diversion from memories of the Great War; during the 1930s, it was psychological relief from the economic depression. For successful fighters, it was a source of substantial income at a time when so many went without work, food, and shelter. Boxers became celebrities, glorified by the masses.

Today, boxing has become an afterthought in an age when team sports reign supreme in the public's mind. In the 1930s, however, boxing was the nation's premier sports attraction accessible to the public, especially at home, where the matches were featured on radio virtually every night. A match for the heavyweight championship of the world always commanded universal anticipation and attention. Boxing news filled the daily newspapers. Upcoming bouts were matters of constant discussion, as well as the basis for innumerable wagers. When one boxer symbolized good and the other bad—something a fight's promoters sought out and, if necessary, fabricated—the political and social implications were paramount and the radio broadcasts would be heard by millions.

MAX SCHMELING

Maximillian Adolph Otto Siegfried Schmeling was an unlikely champion for Hitler's Germany. He certainly did not fit the prescribed blond, blue-eyed Aryan model, but he was a great boxer, the best Germany ever produced. With dark hair, heavy features, and a protruding brow, Schmeling was inaptly nicknamed "The Black Uhlan of the Rhine." (The Uhlans had been the Prussian cavalry in the nineteenth century, and Schmeling was born in Klein Luckow, eighty miles north of Berlin and hundreds of miles from the Rhine.)

Schmeling worked the boxing clubs of Dusseldorf and Cologne during the Weimar Republic, and he showed no particular interest in politics. He was a disciplined boxer with great skills, which he demonstrated as he rose through the ranks of German pugilists. He was sometimes called the "German Dempsey" after the American heavyweight champion of the 1920s, whom he resembled. Over his career, most of his important fights would be in America, the world center for boxing and the source of the highest purses. He called America "my second home."

Although the press would portray Schmeling as a Nazi Party sympathizer, it was Hitler who had first approached the boxer, long before he became a world champion. Shortly after he assumed the German chancellorship in 1933, Hitler summoned Schmeling to the chancellery for dinner with Goring, Goebbels, and other cabinet members. Hitler took a liking to the boxer and encouraged Schmeling to fight "for Germany." Throughout the 1930s, Hitler would meet with his "Maxie." Schmeling was flattered by the attention. Like many Germans, Schmeling passively accepted Nazi dogma as the prevailing canon. He adapted to the circumstances he faced. He said he found Hitler to be "charming." As a result of his prowess in the ring, Schmeling became a national hero, and he welcomed the acclaim of the German press and his prominence in German society. Schmeling's victories in the ring turned Germany boxing-crazy, and he was the idol of the masses. Boxing, in turn, became the perfect symbol for a country that had once again turned bellicose.

Schmeling's personal views remain an enigma. The Nazis offered him the Dagger of Honor and the honorary title of a commander in the Sturmabteilung, Hitler's private army of brownshirts, but Schmeling declined. In fact, early in the Nazi regime, when not in or near the boxing ring, Schmeling and his wife, the Czech film actress Anny Ondra, were involved with the German intelligentsia—including avant-garde Jewish artists, writers, and filmmakers, many of whom immigrated once Hitler assumed power. Those who did not voluntarily depart were eventually sent to concentration camps.

Schmeling's American manager, Joe "Yussel the Muscle" Jacobs, was a Hungarian-born Jew. Schmeling refused Nazi orders to dismiss Jacobs, insubordination that would have been sufficient for Schmeling to be sent to a concentration camp if he were not a Nazi favorite. During Kristallnacht in November 1938, Schmeling picked up two Jewish sons of an old friend and drove them to Berlin. The boxer hid them in his Excelsior Hotel suite for several days until the worst excesses of the Nazi pogrom had passed. Outside, Hitler's brownshirts destroyed Jewish businesses, burned synagogues, and sent thousands of Jews to concentration camps.

Schmeling was the only boxer ever to win the heavyweight title on a foul, a low blow in the fourth round of his June 1930 match in Yankee Stadium against Bostonian Jack Sharkey. It was an unfortunate way to prevail, and certainly not the manner in which the German champion would have preferred to win the title. Sharkey had clearly outboxed Schmeling that night, but the referee had little discretion in disqualifying the champion. He had seen the shot to the groin that incapacitated the German. Returning to his homeland, Schmeling was booed when introduced before a fight at the Berlin Sportpalast. In another controversial decision, Sharkey would win the rematch two years later in a fifteen-round decision to regain the title. When Schmeling lost to Max Baer in 1933, *Box-Sport* said the defeat was "the end of a fortunate career." All of his bouts before 1936, however, were merely a prologue to his two monumental encounters with Joe Louis.

THE LEGACY OF BLACK BOXERS

A child of the segregated South, Joe Louis Barrow (he dropped his last name when he began boxing) was well schooled in avoiding confrontation outside the ring. His family joined the Great Migration and moved north to Detroit in 1926 after the Ku Klux Klan threatened his mother and stepfather. They found downtown Detroit as segregated as Alabama, increasingly so as blacks migrated north from the subsistence farms of the South. Louis had to learn what other blacks in the segregated country knew quite well. As a member of a devalued race, he would have to follow the expected norms of behavior, say little, and fight hard. He learned how awful life was as a person of color in apartheid America. High aspirations were simply pipe dreams in the urban ghetto.

Americans had a distasteful experience with the great black boxer Jack Johnson, who won the heavyweight crown in 1908. Johnson was the first person of color to be allowed to fight for the championship. Once crowned, Johnson proceeded to "misbehave," as far as the white power structure was concerned, thinking quite incorrectly that he now had the right to exercise free will. His wives were white, he had affairs with other white women, and he offered liquor to an integrated crowd of patrons at his Café de Champion in Chicago. This was not approved behavior during the Jim Crow era. One white preacher referred to Johnson from the pulpit as "that black gorilla." He was seen as a danger to public tranquility.

Jack Johnson's brilliant performances in the ring brought out crowds of white fans who rooted for his defeat, particularly in his 1910 championship match in Reno against the "Great White Hope," Jim Jeffries. Jeffries, the heavyweight champion at the turn of the twentieth century, had been called out of retirement to put Johnson in his place. Jeffries explained: "I feel obligated to the sporting public at least to make an effort to reclaim the heavyweight championship for the white race. . . . I should step into the ring again and demonstrate that a white man is king of them all." John L. Sullivan had made his prediction years earlier in an article he wrote for the *Boston Globe*: "They'd need a couple of ambulances to pick up the dark meat when Jeffries pulled off his gloves and called it a day's work."

Yet Johnson prevailed, setting off celebrations among urban blacks across the country. White authorities used force to suppress black revelries that they labeled "riots," causing the deaths of dozens of people. The *New York World* story reflected the reaction of white America: "That Mr. Johnson should so lightly and carelessly punch the head of Mr. Jeffries must come as a shock to every devoted believer in the primacy of the Anglo-Saxon race."

Jack Johnson's golden smile would set his enemies aflame. He fought unafraid, without hesitancy or timidity. He would often finish a match unscarred, never really tested by most opponents, a troubling wonderment in a country that considered blacks a degenerate and debased race. While appalled both by his success and his behavior, America could not ignore Johnson's amazing fighting prowess. The white press saw Johnson's cocky demeanor as unacceptable arrogance, and it worked diligently to make sure Johnson would ultimately pay for transgressing established norms. At the same time Johnson was marrying white women—his first wife committed suicide—other black people were being lynched for even looking at white women. Johnson made plain his state of mind: "I am not a slave, and I have the right to choose who my mate shall be without the dictation of any man. I have eyes and I have a heart, and when they fail to tell me who I shall have as mine, I want to be put in a lunatic asylum." Many Americans were ready to make a reservation for Johnson at the nearest mental hospital.

One significant source of income for victorious prizefighters before the age of radio and television was the distribution of films of championship fights. The first fight film, albeit staged, was shot by Thomas Edison in 1894 at the Edison Laboratories in New Jersey. Heavyweight champion Jim Corbett (who had taken the title from Sullivan) knocked out Peter Courtney just before the film ran out. As technology improved, actual fights were filmed, including the Johnson-Jeffries Reno match, and the film was ready for release within days of the encounter. It was unfortunate to many that Johnson had defeated Jeffries, and many local political authorities, supported by Christian and police organizations, determined it unacceptable for the images of the interracial battle to appear at local theaters. In cities from Baltimore to Havana, Cuba, films of the Reno fight were banned, although bootleg copies were screened in some cities. Two years later, Congress banned all prizefighting films from interstate commerce, a prohibition that would not be reversed until 1939, after Joe Louis's magnificent victory against Max Schmeling.

Johnson's flamboyance and open fraternizing with white women ultimately led to his criminal indictment and (after years of exile) incarceration. Decades later, Joe Louis would emerge as a very different kind of black boxer. He learned not to repeat Johnson's mistakes. He would be polite, respectful, passive, soft-spoken, dignified, and reticent, except, of course, when he was boxing. He would behave, as was often said, as "a credit to his race."

JOE LOUIS

Joe Louis was a natural athlete in the ring, but he needed to be trained to be a prizefighter with an acceptable public image. He had never shown any particular promise or understanding of boxing until he fell into the right management with the correct trainer. He then received the good advice he needed, the manufactured image of respectability that was unobjectionable both north and south, and the training to become a champion. He was cautioned to stay clear of any possible trouble. Louis would never have his photograph taken alongside a white woman. He would never boast over his accomplishments in the ring. His deadpan expression was the opposite of Jack Johnson's broad smile.

Louis married Miss Marva Trotter, an attractive black woman who was a stenographer for the Chicago Insurance Exchange. His manager and trainer had encouraged the match as stabilizing for Louis and the opposite of Jack Johnson's escapades. In a sport that needed a major new figure to attract cash, Louis would serve well as long as he stayed under control. He surely could throw a punch, and he knew how to keep his mouth shut. He would not remind the public of Jack Johnson in any way other than as champion of the world of boxing.

Louis faced Italian Primo Carnera in a filled Yankee Stadium on June 25, 1935. It was Louis's first fight in New York City, the world capital of boxing. This was also Louis's first exposure on the international stage. The *New York Times* estimated that 15,000 blacks attended the event, many from out of town, the most ever to attend a prizefight. They had come to see the "new risen hero of their race." The *Pittsburgh Courier* said that Louis "carried the weight of an entire race on his shoulders." His opponent, Primo Carnera, the tall and powerful former heavyweight champion, was "Mussolini's muscle man." Il Duce's forces were about to attack Ethiopia, and sports columnists quickly turned the Yankee Stadium bout into a symbolic preview. There were doubts in the boxing community whether Louis could prevail against such seasoned competition after only a year in the professional ring. Once the fight began, however, it was clear that Louis was the dominant force. The referee stopped the fight for a sixth round technical knockout when Carnera was unable to protect himself. (Ethiopia was not as fortunate, although the forces of King Haile Selassie fought valiantly.) By besting Carnera, Joe Louis became a national "race" hero, the most famous black man in the country.

Louis bolstered his image in another Yankee Stadium bout in September 1935 against another ex-champion, Max Baer. There were as many as 95,000 in attendance. Gate receipts topped one million dollars. This time, as many as 35,000 blacks attended the bout, filling whole sections of the outfield. The fight was a political event par excellence: Governor Herbert Lehman of New York hosted his fellow governors from Connecticut, New Jersey, Pennsylvania, Michigan, and Maine. New York City mayor Fiorello La Guardia was accompanied by mayors from Chicago, Detroit, Jersey City, and Newark. The nation's sports attention focused on the stadium in the Bronx.

Sports reporters thought the fight was evenly matched, but Baer could not withstand Louis's assault. By the second round, Louis was jabbing Baer at will.

He knocked Baer out in the fourth. Black America exploded in joy. Richard Wright wrote: "It was like a revival." Louis had established himself as the premier heavyweight in the world, the most popular sports figure in America, and the representation of the aspirations of America's marginalized race.

It would be difficult for Louis to maintain his reputation of acceptable moderation as his fame grew across America, especially among people of color and particularly in Harlem, the capital of black America. Louis was the king of 125th Street, and he accepted popular acclaim as the "Brown Bomber." Louis, a gifted tornado in the ring, came to symbolize black hopes. Although that was not his objective—he was a boxer and not a social leader—Louis appreciated the role he now played. His victories in the ring over white fighters inspired celebrations in black America as inhabitants packed the streets as never before whenever he prevailed, which was quite often. In total, he won sixty-six bouts over seventeen years of boxing, losing but three, with one draw.

Millions listened to Louis's fights on radio. In fact, many black families bought their first radios to hear "our Joe" triumph. They could not have prayed for a better role model—polite, dignified, and successful. Louis never spoke ill of any of his opponents, never taunted them as Jack Johnson had done. He played fairly, with humility and pride, all business and dedication. Louis fought to a shower of press superlatives as the champion for almost twelve years. A bout against Louis promised riches for any boxer who could match him. Louis was even invited to meet with President Roosevelt in 1935, a rare honor for a black man.

Louis's public image contrasted with his behavior as a private man. He was a constant philanderer, hardly loyal to his picture-perfect wife, Marva. He had affairs with Lena Horne, Sonja Henie, and Lana Turner. Although a hero to the working class, he made millions from his work in the ring and then spent it all or gave it away, ending up bankrupt after World War II.

1936

Louis and Schmeling met on June 19, 1936, in the roped arena at Yankee Stadium before a disappointing crowd of 45,000, including 700 sportswriters from around the world. The Nazis were not pleased with the bout from the beginning, but candidly admitted there would be no problem as long as Schmeling quickly dispatched the mongrel boxer. While in America, Schmeling was a positive spokesman for the Reich, the most famous German athlete in the world, and Hitler had no doubt as to his loyalty. The risk, of course, was that Schmeling could lose to a member of an inferior race. The *Volkischer Beobachter* wrote that "our patriotic ambitions" were at stake in the match, but the paper was not concerned because Schmeling's strength "sprang from German character" and "this special race feeling."

The fight attracted America's political and entertainment elite. Attendance at the match crossed racial and political lines at a time when mixed crowds were rare in America and around the world. Louis was an 8:1 betting favorite, although most sportswriters were fond of Schmeling as a good-natured and courageous sportsman. Louis was also well liked as a well-behaved black role model who followed the rules firmly set by whites. The winner would likely soon face James J. Braddock for the heavyweight crown.

Hitler had personally given Schmeling his marching orders: promote Germany during the 1936 Olympic year and return to the Fatherland victorious. The coincidence of the Yankee Stadium fight and the Olympics cemented Schmeling's image as a representative of the Nazis and Louis as a democratic hero. Some thought that Schmeling's chances were weak at best, but the Nazi propaganda machine extolled his "fighting morale." However, to be safe, Nazi officialdom ignored his departure from Germany for the trip to New York, and there was no official excursion of spectators planned for the event.

The world's press portrayed Schmeling as the embodiment of the Fascist threat. Like his fellow countrymen, he offered the Nazi salute on command and enjoyed the acclaim offered by his new admirers. Guido von Mengden, media chief of Nazi sports, said before Schmeling left for the New York bout: "Schmeling is the most famous and best loved athlete in modern German history, and the Reich wishes him well." Although wary of the fight to come, Nazi sportswriters joined Schmeling aboard the Bremen ocean liner to cover the story.

Both fighters prepared for the match, but Schmeling seemed to make better use of his time, and his confidence grew. He insisted that in watching films of Louis he had found a weakness and could down the man people already thought of as the heavyweight champion. Schmeling would prove to be prescient. Louis seemed complacent and, perhaps, overconfident. Training camp seemed to hurt Louis's focus and fitness, as he played more golf than he should have as the fight approached.

Louis was a prohibitive betting favorite. The press reported that there was no "Schmeling money" in evidence. The *New York Times*, in its preview of the week ahead, headlined two radio events of note for June 18, 1936: the total eclipse of the sun in Siberia—the "spectacle" would be broadcast on radio—and the Louis-Schmeling prizefight that would precede the eclipse live from Yankee Stadium. Clem McCarthy, NBC's leading sports announcer, would provide the blow-by-blow account of the fight. Edwin C. Hill would handle the "sidelights." Sixty percent of all American radios would tune in to hear the duo's report. While an unscheduled downpour postponed the boxing match for one night, the total eclipse from Siberia came off as scheduled.

Prefight chatter characterized Louis as inordinately quiet—it was said he even spoke less than "Dummy" Taylor, the New York Giants' mute pitcher—but in the ring, as the *Times* reported, "he displays boxing intelligence tantamount to the stalking instinct of the panther." The German press had genuine difficulty understanding how Americans could support a black boxer. *Box–Sport*, the German boxing tabloid, hoped that white Americans would soon come to their senses: "We hope that the 'white blood' and the spirit of the white race, despite all mixing, will prove to be the stronger and more vital." In fact, the Nazis had used the effective segregation of the races in America as a role model for their reordering of German life. Most white Americans disdained blacks. How then could Joe Louis possibly be an American hero?

What the Nazis could not appreciate was that Americans had always learned to accept the lesser of two evils. Louis might be a black sharecropper's son, but he was an American, and Schmeling was German and the symbol of a potential enemy. Hypocrisy was always a critical component in the American political and social ethos, and the Louis-Schmeling Yankee Stadium fights would provide what had seemed impossible—an opportunity for Americans to rally behind a black athlete.

Newspapers were filled with stories about the fight, and most fans predicted that Louis would make quick work of the German. That was not what happened in the ring that night. Louis seemed unfocused. Schmeling was at the height of his physical powers. Louis would jab and, as Schmeling later related, "I cross my right over and smash him on the side of the jaw."

Throughout the day, Deutscher Rundfunk repeatedly broadcast the following announcement: "It is every German's obligation to stay up tonight. Max will fight overseas with a Negro for the hegemony of the white race!" Many

Germans obediently set their alarms to awaken at 3 a.m. Arno Hellmis, the Nazis' favorite boxing writer, sat at ringside in the Bronx to offer his partisan viewpoint to the German radio audience. Arthur Donovan, America's premier boxing referee, kept control in the ring. As Schmeling landed a hard right, Hellmis would cry out: "Bravo Max! Bravo Max!" Schmeling's confidence continued to grow with his punching prowess, and Louis was lost in the ring. The outcome was no longer in doubt.

Sixty million people listened to NBC radio as Clem McCarthy told the tale at the end of the fight: "And Donovan broke them. Schmeling got over two more hard rights to Louis's jaw and made Louis get down, and Schmeling straightening up Louis with hard rights and lefts to the jaw. . . . He has puffed up Louis's cheek, and Louis is down! Louis is down! Hanging to the ropes and hanging badly! He's a very tired fighter, he is blinking his eyes, shaking his head and the count is TEN, THE FIGHT IS OVER! LOUIS IS COMPLETELY OUT!"

Schmeling knocked out Louis in the twelfth round: "It is over! Yes," Schmeling said, "I jump high into the air and wave my arms. . . . I tell you, so happy I have never been before." On German radio, Hellmis announced to the Third Reich that the champion stood in the ring giving the Hitler salute. (No one else in the Stadium saw Schmeling raise his right arm.) Hellmis reported that all the white spectators at the Stadium that night wildly cheered the Schmeling victory.

In his dressing room, Schmeling called his wife by transatlantic telephone. She had been listening to the bout at the home of Josef and Magda Goebbels. When Joe Louis's mother later asked her son what had happened, he responded: "He just whupped me, Ma." The nation's black newspapers reported that Harlem was "in mourning." It was a morality play for black Americans. When you rise too high too quickly, you fall just as quickly.

The Nazis wallowed in the victory of their countryman. Goebbels cabled Schmeling within minutes of his triumph: "To your wonderful victory my best congratulations. I know you fought for Germany; that it's a German victory. We are proud of you. Heil Hitler." A telegram from the fuehrer followed shortly thereafter: "Most cordial congratulations on your splendid victory." The German magazine *Der Weltkampf* wrote: "Max Schmeling's victory over Joe Louis is a cultural achievement for the white race. It clearly demonstrates the superiority of the white intelligence." The newspaper of the SS, the *Schwartze Korps*, swooned over "unser Max"—our Max. His "shattering fists had smashed all adversaries of National Socialism in the face" and had "saved the prestige of the white race."

Schmeling was surprised by the acclaim he received upon returning to the Fatherland. He was welcomed home as a national hero. Air force planes circled the Hindenburg dirigible as it landed in Frankfurt three days after the fight. Schmeling stood on the balcony outside his suite, acknowledging the adoring crowd and offering them a Hitler salute. The next day, he flew to Berlin on Goebbels's private plane to meet with the fuehrer and dine with Goebbels. The greeting party at Tempelhof Field included 500 amateur boxers standing at attention. The Nazi press declared Schmeling's victory a critical event in the "fight for white supremacy," as he received what was, in effect, a state reception. Within days, film of the fight was shown in cinemas throughout the Reich and in Austria, with crowds shouting "Heil Hitler" and "Heil Schmeling." The fight film offered the public the opportunity to feast in the frenzy.

For ordinary people, Schmeling's boxing triumph finally redressed the national humiliation of the Versailles Treaty. Germany needed a hero and Schmeling would serve well in that role. He enjoyed all the public attention. By all accounts, he appeared to be comfortably aligned with the Nazis, who felt triumphant. Schmeling basked in the glory of Hitler's adoration. His success, considered a major societal achievement, was attributed to Hitler's support, part of the triumph of the master race. A grateful fuehrer waived all taxes on Schmeling's earnings from the fight.

Embraced by the Nazis, Schmeling quickly became the object of protests by those who found the German regime to be an abomination. As his managers maneuvered to arrange a championship fight against Braddock and later a rematch against Louis, the American-based Non-Sectarian Anti-Nazi League campaigned for a boycott of all Schmeling bouts. The disdain for Schmeling, however, could not overcome the marketability of a second matchup between the Nazi hero and the sharecropper's son. For that bout, it would be business as usual.

The unexpected outcome of their 1936 fight confirmed preexisting prejudices and the established social norm. The upset had reset the American political scales back to normal—white over black. Disappointment was what blacks had learned to expect from their lot in American life. The southern press celebrated the German's victory. Louis would not make excuses. Insiders knew, however, that he had not trained well. Louis explained that in the ring "everything was in a fog." He had learned many lessons from his humiliating defeat, and it would not happen again. He would not lose another fight for fifteen years.

1938

Although he was mostly forgotten in the clamor over Louis and Schmeling, James J. Braddock remained the reigning heavyweight boxing champion, although he rarely fought to defend his title. (Braddock had won the title from Baer, who had won it from Carnera, who had won it from Sharkey after Sharkey had beaten Schmeling.) Schmeling and Braddock signed to fight for the championship belt, but Louis was the only popular attraction who could fill Yankee Stadium. When Louis's people offered the champion a fight against their man, Braddock dumped Schmeling. Although they had signed a contract to box for the title, the likelihood of an effective boycott made the Braddock-Schmeling matchup unattractive. Braddock broke the agreement with Schmeling in order to fight Louis, certainly the more lucrative option. The Nazi press exploded in hyperbolic rage against the Jews of America, who it blamed as the culprits in this outrage.

Schmeling sued to enforce his contract with Braddock, but lost in court. He was fortunate in one significant regard, however. The contretemps over the canceled fight caused him to change his travel plans. He had been scheduled to be a passenger on the Hindenburg on its ill-fated voyage in May 1937 when it exploded over Lakehurst, New Jersey, killing thirty-four passengers. Schmeling had taken an earlier ocean liner to travel to America for his court action.

Louis won the heavyweight crown from Braddock in a fight in Chicago's Comiskey Park in June 1937 and became the youngest heavyweight champion in history. When Louis was done with him, it took four men to carry Braddock to his corner, where he remained unconscious for several minutes. The Nazi press declared the date of that fight "the darkest day in the long history of American boxing" and a great victory for the gangsters and the Jews of the world, who had engineered the travesty. Even among more rational observers, the excitement over Louis's championship victory seemed muted except for the exultation in the black community. Although he fought diligently, Louis had turned dull in the ring. Only a rematch and a victory against the Nazis' hero could reignite the fire that had made Louis unique among the world's boxers.

Not everyone appreciated the global importance of a rematch against

Schmeling. John Kiernan, writing for the *New York Times*, opined, "the notion of making a prizefighter stand forth as the shining representative of a race, a creed or a political program verges on the fantastic." Kiernan was wrong. The fight would stand the test of history as a political event of prime importance. Louis had become a symbol of the aspirations of one-tenth of the American population, while remarkably not exacerbating problems of race relations within the United States. For the first time, a person of color had been anointed to defend the American way of life under the bright lights of the world's press. The Brown Bomber had the power, by using his two fists, to crush the myth of Aryan supremacy. That was a fight worth making at a time when America and much of the rest of the world had finally begun to recognize the lethal threat posed by the Fascist regime. Louis had no pretensions about the import of the fight. He knew the role that had been thrust on him. Yet, for Louis it was just part of his responsibility as the new heavyweight champion and a means to earn a considerable paycheck.

Although Hitler was furious about how America had treated his boxing hero, he had other more pressing political issues to address as he continued to implement his plan for world domination. On March 12, 1938, Hitler annexed the land of his birth, Austria, to its "proper place" as part of the Third Reich. Troops and tanks rolled into Vienna. The *Anschluss* was met by cheering crowds and Nazi salutes. Civil war raged on in Spain, with Germany's military actively supporting fellow Fascist Francisco Franco. Hitler next pressed his claim to the Sudetenland provinces of Czechoslovakia. He did have time, however, to wish his "Maxie" well in his rematch against Louis.

REVENGE IN THE RING

As Machiavelli wrote in *The Prince*: "Upon this, one has to remark that men ought either to be well treated or crushed, because they can avenge themselves of lighter injuries, of more serious ones they cannot; therefore the injury that is to be done to a man ought to be of such a kind that one does not stand in fear of revenge." Under this precept, Max Schmeling should have beaten Joe Louis so badly in 1936 that he could not avenge his defeat. Instead, the combatants would meet again in 1938 for a historic match that was more than just sport. It was global politics in the ring.

Politics are often motivated by revenge. Starting deep in the Middle Ages,

European nation-states rotated in avenging the last military defeat at the hands of their archenemies. Germany's rush to prepare for war in the 1930s was driven by the humiliation it had suffered at Versailles. Hitler had experienced the indignities of personal defeat his entire life, and he would never be satisfied until all real and imagined slights were redressed. Germans, battered by the worldwide depression, shared Hitler's deflated self-image and his motive for revenge.

Between the two Louis-Schmeling fights, the Nazis had accelerated their program of internal "purification," showing the world more of the true nature of their political program. At first, the Nazis sought to chase the Jews from Germany by persecuting them. Smashing windows in Jewish stores, attacking shop owners, rounding up whole neighborhoods, and transporting the outcasts to work camps, the atrocities escalated throughout 1938, culminating in Kristallnacht on November 9, 1938, when Jewish properties were torched and thousands of Jews were rounded up for transport to concentration camps. The Nazis' Final Solution—the elimination of the Jews—would follow the outbreak of the war.

Politics, however, requires a careful balance of calculation and ruthless emotion. Because information is never complete and predictions of the future are necessarily uncertain, great politicians must be risk takers. Much the same is true in boxing, a speculative and risky enterprise, like war, where defeat can be fatal. The emotional part of the balance overcomes the uncertainty and drives politics forward. Those unwilling to take a chance will suffer with past indignities. Louis was not debilitated by his defeat, although he had been embarrassed. From 1936 until 1938, he rebuilt his career, besting all opponents and winning the heavyweight crown from Braddock. He remained the most popular sports figure in America. What he needed to do, of course, and what would make him a historic figure, would be to defeat Max Schmeling.

Although certainly not a professional politician, Louis was thrust into the vortex of international politics as a symbol of the Western democracies. President Roosevelt again invited him to the White House. Feeling the bulging muscles in Louis's right arm, FDR declared for the cameras, "Joe, we are depending on those muscles for America." Louis later commented: "Now, even more, I knew I had to get Schmeling good. I had my own personal reasons, and the whole damned country was depending on me."

As a boxer on the world stage during a time when every human activity was heavily politicized, Louis's rematch against the German champion would pit nation against nation, democracy against totalitarianism. More was at stake than a mere championship belt. National pride, international reputations, conflicting economic and social systems, and the prospects for war would turn on the performance of the two men in the "squared circle" at Yankee Stadium.

For weeks before the return match, the German press had predicted Schmeling's certain victory "on the basis of the blood." While Schmeling insisted he was not in the ring to represent the "master race," the German media had transformed him into an Aryan icon. *Box-Sport* devoted an issue to proving the "utter impossibility" of Schmeling's defeat by the Negro, using the research of Nazi "race scientists" in support of its confident prediction. Louis, however, predicted a quick knockout, although he never specified which boxer would do the "knocking out." (He did tell sportswriter Jimmy Cannon, however, that he intended to knock out Schmeling in the first round.)

The experience in training camp for the return match would be different from their first encounter. Louis played no golf and focused on his preparation. By 1938, all Americans, north and south, had seen the perfidy in Hitler's schemes and his vile oppression of the Jews and his political foes. This time white America fully supported Louis, a truly remarkable event for a nation steeped in separation and race discrimination. Schmeling's own racism, quite temperate for the time, was summarized in his remark reprinted in the *Chicago American*: "The black dynasty of pugilism must come to an end." He lauded Hitler for what he had accomplished for the German economy and public safety. He correctly assessed Hitler's high level of support among ordinary Germans. Hitler, in turn, rallied behind "Maxie," and Nazi Germany joined in his love for the pugilist.

The fever attendant to the scheduled boxing rematch mirrored the cataclysm that was soon to befall the world. All the obvious stereotypes were reinforced. No press story in America or Germany about Louis failed to mention his skin color. It was to be Negro versus Nazi. Race and nationalism were the ordained leitmotif for the rematch, and Louis and Schmeling would battle only months before the real war was to start.

Black newspapers appreciated the significance of the boxing match. The *Pittsburgh Courier* ran a half-page photo of Schmeling under the headline: "THE NAZI-MAN WHO WOULD BE KING." Schmeling fed the racism. Louis, he explained, would be afraid simply as a result of Schmeling's "white presence." Louis would be haunted by the beating he had received two years earlier. Hitler cabled Schmeling: "To the next world's champion, Max Schmeling. Wishing you every success." Franklin Roosevelt, however, bet $20 on Schmeling to win.

THE FIGHT: JUNE 22, 1938

Once again, Louis was the favorite to beat Schmeling, although this time the odds were narrower than before the 1936 bout. New York's *Amsterdam News* reported: "Harlem is tense," but it will "burst wide open after the fight."

Arthur Donovan, once again the referee, told both boxers to give the crowd a great fight: "I want to impress upon you men now of the terrific responsibility that you have in this ring tonight." All in attendance and listening by radio appreciated that the boxers' struggle would have social and political implications far beyond the confines of boxing and Yankee Stadium. It would not take much prescience to know that the Fascists and the democracies would soon clash, however much British prime minister Neville Chamberlain promised three months later that there would be "peace in our time." By the time of the second Louis-Schmeling fight, Hitler had put into motion his plan for conquest, accompanied by the purification of the expanding German homeland. Nazi Germany had already taken over Austria, and within months it would reoccupy the Sudetenland. The Yankee Stadium boxing match would stand as a surrogate for all-out war.

Schmeling later claimed that as he walked to the ring he was hit by a barrage of garbage thrown from the stands, although that appears unlikely. The 70,000 spectators fortunate enough to have obtained a ticket to the rematch knew that they were about to witness an extraordinary event that involved equal parts athletic skills and raw international politics. Yankee Stadium was bathed in American flags, without a swastika in sight. A hundred million people would follow the fight worldwide by radio, believed to have been the largest audience in history for a single radio broadcast. More than half the population of America, some seventy million, tuned in to NBC radio to once again hear Clem McCarthy relate the tale. Arno Hellmis again traveled from Berlin to do the German play-by-play. Hitler had closed all movie theaters in the Third Reich so people would listen to the fight as the fuehrer would do from his Bavarian retreat. The fight was also broadcast to South America in both Spanish and in Portuguese, although the feeds got crossed and millions of listeners heard the call of the match in the wrong language.

The "Fight of the Century"—it might actually have been "The Battle of the Ages"—began with an explosion of attacking fists, but by only one of the two combatants. Louis erupted into his opponent from the opening bell at 10:08 p.m. He landed his first punch in seven seconds, landed forty more punches, and did not stop until Schmeling was a beaten fighter. Louis had appeared as an avenging angel in the ring, demonstrating an uncharacteristic anger, something that would rarely occur in his stellar career. Nat Fleischer wrote in *Ring* magazine: "The revenge for which he had been looking for two years was now within his grasp, and he had no intentions of letting it slip away. Like a tiger, Joe was at him. He wasted no time and only a few punches. Those that missed didn't matter much. Too many were landing with telling effect."

Bob Considine wrote for the Hearst wire service that Louis appeared to be a "package of coiled venom." The crowd screamed: "Kill the Nazi!" Some thought Louis was just responding to the memory of the prior match. Others believed that Louis saw Schmeling as the embodiment of all things evil about Nazism, that he had been politicized in the interim between the battles. In any case, he dominated the fight as he never had before.

Clem McCarthy related to America what he saw: "Louis, right and left to the head, a left to the jaw, a right to the head, and Donovan is watching carefully. Louis measures him. Right to the body, a left up to the jaw, and Schmeling is down! The count is five! Five, six, seven, eight—the men are in the ring! The fight is over, on a technical knockout. Max Schmeling is beaten in one round!"

The fight would last two minutes and four seconds, the second-fastest heavyweight championship fight ever up to that time. Arno Hellmis screamed "Steh auf, Maxe!" ("Get up, Max!"), but he was down for the count. The Nazi hero would be helped to his corner, an international embarrassment to Herr Hitler and his Aryan super-race. Schmeling sat there weeping. Within a few seconds, Goebbels pulled the plug on the radio broadcast from New York.

The response to the fight across America was joy at the victory against Hitler, even if it was only a symbolic one in the boxing ring. For black America, it was "heaven on earth." America's political and economic system had been shocked by the Depression and revitalized by a "New Deal" for everyone. The established social system, however, remained unaffected until a boxer happened on the scene. Joe Louis had come to represent all Americans who wished to be free. Some would refuse to accept the inevitability of change and would hang onto prejudices that offered them short-term advantages. Most, however, would adopt Joe Louis as their standard-bearer and, in the process, would begin to recognize the American founding promise of equality. Louis's triumph in the ring was America's greatest moment of the decade. During a period when economic catastrophe was followed by military disaster for America's allies, one remarkable son of a sharecropper showed the way to America's redemption.

The fight was as short as the coming war would be long. How the Allies would have wanted the opportunity to K.O. Hitler as Louis had knocked out Schmeling—with a vicious, unceasing attack to the chin and the body. It was sweet retaliation for the Detroit fighter, a potent personal and political revenge, but it was more than that. It was an auspicious victory over a symbol of the worst expression of human malevolence the modern world had ever known. For the first time in its history, America had chosen country over race and had transformed a poor black from the South into the standard-bearer for American values and identity.

The 1938 rematch was certainly Joe Louis's greatest performance. He was not merely victorious, he was dominant. In the process of taking his revenge, Louis gave hope to millions of his fellow countrymen and served as the spearhead of a black consciousness that, over the coming decades, would change the face of America. The *Pittsburgh Courier* wrote that Louis "lifted an entire race out of the slough of inferiority, and gave them a sense of self-importance." Louis had confirmed their humanity. The *Courier* editorialized:

There is no doubt that German Nazis, and their kind in this country and elsewhere, looked upon the Louis-Schmeling fight as a racio-political contest which would end in greater glory for Nazism and Aryanism. So eager was the maniac Hitler to show how Nazidom viewed the bout, that on the eve of the historic battle in Yankee Stadium, he sent the Black Uhlan a wire referring to him as "the coming champion." Such things are not done by first class people with a sense of dignity and responsibility. But what can be expected from a man like Hitler?

Since the Nazis viewed this pugilistic contest as a fight between the so-called Aryan race and the colored race; between totalitarianism and democracy, the colored people may be excused for celebrating Louis' victory from the same viewpoint. It is true that men are the symbols of events; that individuals are the instruments that implement historic social changes; that Man is led by men. Accepting that viewpoint, the Brown Bomber's devastating victory has social, psychological and even political significance. . . . It was redemption for a subjugated community not yet fully free and equal. It was great sport.

The celebration in Harlem of more than 100,000 joyous participants was a testament to the political impact of Louis's victory. Richard Wright wrote for *New Masses* magazine: "They shouted, sang, laughed, yelled, blew paper horns, clasped hands, and formed weaving snake-lines, whistled, sounded sirens, and honked auto horns. From the windows of the tall, dreary tenements torn scraps of newspaper floated down. With the reiteration that evoked a hypnotic atmosphere, they chanted with eyes half-closed, heads lifting in unison, legs and shoulders moving and touching: 'Ain't you glad? Ain't you glad?'"

American Jews rejoiced at Louis's triumph over the Nazi standard-bearer. Louis became a hero in the battle against anti-Semitism. The *Jewish Times* editorialized: "If only Schmeling's collapse can be taken as a portent of the weakness of Nazism as a whole, our troubles are almost over." Regrettably, this prayer would not soon be answered.

There had been considerable speculation in the press about how the Nazi regime would respond to a Schmeling defeat, especially at the hands of an African American. Would Schmeling return to the Fatherland in disgrace? The Associated Press reported that the Germans were "disheartened." Hitler sent a message of sympathy to Schmeling's wife, and Goebbels added flowers. Neither man made any public comment, however. The German press was astonished by the outcome and blamed the Americans, especially the Jews, who were prominent in the fight game, for making the fight "a political question." German cinema replayed the film made of Schmeling's 1936 triumph over Louis, claiming that the film of the 1938 bout arrived "too late to have any topical interest."

Goebbels appreciated the debilitating effect the fight's outcome could have on Germany. He wrote in his diary that it was a "crushing defeat. . . . Now the entire nation is depressed." There would be no public talk about any loss of international prestige. The story of Max Schmeling simply disappeared from the Nazi press.

THE WAR YEARS

Although America's black newspapers had predicted that Schmeling would be sent to a concentration camp upon his return to Germany, he was not. Instead, for the most part Schmeling was simply ignored. The *New York World-Telegram* reported that a small crowd met his ship at Bremerhaven. He was no longer the national hero of two years earlier. There was no "screaming throng of worshippers." He was not arrested, however. Schmeling remained a marginal public figure and even traveled once again to America before the war broke out. He avoided talking politics and spoke only of boxing. Hitler would not allow him to fight in America, afraid of further humiliation. Schmeling did fight Germans in Germany and won every bout.

Schmeling "volunteered" for the German Army as a "parachute trooper." (He was likely drafted by the direct order of Goebbels. Schmeling had been reluctant to serve.) The Nazi press followed his exploits in the military, and he became the face of the Wehrmacht at war. Schmeling was falsely reported to have been killed in Crete while trying to escape his captors. Although Goebbels tried to have him court-marshaled, Schmeling returned to Berlin, where he received the Iron Cross for his bravery in battle. He was later incorrectly reported as having been captured by the Russians. For the rest of his service, he entertained German troops with boxing exhibitions and visited POW camps. In late 1943 or early 1944, Schmeling was released from the army and retired to his farm outside Cologne. Later reports had him imprisoned by the Nazis in the last days of the war as a deserter. Finally, the British took him into custody after the war when he was recognized walking the streets of Hamburg. On November 24, 1946, the Hamburg "denazification" court declared Schmeling "free of Nazi taint."

Joe Louis, who had earned $321,345 for his two minutes of work in Yankee Stadium against Schmeling, signed up for the draft even before Pearl Harbor. When notified in September 1941 by his local Selective Service Board 84 in Chicago that he had been classified 1-A, Louis indicated his willingness to serve: "I don't want any favors." He enlisted in the army in March 1942, passed his physical examination in October, and was summoned for service the following January. The fighter who had earned $2,263,784 in the ring signed with the army for $21 a month. He listed his occupation as "fighting" and moved into the segregated barracks at Camp Upton on Long Island for basic training. He continued to box professionally while in the service, but donated his earnings to the war effort. At a rally to raise funds for the Navy Relief Society, Louis was asked to speak about the war effort. He extemporized: "[W]e'll win 'cause we are on God's side," which became a battle cry for the Americans. Over forty-four months of service, Louis toured army camps in America and in overseas theaters of operation to raise the morale of the troops, covering 30,000 miles. He was seen by two million troops.

Near the end of the war, Marva divorced Louis. The champ, discharged from the army in October 1945, was deeply in debt and owed the Internal Revenue Service hundreds of thousands of dollars in unpaid taxes. Louis fought Billy Conn and Jersey Joe Walcott for good paydays and then retired with the remarkable record of fifty wins in fifty-one fights. He had defended his title twenty-five times. Louis returned to the ring and lost in 1950 to Ezzard Charles and in 1951 to Rocky Marciano. There was sadness in his final performances, but he needed the money to pay back taxes. Louis had earned a total of $4.6 million in the ring, but now he was broke financially and broken physically. When he died, he still owed the IRS two million dollars.

Both Schmeling and Louis boxed as long as they could, but their legacy was written in Yankee Stadium in 1936 and 1938. In the mid-1950s, they met in a Chicago nightclub as friends to talk about boxing, which had been their lives together. Schmeling left America with a Coca-Cola franchise for northern Germany that would make him a millionaire. The Atlanta-based company never offered anything to Louis.

CONCLUSION

Joe Louis's one-round triumph against Max Schmeling had obvious importance in the chaotic world of 1938, and it would also foreshadow changes in American political society that would commence shortly after the Second World War. Louis was the forerunner of Jackie Robinson and his fellow black pioneers on the baseball diamond who charted new territory in the national pastime. Change in popular sports in time helped remake American life.

Athletes of color have stood up to the status quo, but were only effective when their abilities were exemplary. A straight line of black athletes—from Jack Johnson to Joe Louis to Jackie Robinson to Tommie Smith and John Carlos to Muhammad Ali—triumphed in sports and symbolized the changes in the status quo that were coming, albeit slowly, in society. Publicly nonviolent, stoic, competitive, challenging, spirited—they stood strong to the end. Their narrative—real or imagined—catalyzed the reconstruction of American society. We are better for what they did as athletes and as fellow Americans. As Jimmy Cannon famously wrote about Joe Louis: "He was a credit to his race—the human race."

El Salvador and Honduras fought a bloody four-day war in 1969 that was triggered by soccer game violence among partisan spectators. With qualification for the World Cup at stake, a three-game playoff was scheduled. Although the two neighboring countries had long-standing differences about economic and migration issues, it was "futbol" that would spark the conflict. Sports and war could not be disentangled. *AP Images*

Some people believe football is a matter of life and death. I'm very
disappointed with that attitude. I can assure you it is much, much more
important than that. —*Bill Shankly, English soccer manager*

Serious sport has nothing to do with fair play. It is bound up
with hatred, jealousy, boastfulness, disregard of all rules and sadistic
pleasure in witnessing violence: in other words, it is war
minus the shooting. —*George Orwell*

[4]
THE "FUTBOL WAR"
OF CENTRAL AMERICA

On July 15, 1969, the *New York Times* reported that an armed conflict had broken out between Honduras and El Salvador, neighboring Central American
countries. Salvadoran aircraft—the country had only fourteen propeller-driven
planes—bombed southern Honduran cities. Honduras and El Salvador had
broken diplomatic relations two weeks earlier "after a series of violent incidents that followed soccer games between the two countries' national teams."
The *Times* offered long-standing and fundamental reasons for the outbreak
of hostilities: "deep-rooted economic, social and territorial disputes [that]
divide the two Central American countries." By the following day, however,
the *Times* began referring to the armed conflict as the "soccer war," and so the
world media applied the sports reference. Indeed, it was soccer game violence
among the partisan spectators that had triggered attacks by Honduran nationals
against thousands of Salvadorans who had squatted on Honduran lands. The
Salvadorans responded with armed force in a war that would last only four
days but would be costly in lives and property.

The Central American region has a long history of warfare, politics, and
sports. The Mayan or Mesoamerican ball game called *tlatchtli* was a team sport

played for centuries on stone courts in villages of what is now Mexico and Central America. A combination of handball, jai-alai, and volleyball played with a hard rubber ball struck by racquets, bats, stones, hips, and forearms, this dangerous game took on religious and martial significance, not unlike the ancient Olympics. The ball game served as a way to defuse or resolve conflicts between clans, families, and regions without genuine warfare. Failure in the game, however, was particularly risky, sometimes penalized by the decapitation of the losing team's captain. In this deeply ritualized activity, rivals would play the sport in lieu of battle. In the 1969 "soccer war," Central American sport escalated into open transnational conflict.

ON WAR

Carl Philipp Gottlieb von Clausewitz, a nineteenth-century Prussian military philosopher, described politics as war by other means. He would likely have found a similar relationship between sports and politics, in particular the sport of soccer, the world's most popular athletic pursuit and the source of abundant national and regional fervor. The Prussian theorist recognized in his dialectic masterwork *On War* that one cannot rely for analysis merely on "theoretical sophistries." For Clausewitz, actual experience—in the case of Honduras and El Salvador, the congruency of sports and war—would tell the tale. While politics and social custom can unite a people in pursuit of the safety of the political state, at times ructious friction between nations can be the only rational response to circumstances. When combined with what Clausewitz would refer to as "violent emotion," the result would be war, death, and destruction. There is a striking similarity between sports and war, and the actual experience on the soccer pitch and among the spectators of the sport that demonstrates the transferability of Clausewitz's insight. At times, sports and war cannot be disentangled.

When sports began in prehistory, they were closely aligned with warfare. Athletics constituted a preparation for the hunt and for the defense of the clan or tribe. The ancient Greek Olympics were recognized by contemporaries as war training. It would not be surprising, therefore, to find variations of this antediluvian experience replayed in modern times. Anyone who has attended an international soccer match, traditionally carrying the misnomer of "friendly," has witnessed a full measure of what Clausewitz termed "violent emotion." For spectators watching the symbolic combat of a soccer match between teams representing two nation-states, passion can easily escalate beyond rationality. Much like politics, it can escalate into war, pitting tribe against tribe, class against class, country against country.

Clausewitz saw politics, war, and sports as encapsulating much of human experience. He stated that war is "an act of force to compel our enemy to do our will." Sports, based on mutually understood rules, provides the arena in which to accomplish a tribal triumph, but it may prove insufficient to assuage the full range of irrational emotions. Human nature may demand more by way of conquest or revenge than sports can provide. Even when reasonable people are in the control of politics, sports may not be able to stem irrational chaos. In fact, sports might even exacerbate the animosity and trigger further chaos.

Clausewitz wrote of the "real shock upon the nerves which one of the two athletes receives by the electric spark of victory." Even without victory, the contest itself may provide "the electric spark," the rush of adrenaline that increases the heart rate, constricts blood vessels, dilates air passages, and stimulates the sympathetic nervous system. Alternatively, sports may dull human pain by diverting attention during an uncertain contest. The human need to commit to one side in a partisan affair of sports may entail a narcotic effect, and thereafter require more forceful stimuli to achieve congruent relief.

The relationship between sports and war has been part of the American experience for centuries. Supreme Court justice Oliver Wendell Holmes, Jr., a Civil War veteran, told the Harvard graduates in 1895 that their struggles on the field of play were a way to keep actual battles from occurring. "Rugged athletics" would be the best way to prepare for conflict. Reflecting on the brutality of contemporary football, he said: "If once in a while a neck is broken, I regard it not as a waste, but as a price well paid for the breeding of a race fit for hardship and command."

Theodore Roosevelt was the most prominent proponent of the sports field as the training ground for war and peace. He promoted "good, healthy play" as essential in human development, but "no bodily vigor will make a nation great if it lacks the fundamental principles of honesty and moral cleanliness." As he wrote to his son Ted, an undergraduate at Harvard in 1903: "I am delighted to have you play football. I believe in rough, manly sports. But I do not believe in them if they degenerate into the sole end of any one's existence." Unfortunately, sports does not always come defined by such limitations.

Others, like George Orwell, perceived sport as being wholly insidious. It was not a suitable substitute for war but war itself: "Football, it seemed to me, is not really played for the pleasure of kicking a ball about, but is a species of fighting." Orwell saw no redeeming social value in such competitive athletic activity. "Sport is an unfailing cause of ill-will," he wrote in 1945 in *The Sporting Spirit,* and "international sporting contests lead to orgies of hatred." He ridiculed those who thought that "running, jumping and kicking a ball are tests of national virtue." Although his ultimate conclusions may be questionable, his insight into how many humans perceive sports was quite accurate. While Orwell would have chosen to ban athletic contests as pernicious, sports' organic and ethological appeal made them universal, even if they led to "orgies of hatred." In any case, war without shooting is preferable to war with shooting.

War has certainly interfered with the normal conduct of sports. The Olympic Games were suspended during the first and second World Wars. The 1942 Rose Bowl was moved from Pasadena, California, to Durham, North Carolina, out of fear of a Japanese sneak attack on the West Coast a month after Pearl Harbor. The Rose Parade was canceled for the only time since 1890. Although Duke University had a distinct home-field advantage in the relocated "granddaddy of them all," the home team lost the bowl game to Oregon State, 20–16. During the Second World War, however, President Roosevelt declared that all sports, professional and amateur, should continue given their inherent "morale benefits." In his "green light letter" to Commissioner Kenesaw Mountain Landis, FDR said "it would be best for the country to keep baseball going. Everybody will work longer hours and harder than ever before. And they ought to have a chance for . . . taking their minds off their work even more than before."

Sports do not always trigger conflict. In fact, the opposite is often true. In the ninth century BC, the "Ekecheiria" truce allowed the ancient Olympics to proceed despite the incessant Hellenic wars. Athletes, artists, and their families had immunity to travel to and from the athletic sanctuary at Olympia. In 1969, the same year as the Central American soccer war, a three-day cease-fire was declared during the Nigerian civil war that allowed international players to play a soccer match in Nigeria. Pakistan and India, longtime foes who have fought three wars, have used sports, in particular their mutual national sport of cricket, as a medium to generate dialogue, although not yet successfully achieving lasting peace. Two world-class tennis players—Indian national Rohan Bopanna and his Pakistani doubles partner Aisam-Ul-Haq Qureshi—won acclaim and international peace awards for their message "Stop War, Start Tennis." Orwell would be confused by such national archrivals attempting to bridge such a wide political gap with racquets, bats, and balls.

SOCCER

The "beautiful game"—called "football" and not "soccer" in most nations of the world—is the world's premier sport, its lingua franca. It is played regularly in every country by an estimated 265 million people. (By comparison, only about a million people play tackle football, the American spinoff of the game first played by college students in the nineteenth century, which combined elements of soccer and rugby.)

The professional sport of soccer is played at its best by the twenty clubs of the English Premiership League, which has evolved into an international circuit attracting (and handsomely paying) the best players in the world. Although all its regular-season games or "fixtures" take place in England, they are televised around the globe to huge and attentive audiences. Virtually every country has its own professional soccer league with clubs representing local towns and cities. Some of those national leagues, such as the ones in Germany, Spain, and Italy, include clubs of international stature.

Much like professional sports teams in America, the Premiership clubs are filled overwhelmingly with working-class players. Although they generally have little formal education, they are extraordinarily skilled at soccer. The game they play is rough, played under rules enforced, sometimes unevenly, by a referee. The players have all learned the truism pronounced by Phil Woosnam, a Welsh soccer player and manager: "The rules of soccer are very simple, basically it is this: if it moves, kick it. If it doesn't move, kick it until it does."

England rightfully prides itself as the birthplace of soccer. Association football was first played under standardized rules in the mid-1860s. The first professional league, the English Football League, was founded in 1888 by William McGregor, a Scottish draper who was the director of the Aston Villa club.

However, the core of the game itself—kicking a ball through a goal—can be traced back to ancient China. The game as played in medieval England pitted entire villages against one another in contests that approached open warfare. King Edward III banned the "game" in 1331, and Queen Elizabeth I imposed a one-week jail sentence on anyone who was caught playing soccer. Notwithstanding these efforts, the game remained a popular pastime.

Commentators and spectators alike wax poetic when discussing the importance of soccer. In most countries, it is the primary sports pastime, and in some it is the only athletic pursuit, with professional leagues that run eleven months of the year. Arthur Hopcraft explained the role of the sport in *The Football Man* in 1968:

> The point about football in Britain is that it is not just a sport people take to like cricket or tennis or running long distances. It is inherent in the people. It is built into the urban psyche, as much a common experience to our children as are uncles and school. It is not a phenomenon; it is an everyday matter. There is more eccentricity in deliberately disregarding it than in devoting a life to it. It has more significance in the national character than theatre has. Its sudden withdrawal from the people would bring deeper disconsolation than to deprive them of television. The way we play the game, organize it and reward it reflects the kind of community we are.

While soccer is played on the green expanse of the "pitch," it is difficult to ignore the role of the spectators, who have often brought disgrace and sometimes tragedy to the sport. The Heysel disaster of 1985 is often cited as the nadir. The European Cup final at Heysel Stadium in Brussels pitted the Liverpool club of England against the Juventus club of Turin, Italy. Sensing trouble was in the offing, spectators favoring the competing clubs were fenced in to avoid a confrontation. An hour before kickoff, the Liverpudlians, as the inhabitants of the Lancaster city on the Mersey are called, broke free and attacked supporters of their Italian rivals. While retreating from the onslaught, hundreds were injured in the melee and thirty-nine died. As a result, the European soccer federation banned all English clubs from European competition, a ban not lifted for five years. Despite the loss of life, the match proceeded. Juventus won 1–0 on a penalty kick.

Violence connected to international soccer matches is not an unusual phenomenon. On May 24, 1964, a riot broke out during a pre-Olympic soccer match in Lima between Peru and Argentina after a referee disallowed a late Peruvian goal. After a few spectators rushed onto the pitch, the police panicked and fired tear gas directly into the stands. Over 300 people were killed and more than 500 injured. When Romania qualified for the 1990 World Cup, the celebrations in Bucharest carried over into the streets, culminating ultimately in the execution of ousted dictator Nicolae Ceausescu and his wife. In the November 1997 "football revolution," women of Iran, who had been banned from all celebrations, stormed into the Tehran stadium to celebrate Iran's victory, which qualified it for the World Cup. Soccer can at times even be a counterbalance to religious oppression. At least on that one occasion, the heavy hand of the mullahs had met its match.

The most recent mass murder on the soccer pitch occurred in Port Said, Egypt, on February 1, 2012, during a contest between historic rivals El Masry of Port Said and Al Ahly of Cairo. Visiting fans, referred to as "ultras," displayed signs that questioned the manhood of the local faithful, and fights broke out in the stands. After the home club rallied to an upset victory, the spectators stormed the field, attacking opposing loyalists with knives, clubs, and stones. Police stood by as the massacre of the spectators proceeded. Al Ahly star midfielder Mohamed Aboutrika said: "People here are dying, and no one is doing a thing. It's like a war." At least seventy-four fans died in the brawl, some thrown from high in the stands, others trampled by the stampeding crowd. At least a thousand were injured, many seriously. Egypt's military government characterized the melee as part of the effort to halt the transition to civilian rule in a country still reeling from the 2011 revolution. Soccer ultras had joined in that historic revolt from its beginning, helping to beat back supporters of President Mubarak in a daylong battle at Tahrir Square. The president of the Masry club commented that the deaths at the soccer match in Port Said were political: "This is a plot to topple the state."

THE WORLD CUP

A quadrennial soccer competition among the nations of the world offers numerous opportunities for sports and politics to intermix. The World Cup is a momentous event. Qualifying matches often become international competitions of significant national importance. The World Cup is a vehicle for national pride and international rivalries. For some countries, merely qualifying for the World Cup is a meaningful national accomplishment and a matter of personal and community self-esteem. Only one nation, Brazil, has qualified for all nineteen World Cups. Even success has its price, however. In July 1950, Uruguay faced Brazil for the World Cup championship in Rio de Janeiro. The surprise victory by the Uruguayan visitors to Maracana Stadium, before a crowd estimated at a record 200,000, caused such shock in Uruguay that eight rooters for the victors reportedly died of heart attacks upon hearing the news.

There is also the often-unexpressed feeling that the World Cup is special because it is one arena—either in sports or otherwise—in which the United States does not dominate. The U.S. team has advanced to the semifinals only once—at the first World Cup, in 1930. Since that event, it has progressed to the round of sixteen only twice. From 1954 through 1986, the U.S. national team did not even qualify to participate.

Qualifying for the World Cup can come at a price. In 1982, Sheikh Fahid Al-Ahmad Al-Sabah, the president of the Kuwaiti national team and the brother of the Kuwaiti emir, offered each player a $200,000 bonus for besting the French club in the qualifying round. There may have been other money offered for a favorable outcome. With France leading 3–1 in the match at Valladolid in Spain, French midfielder Alain Giresse scored a goal that the Kuwaiti team protested. Many thought Soviet referee Miroslav Stupar had blown his whistle, causing the Kuwaiti team to stop playing. Stupar denied he had sounded a stoppage in play. Sheikh Al-Sabah rushed onto the pitch to complain. Remarkably, the Soviet referee changed his decision and disallowed the goal. The French proceeded to score another goal a few minutes later and won 4–1. Stupar had disallowed five goals by France during the match, suggesting perhaps that he might have been favoring the Kuwaiti squad. As a result of his performance, referee Stupar lost his international refereeing credentials, and Al-Sabah was fined $10,000, a mere slap on the royal wrist.

A loss in World Cup competition can have serious consequences. Colombian player Andres Escobar inadvertently deflected the ball into his own net during the 1994 World Cup, leading to his team's loss to the United States. After returning home to Medellin after his "own goal," Escobar was assassinated. His killer, Humberto Munoz, confronted him in a parking lot, saying "*¡Gracias*

por el auto gol en la propia puerta!" (Spanish for "Thanks for the own goal"),
and then shouted "Gol!" (Spanish for goal) each of the twelve times he shot
Escobar. He was sentenced to forty-three years in prison but had only served
eleven at the time of his release in 2010.

CENTRAL AMERICA

Demarcated by mountain ranges and bordered by two oceans, the countries
of Central America, like the Balkan states, have experienced years of warfare,
political instability, abject poverty, and absolute dictatorships. Both Honduras
and El Salvador gained their independence from Spain in 1821, and both have
suffered profound economic misfortune for most of their history. For almost a
century prior to their armed conflict in 1969, the two nations had been disput-
ing their common border. The two nations and their neighbors made various
attempts at economic reform and political unification, but all efforts proved
unavailing. Revolutions, anarchy, rivalries, and human hardship prevailed
instead. Both the political and business leaders of Honduras and El Salvador
faced considerable economic and social problems without ready solutions. A
war, however, could be a convenient diversion for the political leadership of
both countries. Based on long-standing grievances and true economic hardship, a war would boost national honor and pride.

El Salvador is a small country, about the size of New Jersey, with an economy that throughout the twentieth century relied on agricultural exports of
coffee, sugar, and cotton. The nation was run by an oligarchy of elites that captured most of its national wealth and held all the political power. Population
growth, which had resulted from improved medical treatment, created another
export—Salvadorans. Starting at the turn of the twentieth century, Salvadoran immigrants began to cross the border into Honduras, and by 1969 some
300,000 were living there, making up 20 percent of its peasant population.

Ultimately, it was the problem of Salvadoran immigrants squatting on Honduran lands that would be the root cause of the armed conflict. El Salvador
would have had sufficient land for all its people if land had been distributed
equitably instead of concentrated in the hands of a few autocratic families.
Impoverished but ambitious, Salvadorans crossed the border for decades to
work in the mines not far from the Salvadoran border. Some headed to the

Honduran north coast, where there were jobs offered by the banana companies. Others simply settled down to farm on public Honduran lands. The Honduran government and press focused the nation's hatred on these Salvadoran peasants.

Although it experienced political instability similar to El Salvador's, Honduras had a much smaller population and an economy based almost exclusively on banana exports, operated by the American-controlled United Fruit Company, which owned 10 percent of the country's land. Honduras's history had been filled with instability caused by boundary conflicts with its neighbors. Civil unrest fueled by labor strife, national debt, and North American interference, as well as a large influx of Lebanese Christian immigrants, led to revolving governments, military coups, elections, and purges. Honduras became, in large measure, an economic colony of the United States. By the mid-1960s, United Fruit joined with other large landowners in an association to pressure the Honduran government to protect their property rights by addressing the issue of Salvadoran immigrants. The country's press, remarkably uncontrolled, abused its freedom by exaggerating real problems into catastrophic dilemmas in order to increase circulation. The Salvadoran press, of course, would not be outdone and followed suit, reporting stories of the hardships inflicted on Salvadoran immigrants in Honduras. Journalists in both countries spewed outrage about the situation, inciting action if not violence itself.

Both El Salvador and Honduras tried without success to address these immigration problems peacefully. Ultimately, Honduras announced it would apply the existing (but previously unenforced) agrarian reform law that limited land ownership to native Hondurans. As a result, in 1967 the government confiscated the land Salvadoran immigrants had worked, sometimes for decades. It then announced it would expel 80,000 Salvadorans. Honduran peasants and government-sponsored thugs attacked the Salvadorans, and there were sporadic clashes across the border, with "provocations" committed by both sides. Hostilities grew as the exploitative press of both countries fanned suspicions and denounced their neighbors.

In the middle of this boiling political and potentially military cauldron, the two countries were scheduled to play important soccer matches. While the underlying and fundamental conflicts between the nations certainly explain the hostilities that followed, it was the soccer matches that ignited a war. The countries were scheduled to play three elimination matches. The first to win two games would move on to the World Cup. The first match was held on June 8, 1969, in Tegucigalpa, Honduras. The arriving Salvadoran footballers were greeted at their hotel by a hostile crowd. Hooligans shot off fireworks and promised trouble. Local fans kept the El Salvador team awake by making an infernal din outside their hotel. The next day Honduras beat sleepless El Salvador 1–0. The second match was scheduled for San Salvador, the Salvadoran capital, a week later.

The loss to Honduras in the first game, it was said, drove an eighteen-year-old Salvadoran girl, Amelia Bolanos, to commit suicide. After the winning goal was scored, Bolanos, who was watching on television, ran into the adjoining room, found her father's pistol, and shot herself through the heart. At her funeral, which was televised nationwide, El Salvador's president, a military honor guard, and the national soccer team walked behind her flag-draped casket. A local newspaper reported: "This young girl could not bear to see her nation brought to its knees." The Salvadorans blamed Honduras for Bolanos's death, further inflaming the relationship between the two countries.

The second match was held in San Salvador on June 15, 1969, and the Salvadoran crowds greeted the Honduran squad with revenge in mind. Local fans kept the Honduran squad awake all night, hurling rotten eggs and dead rats through their hotel windows. The visiting Honduran team was taken to the stadium in armored cars. Instead of raising the Honduran flag before the game, the hosts ran up a dirty old rag. At the stadium, the partisan crowd hurled balloon "bombs" filled with urine at those Honduran fans who had braved the trip. El Salvador prevailed 3–0. The Honduran players were just glad to get out alive. The same could not be said for two of the visiting fans, who were killed near the stadium. In retaliation, a number of Salvadorans living in Honduras were killed, and Honduras broke off diplomatic relations with its neighbor. The press on both sides was aflame.

The third and deciding match was played on a neutral pitch in Mexico City on June 26, 1969, and El Salvador prevailed in extra time, winning the World Cup invitation. Following the matches, incidents continued to multiply in both countries, sometimes at the urging, or with the participation, of the security forces of the two countries. Salvadoran newspapers alleged episodes of "barbaric terrorism" against Salvadorans in Honduras, including hangings, castrations, mutilations, and lynchings. El Salvador cut off diplomatic relations with Honduras, stating that "the government of Honduras has not taken any effective measures to punish these crimes which constitute genocide, nor has it given assurances of indemnification or reparations for the damages caused to Salvadorans." The Organization of American States (OAS) investigated and confirmed that some of these incidents had taken place.

To avoid further injury, a flood of Salvadoran refugees headed back across the border. On June 24, 1969, the Salvadoran National Assembly passed a resolution censuring these "outrages," noting in the legislation that Honduras apparently was instigating these atrocities "as a result of the recent international football games." The World Cup qualifiers had detonated the explosive situation between the two countries.

Ultimately, international news began to report the incipient conflict. The *New York Times* wrote that some 300,000 Salvadorans had entered Honduras seeking land because their tiny country could not accommodate their needs. Honduras, it explained, with five times the land mass of its neighbor, had fewer nationals than El Salvador. The Associated Press reported the political conflict's connection to sports: "These feelings came to a head last month during a three-game soccer match to determine which team would play in the world cup matches. A wave of violence flared against Salvadorans after charges of mistreatment of Honduran fans at a game in San Salvador." In response, it said, Honduran police and irregulars attacked the Salvadoran foreigners who had squatted on Honduran land.

El Salvador was better prepared for the war, with 8,000 well-trained regular troops and adequate armament. Both governments enjoyed the support of their populace, and the local press had turned rabid. Both countries charged aggression by their enemy, although it was the Salvadorans that invaded on July 14, 1969, after first using the meager air power it possessed. El Salvador did not have sufficient military aircraft to continue its attack, however. It appropriated propeller-driven passenger airplanes and, with bombs attached to their fuselages, attacked targets inside Honduras, including the airport facility at Toncontin and other strategic locations, leaving the Honduran air force unable to react effectively. El Salvador announced that it simply sought to protect its nationals who had immigrated to Honduras. In turn, Hondurans rallied to support their territorial integrity. Its weaker air force set Salvadoran oil tanks ablaze. However, its smaller army of 2,500 trained men quickly faltered.

The advent of the rainy season helped stem the advances of both armies, which were bogged down on muddy roads. The World War II aircraft on both sides were either lost or grounded by lack of parts or fuel. The Organization of American States offered a way for the combatants to save face after both armies staggered. The OAS intervened with a resolution calling for the withdrawal of troops and with guarantees for the protection of the remaining 200,000 Salvadorans within Honduras. Within a few days, the two countries declared a cease-fire, mutually withdrew their troops, and pledged to protect the safety of the other country's nationals. It took years, however, for the warring parties to reach a final peace treaty.

The soccer rivalry between Honduras and El Salvador had been intense; their war was, for the most part, not quite as intense, but it was bloody. The four days of hostilities resulted in as many as 2,000 deaths, with twice that number wounded and many times that number left homeless. Eleven years later, the two nations signed a peace treaty and resolved the continuing dispute over their border through international arbitration.

Although the economic and social underpinnings of the conflict have been well documented, it was the soccer riots that triggered the conflict. Wars are not fought over soccer matches, but emotions evoked by soccer matches can light the fuse of conflict.

In the 1970 World Cup, El Salvador lost its three matches, against the Soviet Union, Mexico, and Belgium, scoring no goals. Both Honduras and El Salvador qualified for the 1982 World Cup. Neither won any matches, but Honduras tied two national teams before being eliminated in the first round. El Salvador scored no goals, losing all three matches. On October 14, 2009, Honduras qualified for the 2010 FIFA World Cup after a 1–0 win against El Salvador. There was no war this time. In the games held in South Africa, it tied one match, but did not score a goal in that game. In both countries, soccer remains the national passion.

SOCCER AND CONFLICT

While the Honduras–El Salvador conflict is generally referred to as the "soccer war," the "beautiful game" has been the source of other violent struggles between nationals of competing nations. On September 24, 1962, the president of the Congo Republic declared a state of emergency to try to stem attacks against

Gabonese citizens living in Brazzaville. The source of the mob violence was a soccer match that had occurred eight days earlier. Congo had won the match against Gabon. Rumors spread in Gabon that its club and supporters had been attacked, leading mobs in Libreville, Gabon, to seek out Congolese for retaliation. Gabon's premier severed all sports contacts with Congo and ordered the expulsion of all Congolese from Gabon. Thousands were rounded up and placed on ships that would take them to their home country. The Congolese quarter in the Gabonese capital was burned to the ground.

Two years later, in 1964, in Lima, Peru, in the final qualifier for the 1964 Tokyo Olympics, Peru faced Argentina's vaunted soccer team. With two minutes remaining, a goal by Peru's Bertolotti Andrés was annulled, sparking an outbreak of violence. The police hurled tear gas into the northern grandstand to pacify the crowd and then padlocked the stadium. Three hundred eighteen of the stunned and locked spectators died, many from asphyxia. In the street, a mob destroyed private property around the stadium. The incident prompted the Peruvian government to institute martial law for thirty days.

A November 2009 soccer playoff between Egypt and Algeria would determine who would participate in the 2010 World Cup in South Africa. Algeria had won the first match, in June, and Egypt had to win at home to have a chance to attend the quadrennial event. As the Algerian team bus passed through the streets of Cairo, it was stoned, and three players were injured. The Egyptians won the match, necessitating a deciding fixture at a neutral site in the Sudan. Algerians responded with outrage by looting and burning the offices of Egyptian companies in Algiers, including Egypt Air, causing millions of dollars in damage. An Egyptian plane was dispatched to Algeria to rescue its citizens, but it was refused permission to land. In Marseilles, 500 police were deployed to quell disturbances by Algerian youths, making eight arrests. The Algerian embassy in Cairo was then attacked. Egypt recalled its ambassador from Algiers. Algeria emerged victorious in the Sudan rubber match 1–0, but only managed one tie in three matches in the South African World Cup.

PARAMILITARY SPORTS

Franklin Foer, in his remarkable book *How Soccer Explains the World*, tells the story of Serbian warlord criminal Željko Ražnatović, nicknamed Arkan. Arkan led the hooligans of the Ultra Bad Boys of the Belgrade Red Star soccer club into the paramilitary hostilities of the Balkan Wars of the 1990s. Before the wars, the Ultra Bad Boys had intimidated both opposing soccer clubs and their followers. Fans came to the soccer matches of clubs that embodied their nationalist aspirations carrying arms and prepared to start trouble. The violence soothed their desperate sense of historical injustice, if only temporarily.

At about the same time, Croatian football hooligans, fans of Dynamo Zagreb, known as the Bad Blue Boys, became the core of the new Croatian army. Many date the origin of the breakup of Yugoslavia and the resulting Balkan Wars to the May 13, 1990, soccer match between Dynamo Zagreb and Red Star Belgrade. The riot that ensued in the stadium and on the streets of Zagreb sparked a political and military convulsion. Three thousand of Arkan's Serbian followers had traveled to the Zagreb match, and their chants—"Zagreb is Serbian" and "We'll kill Tudjman," the newly elected Croat leader—incited the violence. The combat that took place on the soccer pitch between the armed mobs lasted for over an hour.

The Balkan football thugs demonstrated with nihilistic proficiency how war did not require actual nation-states or uniformed armies. These were ultranationalist gangsters pursuing the goals of the elected thugs without restraint. Arkan vowed to "defend the nation to the last man." As soccer skirmishes became total war, his soccer hooligans turned paramilitary avengers. Starting with the rape of Bijelijna, Zornik, Bratunak, and later Sasina, Arkan's troops looted Muslim homes, murdered families, and buried them in mass graves. With his booty of war, Arkan purchased his own soccer team, Obilic of Belgrade, and built it into a major soccer power by systematically intimidating opposing players and referees. Arkan was placed on Interpol's most wanted list.

On January 15, 2000, Arkan was murdered by a junior policeman in the lobby of Belgrade's elite InterContinental Hotel, perhaps at the direction of Serbian nationalist authorities. Although some minor figures were convicted, no one knows for sure who had planned the assassination. There were many who would have wanted Arkan dead.

The Croat soccer gangs followed a similar path. Once open war had broken out, they wore the emblem of their soccer club, Dynamo Zagreb, on their sleeves. Today, there is a statue of soldiers at the entrance to the Zagreb stadium with this dedication: "To the fans of this club, who started the war with Serbia at this ground on May 13, 1990," the date of the Belgrade-Zagreb match.

RELIGION AND SOCCER

It was soccer that gave birth to the Balkan gangs, but it was the illness of re-venge, violence, and religious conflict that converted their soccer hooliganism into armed militarism. Not all soccer fans, of course, fall off the same cliff, but many lose control over normal, everyday restraints on behavior. Soccer can reveal what rational people will not say in public. Soccer will catalyze behavior beyond the pale.

Nationalism is matched in its role as a catalyst for violence only by religion. Foer tells the story of the divide between the two most important soccer clubs in Glasgow, Scotland, the Protestant Rangers and the Catholic Celtics. Although their conflict never reached the extremes of that in the Balkans, there was plenty of violence and some murders connected with each "Old Firm" match between the clubs. Even as England fought for its life against Hitler's blitzkrieg, Rangers and Celtics fans rioted.

Religious differences reflecting modern tribes have always spurred violence. Adding sports to the mix offered a forum and an excuse for the pitched battles between gangs of hooligans, with the participants wearing their symbolic shirts and scarves. Vile and drunken adherents of the Rangers and Celtics clubs still continue a battle over a half-century old. Much of the conflict is based on eth-nic rivalry. Perhaps the connection to sports is just a matter of chance. More likely, sports provide the sod in which violence may grow.

CONCLUSION

Although the Rangers-Celtics truculence offers an extreme example, intense rivalry is part of politics and sports. The English Premier League (EPL) offers the best soccer in the world, and the EPL clubs have adherents worldwide, although matches no longer end in a bloody confrontation. Sports fans love the sense of belonging that comes from commitment to the fortunes of eleven men on a soccer pitch. If that requires, at times, some direct action by follow-ers, then so be it. It certainly requires some sacrifice. Every Brit follows his favorite team, and the fortunes of that club reflect on how he sees his status in the world. The devoted know the history of their club as if it was written in that morning's newspaper. Revenge can take decades, but the hating has no end.

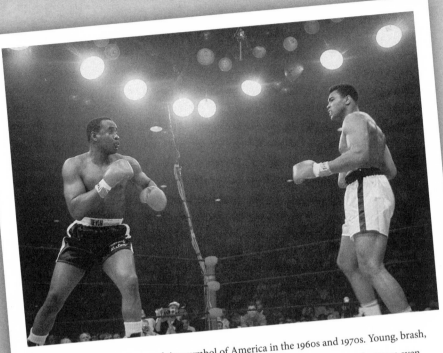

Muhammad Ali was an evolving symbol of America in the 1960s and 1970s. Young, brash, and graceful, the Louisville boxer elicited strong negative feelings from observers even after he had proven his prowess in the ring by twice knocking out the reigning heavyweight king, Sonny Liston. When Ali refused induction into the armed forces during the Vietnam War, claiming conscientious objector status as a minister of his Nation of Islam faith, he became a symbol of resistance. He would end his career as a universal icon, beloved by millions across the globe. *AP Images*

I ain't got no quarrel with them Viet Cong.

—*Muhammad Ali*

[5]
MUHAMMAD ALI
AND THE SYMBOLS
OF POLITICS

Never a man of a few words, Muhammad Ali used but nine of them to express his reason for declining the U.S. government's invitation to fight on one side of a civil war between two political factions in South Asia. He had no personal "quarrel" with the peasants he would be expected to kill as a member of the fighting forces. Unconquerable and unyielding, by his simple act of resistance Ali became a symbol of political opposition to a contemptible war. America was torn between two visions—the predominant ethos of an international enforcer of hegemony in world politics and a subordinate culture committed to the defense of human rights and dignity. Ali may not have thought of himself in such grandiose terms, but, when he refused to take the step forward to accept induction into the armed forces, he galvanized the forces of dissent in a country more divided than at any time in a century. Never has an athlete been more reviled by the forces of the American establishment. Never would an athlete take on a role of such symbolic political importance to those who would resist the dominant ethos and challenge the status quo.

If this were not sufficient, Ali would also become a major actor in the passion play of the civil rights movement. Although not a direct participant in the peaceful campaign for justice, Ali played a critical role in the second wave of black resistance, the phase of black pride, black power, and black consciousness. Some blacks, like those in the Black Panther movement, rejected the nonviolent credo of Dr. Martin Luther King Jr. by encouraging direct, and often violent, action in the urban ghettos. Others, like those in the Nation of Islam, sought to bolster black self-improvement and community development through the rhetoric of self-awareness and separatism. Here is where Ali would find his mission and his ardor, as the most public symbol of the group that became known as the Black Muslims.

Ali, a boxer by trade, would be a principal actor in these two central dramas that would define America in the second half of the twentieth century—war and race. Unschooled in traditional ways, Ali would eventually win over the American public and press, but only after suffering decades of marginalization and outright hostility. By the end of the millennium, Ali would become the most famous American in the world, known by 98 percent of the world's population.

Although clearly influential, Ali would be the first to admit that he was not an original political thinker or a particularly humanistic figure. He was certainly a remarkable athlete. His adoption of the teachings of Elijah Muhammad demonstrated a need to resolve his genuine confusion over spiritual matters. However, Ali deserved the acclaim he eventually received for the actions he took that flowed directly from his newfound religion. He was a stalwart adherent of his faith, and, once he made up his mind, he did not waver.

Ali was as unconventional in the ring as he was outside it. He was not a classic pugilist of the Damon Runyon variety with hands held high, sticking a left jab followed by a right cross. Ali was always on the move during a fight. He would jab and move in time to avoid his opponent's punch. As his doggerel explained:

Float like a butterfly.
Sting like a bee.
Your hands can't hit
What your eyes can't see.

He was a master at invention. He would lean against the ropes in his later fights, letting his opponent punch himself out, a move Ali termed the "rope-a-dope." He used it most effectively in his 1974 fight in the Democratic Republic of the Congo (then known as Zaire) against George Foreman, known as the "Rumble in the Jungle." Ali knocked out Foreman in the eighth round to regain the world heavyweight championship for a second time. Ali's footwork made him the fastest heavyweight of all time. Included in his repertoire was a quick scissor step termed the "Ali shuffle." It would incense his opponents, part of Ali's plan to gain the emotional upper hand in every bout.

AN EVOLVING SYMBOL

Symbols as shorthand images play an indispensable role in political discourse and serve as critical instruments in the exercise of governmental power. Although Ali thought of himself as beyond imposed stereotypes, he was in fact an evolving political symbol. We first saw him as the young, brash, graceful, and "pretty" Louisville boxer, the 1960 Olympic light heavyweight champion with the Romanesque name of Cassius Marcellus Clay, who announced upon his return to the States: "I'm king of the world!" He was king of the amateur boxing world, but he had plans to extend his jurisdiction, as he repeatedly told us. He was decidedly outrageous and offensive to many, especially to members of the boxing press, who at first considered him simply a blowhard and later castigated him as a religious zealot and a traitor to his country.

Ali was a contradiction. He conquered the "mobbed up" Sonny Liston in the ring and showed the world he was a pugilist unlike any in memory. But Ali also had a cruel side. His poetry and clowning outside the ring conflicted with his occasional depravity inside the squared circle. His ferocious batterings of Floyd Patterson and Ernie Terrell (both of whom had refused to call him by his Muslim name) displayed Ali as a vindictive and brutal gladiator. (While thrashing Terrell on his way to winning a fifteen-round decision, Ali punctuated his flurries with taunts of "What's my name?" to express his anger at the slight.) When Ali's devotion to Islam, at least the version espoused by the Nation of Islam, became his life's lodestar, the public was simply confounded. As the most visible representative of a little-known, separatist religious group, Ali symbolized the "other" in American life. During a period of precipitous change and widespread public apprehension, Ali's adherence to the eccentric teachings of Elijah Muhammad was strange and frightening. He was, as sportswriter Alex Poinsett wrote in 1963 in *Ebony* magazine, a "blast furnace of race pride." As Ali said after he had become the world heavyweight champion: "I know the truth, and I don't have to be what you want me to be."

When Ali refused induction into the armed forces during the Vietnam War, claiming conscientious objection as a minister of his Nation of Islam faith, he became a symbol of resistance and, for many, he gained a new dignity. For others, he was simply a coward and a traitor, although throughout his boxing career he had demonstrated he was fearless. Ali saw his refusal as simply a matter of his religious obligation. At a time when a growing percentage of the American public had just begun to rethink its blind support for the military adventure in Southeast Asia, Ali had become a dangerous antagonist to those who were committed to fighting "godless" communism. To others, Ali's sacrifice of his boxing career at the height of its glory was a testament to the sincerity and significance of his resistance. The sporting establishment would make him pay a price for his defiance, and he would be barred from boxing for more than three years. In exchange, however, he won recognition from many Americans who would no longer move in lockstep toward induction. He would serve as a continuing and evolving symbol of nonconformity to the expectations of others. It would be the leitmotif of his life.

After his exile from the ring, in his second coming as a heavyweight champion, Ali became another symbol—one of personal triumph over victimization, an inspiration not only for persons of color but for a worldwide population of disadvantaged humanity. Few athletes could reengage in such a dangerous sport after an imposed layoff, but Ali did. His three fights against Joe Frazier, culminating in the "Thrilla in Manila," showed an aging, but courageous, Ali adopting a revised style of boxing that fit his diminished physical talents. No longer the Louisville "butterfly," Ali would simply outthink his opponents.

Ali's final metamorphosis into an internationally recognized symbol of peace and goodwill was by far his most remarkable transformation. Ali became what sportswriter William Nack called "a cultural saint." He became a hero not because of what he had accomplished in the ring but because he had willingly given it all up for his beliefs. While Ali was in exile from the ring, the world changed and would continue to change over the coming decades. Although he would never win over those who saw his resistance to conformity as "uppity" and his religion as shocking, Ali became for others a champion of human values. His debilitating Parkinson's disease—the tremors, the mask-like face, the halting speech—made his final public representation even more telling.

When to the surprise of a worldwide audience he was chosen to light the Olympic flame at the 1996 Olympic Games in Atlanta, Ali became a symbol of mankind for all time. He had always been an American original, but he had become a global political icon. When Ali stood alone on the platform at the Olympics, carrying the torch in his shaking left arm, he washed away the hate of many who had not forgiven him his transgressions. Although Ali's Parkinson's disease enfeebled him in many ways, it added to his persona as a stoic and symbolic figure. As the crowd of 80,000 chanted his name, Ali lit the Olympic flame for all mankind.

SYMBOLS AND POLITICS

Symbols—both objects and people—have always had potent political significance. Kings and queens carried scepters and wore crowns as symbols of their authority. Priests in all cultures possessed relics of significance that often were said to have originated with the gods. Persons born into influential castes needed no physical representation of their power, which came as a matter of their birthright. Society, whether ancient or modern, had always been segmented by dominance and influence, where symbols played a prominent, differentiating role.

Hitler's twisted cross, the swastika, was the powerful representation of his savage regime. The future fuehrer had selected the Bronze Age symbol for his new Reich while incarcerated in the Landsberg prison after the failed Beer Hall putsch in 1923. The symbol became ubiquitous in Nazi Germany. Together with the extended right arm salute and forceful declarations of "Heil Hitler," the Nazis had devised a triad of devotional representations with which to confirm loyalty to the regime and its omnipotent human embodiment. Even after the demise of the Third Reich, the swastika remained so potent and terrifying a symbol that its display is banned by law in Germany. It remains a crime to publicly display the swastika and other Nazi symbols, salutes, songs, pictures, and slogans.

Not all symbols represent evil. Churchill's "V" symbol of eventual victory rallied the British people to the cause. It was borrowed later by antiwar protesters as a symbol of triumph over militarism. The greatest symbol of all time, the simple cross, unites the world's millions who believe that God's son sacrificed his earthly life to save us from sin. People fight for their country as represented by its flag, more than a designed piece of cloth, a telling representation of a nation and its people.

Over recent decades, millions of Muslim immigrants have been drawn to the European continent seeking economic opportunity. Muslim religious law requires that women dress modestly in public, and that means being covered from head to toe. Europe now faces the challenge of integrating these newcomers into societies that have become overwhelmingly secular in nature. In 2009, the president of France, Nicholas Sarkozy, denounced the wearing of the burqa by Muslim women. He said: "In our country, we cannot accept that women be prisoners behind a screen, cut off from all social life, deprived of all identity." The following year, the French National Assembly officially banned wearing the Muslim garb. Other European countries have considered similar actions.

In 2009, Poland joined the symbol censorship parade by enacting a law that criminalized the possession, purchase, or distribution of any material containing Communist symbols. Hungary, Latvia, and Lithuania have similar strictures. Having suffered under the Soviet "hammer and sickle" for decades, these Eastern European countries continued to worry about the disruptive effect such symbolic representations could have on their societies.

Not only signs and clothing but men and women also can become powerful symbols of good and bad. Every nation has its djinni, those mystical and mythical creatures who must be faced down. Hitler's demonic obsession with the Jews was only the most devastating of these lunacies. Every nation also has its exemplars. Often that person is an athlete who has captured that nation's imagination, hopes, and aspirations.

RACE AND SPORT

For black Americans, freedom from slavery did not produce economic opportunity. In fact, for most blacks, emancipation did not even mean leaving the county of their birth. Most continued to toil in the fields of the South, earning subsistence wages for their work. While political rights were guaranteed by Congress and amendments to the Constitution, social rights were not. Within a very short period of time, the promise of participation in governance was nullified. Jim Crow laws embodied a separate and unequal status for persons of color in America. As recently as 1956, Louisiana enacted a law that outlawed "athletic training, games, sports or contests . . . in which the participants or contestants are members of the white and Negro races."

Some sports, however, would offer talented athletes a narrow avenue of success, where merit and excellence would be rewarded. For example, most jockeys at the turn of the twentieth century were black, and black jockeys won fifteen of the first twenty-eight Kentucky Derbies. Blacks played integrated professional baseball at the Major League level until the 1880s. As American apartheid became the national ethos, however, persons of color were systematically excluded from the public arena. After 1921, for example, no black jockeys would ride in the Kentucky Derby until 2000. Organized baseball would enforce a strict color line dividing the white Major Leagues from the black Negro Leagues until 1947. It would be 1957 before all Major League clubs had at least one player of color on their rosters.

Blacks were also segregated in the boxing ring. Many white fighters would refuse to fight any black boxer. The most prominent example was John L. Sullivan, who stated: "I will not fight a Negro. I never have and I never shall." Although the black community supported prizefighting, the white champions staunchly refused to integrate the ring, lest they fall short of the competition. Only with the coming of Jack Johnson and the championship he won fighting Tommy Burns in Australia in 1908 did the white establishment have to contemplate a black competing on equal footing.

BLACK PROTESTS

Although Ali was certainly the most famous athlete to enter the political cauldron, he was not alone. The solemn black power salute offered by Tommie Smith and John Carlos atop the medal stand in Mexico City at the 1968 Olympics subjected them to public scorn and commercial catastrophe. Wearing black socks and one black glove each, the two athletes bowed their heads while the national anthem played. They raised their black fists to the sky. The most famous black power demonstration ended the Olympics for these splendid and courageous athletes, who were immediately suspended and expelled from Mexico City. The families of both received death threats.

Denver Nuggets guard Mahmoud Abdul-Rauf, who had changed his name from Chris Jackson when he became a practicing Muslim, refused to stand during the national anthem during the 1996 season. He would either stay in the locker room or sit on the bench at courtside. He explained that he saw the flag as "nationalistic ritualism: You can't be for God and for oppression." After his suspension by the National Basketball Association, Abdul-Rauf agreed to stand during the anthem, but he would look down and recite a prayer. He had made his point.

Bill Russell was among the greatest athletes ever to play basketball. He was such a dominating force in college that the NCAA expanded the width of the foul lane from six feet to twelve. It was his bad fortune to have played professionally in Boston, a city that had real difficulty coming to terms with its institutional racism. Russell learned not to trust whites based on a history of being subject to discrimination, despite his remarkable talents on the court. Vandals invaded his house, covered the walls with racist graffiti, damaged his trophies, and defecated in the beds. Russell spoke out, describing Boston as a "flea market of racism." Only decades later, as the city shed its tarnished image, would Boston recognize that Bill Russell had been a hero as an athlete and a person.

CASSIUS CLAY

Young Cassius Clay was America's most unconventional sports figure. A maestro of braggadocio, Clay exploded on the public scene as a brash youngster. Born in Louisville in 1942, a child of the black middle class, the son of a sign painter who aspired to be an artist, Clay was named for an abolitionist who had inherited forty slaves and then freed them. The original Cassius Marcellus Clay was a Kentuckian who was Lincoln's ambassador to Russia. The boxer's great-great-grandfather had been a slave to the diplomat and had taken his name after his liberation.

A beautiful child, Clay suffered the insults of Jim Crow but not the abject poverty that was the common experience for many young boxers. When he was twelve, he vowed to learn how to box so he could punch the nose of the miscreant who had stolen his bicycle. He found his way to Louisville's Columbia gym and soon matured into a fine amateur boxer. He avoided the perils of smoking and drinking, although he never mastered school skills. As he later would say: "I never said I was the smartest; I said I was the greatest."

While Clay's boxing talents were evident, his outrageous rants, raves, and self-promotion were more than just unorthodox. They were disturbing. Fans had never witnessed such a consummate windbag. His poems and predictions began early in his amateur career: "This guy must be done. I'll stop him in one." This was certainly bizarre behavior for a fifteen-year-old, but Clay proved to be a natural performer—David Remnick has called him America's first rapper—with a distinctive touch likened to a circus barker calling out to the crowds. He was a brash, confident performer. There has never been anyone like him before or since. Ali would make the sport of boxing once again an international attraction.

There had been black fighters before, of course, the most prominent of whom were Jack Johnson and Joe Louis. Johnson paid the price for challenging the social status quo. Unconstrained by custom or any imposed versions of propriety, Johnson lived a public life that scandalized white America, marrying white women and carrying on in front of the media. He pounded former heavyweight champion Jim Jeffries, the "Great White Hope," in 1910 even as the crowd chanted "Kill the nigger." Finally, Johnson fled the country ahead of a specious indictment for transporting a white woman across state lines for prostitution. He later returned to the States and served jail time. And, as we have seen, when Joe Louis began his rise in boxing circles, his handlers made sure he would not offend the establishment. He was quiet, respectful, and, at times, dull. He would be the antithesis of Jack Johnson.

Cassius Clay would follow his own distinctive path. Like Jack Johnson, he was unwilling to be controlled by imposed norms, and he rejected the stereotyped role of the obedient Joe Louis. His behavior seemed eccentric, peculiar, audacious, and even dangerous to observers. He was a splendid showman. He would prevail in the ring, he said, because "I'm too pretty to be hit." His prose and poetry seemed to many the ravings of a lunatic. To those still mired in racist conventions, Ali was the paradigmatic "uppity" black who would not submit to the dictates of white opinion. Sportswriters were particularly offended by the unconventional Clay, calling him a buffoon and the "Louisville Lip." Still using what he would later call his "slave name," Cassius Clay, after returning to America in 1960 as Olympic champion, the Louisville fighter quickly rose in the professional heavyweight boxing ranks. After nineteen wins—fourteen by knockout—Clay talked his way into a shot at the title held by Charles "Sonny" Liston, whose background as a mob-connected hoodlum and convicted felon apparently did not disqualify him from the boxing ring. Clay had received financial backing from the Louisville Sponsoring Group, a syndicate of local white businessmen. As a result, he did not need to turn to mob resources for financial support as many boxers had done.

The fight for the heavyweight championship was set for February 25, 1964, in Miami Beach. Few genuinely believed that Clay could best Liston and win the crown. Las Vegas odds had him as a distinct seven-to-one underdog, but Clay cautioned "save your money and don't bet on Sonny!" The boxing press detested the brash young boxer, as Clay lectured them: "It's your last chance to get on the bandwagon. I'm keeping a list of all you people." While it is hard to imagine in retrospect, in the Clay-Liston battle it was the golden, pretty-faced young Olympic champion who played the villain.

America certainly did not elevate Sonny Liston to its pantheon of beloved champions. The Big Bear may have been unwanted, but the sporting press hoped that Liston would teach Clay a lesson. Liston had become the heavyweight champion in 1962 by knocking out Floyd Patterson in the first round in Comiskey Park in Chicago. Born in Arkansas to a sharecropping family, Liston spent years in a Missouri prison for robbery. As a boxer, he was a ponderous bully. When he again dispatched Patterson in the first round in the rematch, the crowd loudly booed the champ. Despite his ignoble profile, however, Liston was the public preference in his matchup with Clay.

Clay's brash persona irritated the sports establishment at the same time Dr. Martin Luther King Jr. and others were leading a peaceful racial revolution. Outside the South, it was difficult for political and business leaders to openly castigate the men and women who put their lives on the line in a movement for freedom. It was easy, however, to belittle Clay. Clay may have welcomed his verbal and print adversaries, at least at first. It was part of the game he was playing.

In the buildup to the championship bout, Clay continually harassed Liston. Clay's prematch poetry showed him at his lyrical best:

Clay swings with his left, Clay swings with his right,
Look at young Cassius carry the fight.
Liston keeps backing, but there's not enough room,
It's a matter of time till Clay lowers the boom.
Now Clay lands with a right, what a beautiful swing,
And the punch raises the Bear clean out of the ring.
Liston is still rising and the ref wears a frown,
For he can't start counting till Sonny goes down.
Now Liston is disappearing from view, the crowd is going frantic,
But radar stations have picked him up, somewhere over the Atlantic.
Who would have thought when they came to the fight
That they'd witness the launching of a human satellite.
Yes the crowd did not dream, when they put up the money,
That they would see a total eclipse of the Sonny.

At the weigh-in, Clay shouted and screamed his insults directly at Liston: "You're too ugly! I'm going to eat you alive!" Clay appeared unhinged, which was exactly what he wanted Liston to believe. Upon leaving the weigh-in, Liston commented: "That boy is crazy." The champion was unnerved, angry, and decidedly unprepared for the fight.

The Miami Beach match would prove that Clay's bluster was based on fact, not just poetry. While the crowd jeered and booed, Clay avoided the Big Bear's devastating left hook by dancing clockwise around the twenty-foot square ring. Clay scored with his quick jab and long right, and opened a cut on Liston's face in the third round.

Some reports claimed that after the fourth round Liston told his corner to "juice his gloves" with oil of wintergreen or ferric chloride, stinging substances normally used to seal cuts. After a few of Liston's jabs landed in the next round, Ali's eyes were blinded by the chemicals. In pain, he circled away from Liston until his tears cleared his vision. Now disoriented and frustrated by the failure of his illegal ploy, Liston simply punched himself out as his powerful swings hit open air. Liston did not come out to fight in the seventh round, and the championship had passed to Clay, who quickly and repeatedly announced: "I am the king of the world!" Clay shouted at the reporters at ringside: "I told you, I told you. I shocked the world, I shocked the world!" Robert Lipsyte of the *New York Times* wrote: "Incredibly, the loud-mouthed, bragging, insulting youngster had been telling the truth all along."

The rematch, held on May 25, 1965, at the Central Maine Youth Center, a high school hockey arena in Lewiston, Maine, attracted fewer than 3,000 spectators, but a worldwide television audience tuned in to watch Liston try to avenge his loss. The bout lasted only a little over a minute. The *New York Times* described the action after the "phantom punch" from Ali connected: "Liston collapsed slowly, like a falling building, piece by piece, rolling onto his back, then flat on his stomach, his face pressed against the canvas." Liston was done, and a fighter who soon would proclaim his name was "Muhammad Ali" was indeed the king of the boxing world.

ALI, THE BOXER AND THE POET

Although no sportswriter ever discovered the connection, Ali's famous poetry had an ancient antecedent. Poetry had always been a part of the ancient Olympic Games, with formal victory hymns written to honor those who triumphed. Pindar wrote fourteen "Olympian odes" in honor of victors, extolling the "eternal glory that will never fade." While there is no evidence Ali knew about his sporting predecessors, their work in the ancient arena elevated each athletic triumph to a level of goodness and beauty that Ali would have appreciated. Ali used his whimsical taunts before each match to hype the event and, of course, to sell tickets. He normally predicted the round when victory would be his. (Ali was not the first to make such predictions. Joe Louis, on the eve of his first fight with Schmeling, predicted that the German would fall in the second round. He was very wrong.)

Ali's style in the ring—"floats like a butterfly, stings like a bee"—while distinctive in modern times, also had its counterpart in the ancient Olympics. In the first century, Melankomas of Caria gained fame as a boxer, as he danced around his opponents, avoiding punches while waiting for his foe to tire under the Greek sun. Known for his good looks, stamina, and athleticism, Melankomas also maintained self-control and self-discipline, both necessary because ancient matches continued until one of the pugilists collapsed or conceded. His tactics proved fruitful, and Melankomas was one of the few ancient boxing gladiators to avoid receiving any blows to his face, much like Muhammad Ali, at least in his early fights.

Most found Ali, as the *New York Times* reported, "the most delightful, exasperating, irritating, humorous, serious, boyish title-holder in boxing's up-and-down history." Those who sought to reverse time wanted Ali to return to the ring as Cassius Clay, the respectful and docile fighter who had won the Olympic gold medal. They ridiculed his new persona by invoking his old name. Opinionated and uncontrollable, Ali lampooned his opponents, especially Floyd Patterson, a great black fighter who better fit the model approved by white society. Ali would become furious when Patterson called him "Clay." In return, Ali would humiliate Patterson in the ring.

THE NATION OF ISLAM

Shortly after his unexpected performance in Miami Beach, Clay announced to the press that the rumors about his conversion to the Nation of Islam had been true: "I am not a Christian anymore." Clay was fascinated by the Chicago-based sect led by Elijah Muhammad and inspired by his message of racial pride, self-respect, and separatism: "It is the history of ourselves, the history of our true religion, our nationality and our names." The Nation, Ali thought, "teaches us . . . to be with our own, marry our own, live with our own, clean up ourselves, do for ourselves, quit forcing ourselves on white neighborhoods, clean up our own neighborhoods, makes us proud and makes us identify with our own brothers around the world." Christianity, by comparison, "never taught us our true knowledge."

Although the boxer never bought into some of the more fanciful fables of the Nation, including one involving a spacecraft called the Mother Plane that was to come to redeem mankind, the sect's emphasis on self-sufficiency and black community resonated with Ali. It offered what Ali wanted more than anything else, respect and freedom. Ali denounced drinking, gambling, and abuse of women. He applauded racial separatism and self-reliance: "I want to be happy with my own kind." His adoption of the tenets of the Nation of Islam was genuine and deep-seated, although he never expressed a hatred of whites as many Nation members and leaders had. He stated: "I don't hate nobody, and I ain't lynched nobody."

Elijah Muhammad and his loyal group of followers welcomed Ali to the fold. He would be their greatest public relations asset, although the sect had earlier gone on record against sports, calling it a "filthy temptation" that caused great troubles in the black community. Ali explained his conversion to Islam in his typically hyperbolic terms: "A rooster crows when it sees the light. Put him in the dark and he'll never crow. I have seen the light and I'm crowing."

Called the "Black Muslims" by outsiders, the Nation's rhetoric excited public apprehension during a time when the established social order was already under attack by mainstream leaders of the civil rights movement. The Federal Bureau of Investigation closely monitored the Nation's activities, and Ali would come under government surveillance once he announced his conversion. Now boxing writers had another reason to dislike the outspoken new champion.

On March 6, 1964, Elijah Muhammad announced in a radio address that the name Cassius Clay lacked "divine meaning." The name would be replaced with a Muslim name: "Muhammad Ali is what I will give him, as long as he believes in Allah and follows me." "Muhammad" meant one worthy of praise, and "Ali" was the name of a cousin of the prophet. (Many boxers would follow suit, and subsequently at least fourteen others adopted either the name Muhammad or Ali.)

In 1964, the Nation of Islam was split by the defection of a great leader, Malcolm X, who had befriended Ali. Although the divide was a matter of little concern in established white society, it caused adherents in the black community to take sides. Ali chose to follow Elijah Muhammad, and he split with Malcolm, a decision he would later regret. Malcolm X was assassinated in February 1965 by three members from the Newark Mosque of the Nation of Islam while he was speaking at the Audubon Ballroom in the Washington Heights section of Manhattan.

Ali's affiliation with the Nation of Islam signaled his growing spiritual maturity. His devotion was complete. Ali divorced his first wife, Sonji, because she would not comply with the strict tenets of the religion regarding women's dress. The Nation reinforced his commitment to follow his own path whatever the consequences in dominant white society. Perhaps he was oblivious to the implications of his choice to stand apart. More likely, Ali knew exactly what he was doing but did not care about the impact on his boxing career and his fame as a sportsman.

Ali's choice to follow the Nation would have direct and immediate consequences on his flourishing boxing career as America increased its military involvement in Southeast Asia. His role in domestic American politics and his international reputation would be established by his stance on Vietnam, and here Ali would demonstrate his symbolic power as an individual athlete and the political power of sports in society.

VIETNAM

Throughout the early 1960s, America slid into major involvement in the civil war in Southeast Asia, a conflict that had been raging since the end of World War II. France had controlled Vietnam as a colony since the late nineteenth century as part of its Indochina possessions. It relinquished control in 1954 in the Geneva Accords, shortly after its disastrous defeat by the Viet Minh forces at Dien Bien Phu. Ho Chi Minh's Communist government would rule the northern provinces from Hanoi, and right-wing dictator Ngo Dinh Diem's regime, supported by the United States, would control the southern provinces from Saigon. The two parts of the country were to be reunited by free elections. In 1956, Diem canceled the elections, knowing that Ho Chi Minh would prevail in any free vote.

America's direct military involvement in Vietnam began in earnest in 1965. During that year, President Lyndon Johnson increased the number of American troops in Vietnam to over 200,000. Ultimately, the United States committed a half million troops to the conflict, and a total of 2.6 million men served a tour of duty in Southeast Asia. In order to meet the manpower need, the federal government relied on a draft of America's young men. Protests against the war grew on college campuses, but most Americans believed in the effort, at least at its inception. Sports figures, in particular, expressed their support for the troops and the cause. The opposition needed a symbolic leader, and he came from a most unlikely place—the boxing ring.

THE STEP FORWARD

Ali had registered for the draft when he was eighteen, but in 1962 he failed the Selective Service aptitude test. When the military's manpower needs increased as a result of the escalation of the Vietnam War, Ali was reclassified 1-A. When the heavyweight champion of the world refused induction into the armed services, claiming conscientious objector status, the world took notice. Ali would not fight for a country that would not even recognize the rights of its citizens of color. Young Americans who had never thought about the Vietnam War in anything other than traditional nationalistic terms began to question their beliefs, and within a year politicians would begin to stand up in opposition to the poisonous conflict.

Sports reporters pressed Ali about his views on the war. In fact, Ali knew little about Vietnam and its politics. He finally responded with his memorable line: "I ain't got no quarrel with them Vietcong." In fact, few Americans had any real quarrel with the Vietcong, although many devotedly believed that the war was necessary in defense of the values of Christian America in its global battle against godless communism. For the ever-increasing number of other Americans who questioned the wisdom and necessity of the military adventure in Southeast Asia, Ali's example would lead the way. As he learned more about Vietnam, Ali began speaking out on college campuses. "Why," Ali asked, "should they ask me and other so-called Negroes to put on a uniform and go 10,000 miles from home and drop bombs on brown people in Vietnam while so-called Negro people in Louisville are treated like dogs and denied simple human rights?"

On April 28, 1967, Ali appeared as directed at the U.S. Armed Forces Examining and Entrance Station in Houston. He completed the paperwork and underwent a physical examination. Finally, at 1:05 p.m., the process ended with a ceremony where a young sergeant called his name (actually, he called him "Cassius Marcellus Clay") and told him to step forward, an action that would symbolize his acceptance into the military. Although directed three times to do so, Ali did not step forward. A navy lieutenant then advised him that his refusal was a felony. Ali, in turn, submitted a written declaration explaining he was exempt from military service as a minister of the religion of Islam. He would pay a stiff price for his obedience to his faith and his conscience.

Ali was arrested for refusing induction. Within an hour, the New York State Athletic Commission suspended his boxing license. It was one thing to protest against the war but another to do so as heavyweight champion of the world. On June 19, 1967, an all-white jury in Houston convicted Ali of criminal draft evasion after an hour of testimony and twenty minutes of deliberations. Judge Joe Ingraham sentenced Ali to the maximum term of five years in prison and a $10,000 fine. (The customary penalty for Ali's offense was an eighteen-month sentence.) Ali remained unrepentant and explained: "We don't fight wars unless it's a war declared by Allah himself." That month 449 American soldiers died in Vietnam.

The American press finally had the controversial Ali cornered, and they relished the opportunity to lambast the stubborn and dangerous heretic. Americans remembered the patriotism of Joe Louis, who served in the army for years during World War II, as a symbol of America's struggle against the Nazi menace. More than 500 Major League baseball players, including 32 Hall of Famers, had served in the military during World War II, taking time away from the prime of their sports careers. Now Ali refused to follow their lead.

Ring magazine, the self-proclaimed "bible of boxing," declined to name him its 1967 Fighter of the Year, saying that "Cassius Clay is most emphatically not to be held up as an example to the youngsters of the United States." The respected *Chicago Tribune* accused Ali of treason. The Senate in his home state of Kentucky passed a resolution describing his attitude as "repugnant." Ali, it stated, "brings discredit to all loyal Kentuckians and to the names of thousands of them who gave their lives for this country during his lifetime." Respected sportswriter Red Smith added that Ali was "as sorry a spectacle as those unwashed punks who picket and demonstrate against the war." Even his aunt, Louisville schoolteacher Mary Turner, condemned him. Jack Olsen reported in *Sports Illustrated*, "The noise became a din, the drumbeats of a holy war. TV and radio commentators, little old ladies . . . bookmakers, and parish priests, armchair strategists at the Pentagon and politicians all over the place joined in a crescendo of get-Cassius clamor."

Politicians piled on their scorn. The governor of Illinois found Ali "disgusting," and the governor of Maine said the boxer "should be held in utter contempt by every patriotic American." An American Legion post in Miami asked people to "join in condemnation of this unpatriotic, loudmouthed, bombastic individual."

Ali's act of defiance against an oppressive white government spread throughout black society. The next year, two black track athletes would raise a defiant black-gloved hand of resistance in Mexico City, and black power advocates would speak out about racial pride and empowerment. Julian Bond wrote: "[It is] hard to imagine that a sports figure could have so much influence on so many people. When a figure as heroic and beloved as Muhammad Ali stood up and said, 'No, I won't go,' it reverberated through the whole society. People who had never thought about the war before began to think it through because of Ali. The ripples were enormous."

The United States government understood that Ali's refusal to accept induction constituted a potent symbol with significant political implications. When he refused to take the step forward, the Vietnam War was still relatively popular among the American public. The antiwar movement was at an early stage, but Ali's willingness to sacrifice his career for his beliefs made him a hero. The government also realized the danger Ali posed as the standard-bearer of what was seen as a dangerous religious cult. The FBI ordered its agents to secretly monitor Ali while he appealed his conviction. An internal memorandum complained that Ali "utilized his position as a national known figure in the sports world to promote through appearance at various gatherings an ideology completely foreign to the basic American ideals of equality and justice for all, love of God and country." Public political rhetoric continued to extol the goals of the effort to achieve "freedom" for the people of South Vietnam. At the same time, behind other closed doors in Washington, top American officials had begun to realize that, as a result of growing public opposition to the Vietnam conflict, the primary goal of the war effort had changed from triumph over evil to avoiding a humiliating American defeat.

Ali was martyred and then he was resurrected. He was not afraid of going to jail, saying: "We've been in jail for 400 years." He finally acknowledged the symbolic role he played in American culture and politics: "I'm fighting for me, I'm fighting for the black people on welfare, the black people who have no future, the black people who are the wine heads and dope addicts, I am a politician for Allah."

After extensive litigation in the federal courts, Ali's license to box was reinstated in September 1970. The New York State Athletic Commission had denied Ali a license to box because of his indictment. Among other things, Ali claimed that this action denied him the equal protection of the law since hundreds of other licensed boxers had criminal convictions (not merely indictments) for crimes ranging from burglary and assault and battery to murder. The federal court in New York ruled in Ali's favor. Meanwhile, Ali's criminal case for refusing induction was appealed to the Supreme Court. By 1971, America had turned against the Vietnam War, and Ali's return to the ring after more than a three-year absence was greeted warmly by some who had earlier ridiculed him. However, others would continue to see Ali as a traitor, a blowhard, and a coward.

THE HIATUS

Ali was not sedentary during the time he was forced away from the ring. He preached at Muslim mosques around the country and carried his message to college campuses. Ali loved the crowd, who adored him in return. Although when he talked about the Black Muslims his jargon was extreme, he was always the charming showman who was full of fun. He even met with Dr. Martin Luther King Jr., who was in Louisville to lead an open housing campaign. Ali toured black neighborhoods, churches, and schools, and offered his support for the civil rights effort: "I came to Louisville because I could not remain silent in Chicago while my own people—many of whom I grew up with, went to school with and some of whom are my blood relatives—were being beaten, stomped and kicked in the streets simply because they want freedom, justice and equality in housing."

This was a remarkable shift in thinking for a man who had earlier denounced the effort to achieve integration as contrary to the best interests of people of color.

Ali also dabbled in business during his hiatus away from boxing. He was a shareholder in Champburger Corporation, which franchised burger restaurants run by black entrepreneurs in black neighborhoods. The menu conformed to

Islamic dietary strictures, selling beef hot dogs, fried chicken, fried fish, boiled fish, and Mr. Champ soda. There was no pork or shellfish on the menu. Ali lent his name and image to Champburger—which advertised "We are the greatest!" He made occasional personal appearances at restaurants as they opened.

In December 1969, Ali appeared on Broadway in the musical *Buck White*, which ran for only seven performances. The otherwise scathing review by the *New York Times* said of Ali that he "gentles the night." In an otherwise undistinguished effort, Ali "seems nice." Ali and the cast performed a number from the musical, "We Came in Chains," on the *Ed Sullivan Show* before the show was canceled. He would later cut a record, naturally entitled "I am the Greatest!" and appear as a guest on numerous television shows. Ali, the entertainer, was in his element.

JOE FRAZIER

The second half of Ali's boxing career began in 1970 with victories over Jerry Quarry and Oscar Bonavena, both of which ended in technical knockouts. The matches revealed, however, how much of his boxing prowess Ali had lost as a result of his three-and-a-half-year layoff. His diminished skills were most evident in his first fight against Joe Frazier, who would serve as Ali's foil for the remainder of his boxing career.

Frazier was Ali's counterpoint both inside and outside the ring. Born into a dirt-poor family in South Carolina, Frazier embodied the great American story of success through determination, skill, and hard work. He, too, was an Olympic champion, but his style was dogged, ugly, and awkward, rather than flamboyant. Frazier had worked in a slaughterhouse and then as a janitor before finding success in the ring. He was a determined slugger without finesse, but he was relentless. He beat Jimmy Ellis, Ali's former sparring partner, to capture the heavyweight title. Frazier knew, however, that he would never really be the champ until he bested Ali.

Ali's preparation for his first fight against Frazier was lackadaisical. He had been caught in the web of celebrity, and everyone wanted a piece of him. In addition to his antiwar stand, Ali somehow had become an icon for women's liberation and for ecology, although he never had much to say about those issues, and the Muslims were hardly role models for female empowerment. Frazier, in turn, was seen as an advocate for law and order and the status quo, once again without much basis other than that he was not Muhammad Ali. The March 8, 1971, match in Madison Square Garden, the "Battle of the Century," was a fifteen-round slugfest. Frazier retained his world title by a unanimous decision, reportedly breaking Ali's jaw in the process. Ali felt humiliated, even though the public adoration continued unabated.

Three months after the first Frazier fight, a unanimous Supreme Court decision overturned Ali's criminal conviction for refusing induction into the armed forces. Ali had appealed his local draft board's rejection of his application for conscientious objector classification, and the state's Appeal Board had denied his request without offering any reasons or explanation. Since the government later acknowledged that Ali was sincere in his beliefs and they were the result of religious training, it relied in its Supreme Court case on the sole grounds that Ali was not opposed to all wars since he had admitted he would fight any battle directed by Allah. The court was left to guess whether this was the grounds relied on by the Appeal Board because it had never explained its grounds for its denial of Ali's appeal. This was an adequate basis on which to reverse Ali's conviction. Thus, the prosecution of America's consummate boxer finally ended in a technical knockout of the government's case.

Ali and Frazier signed for a rematch, again to be held in boxing's primary venue, Madison Square Garden, on January 28, 1974. In front of a multitude of cameras, Ali began a nonstop barrage of insults against Frazier, calling him an "Uncle Tom" and a "white man in a black skin." These attacks on his racial bona fides were interspersed with blunt insults directed at his "ugliness." Frazier took them to heart, even though it was once again simply Ali hyping the return match for public consumption. This time Ali was better prepared for the bout and took a unanimous twelve-round decision. It was not an impressive outing by either fighter. Bud Collins, writing for the *Boston Globe*, reported that "the bite and the beat of the past were diminished."

Two more major fights would add a coda to the Ali legend. Although the second Ali-Frazier matchup was a multi-million-dollar success, Frazier had earlier lost his title to George Foreman. Ali would face Foreman to regain the heavyweight crown. The match, called the "Rumble in the Jungle," was set for October 30, 1974, in Mai 20 Stadium in Kinshasa, Zaire. Foreman was a formidable champion with forty victories in forty fights, thirty-seven by knockout, mostly in the early rounds. The press scripted another morality play. To the third-world audience, Ali was the symbol of resistance to white oppression.

He would triumph by knocking out his stronger, and much younger, opponent in the eighth round. Bud Collins was more impressed: "It was a marvelous performance by the inimitable dancing master. . . . Foreman wasn't up to the gavotte." The ex-champ later claimed that he had beaten himself by throwing his potent punches into empty air while Ali circled the ring.

The figurative finality to Ali's story in the ring came on October 1, 1975, when he met Frazier for the third and last time. Ali had taken to calling Frazier "the Gorilla." He would face off against "the Gorilla" in Manila in a fight billed euphonically as the "Thrilla." It would be the ultimate test of courage, skills, and heart for the two longtime opponents. Dave Anderson wrote for the *New York Times*: "They resembled two old bull moose who had to stand and slam each other because they couldn't get away from each other. . . . Ali had not come to dance." The fight ended by a technical knockout of Frazier in the fourteenth round, but both boxers had demonstrated athletic excellence. Ali commented: "That's one helluva man, and God bless him." Eventually, it was Ali who was named athlete of the century, but he would not have accomplished that acclaim without his rivalry with the short, muscular, scowling pugilist from Philadelphia.

Ali then stayed too long in the ring. In his final ten fights, he was a caricature of himself, sometimes out of shape, often left to circle the ring to avoid damage. He lost his title to Leon Spinks in 1978 by not taking his young challenger seriously, then won it back seven months later after preparing for the match, thus becoming the only man to have won the heavyweight crown three separate times. He retired in 1978, only to come out of retirement two years later to fight Larry Holmes: "I'm shooting for immortality, and I'm on the doorstep." He lost to Holmes on October 2, 1980, failing to last the distance for the first time in his career. It was a sad denouement. As Steve Marantz wrote for the *Boston Globe*: "A mountain named Larry Holmes came to the man Muhammed Ali last night, forever banishing him to the ranks of the mortals."

Ali had faded into a mere shadow of himself. Dave Anderson reported for the *New York Times* that when Ali did not leave his corner for the eleventh round, "all around the arena, people stood still the way they do at the funeral of someone who had died unexpectedly. . . . [T]here was no gas in the tank anymore." Dozens of people rushed the ring, not to congratulate the champion but to console the loser.

Ali was wrong in his prebout commentary, however. He had already achieved immortality, and he did not need to fight another round in the ring. He craved attention, however, and that would lead him back to the ring again and again for more punishment and lasting injury. Finally, after the Larry Holmes fight, he recognized "it's too late to come back" (though he would return to the ring one more time, a year later, losing a decision to Trevor Berbick, before retiring permanently).

Ali's performance as a boxer and a showman was unique. He was idiosyncratic, one of a kind, imaginative, outrageous, inventive, jocular, mischievous, and joyous. His performance as a political symbol was equally singular. There were no binding rules or limitations that would apply to the Louisville pugilist. As a result of adhering to his own principles, he forfeited his status and stature in society, only to regain it later when society realized that Ali had been a hero because of his principles. He became a noble figure. As Marc Antony said in eulogizing Julius Caesar, "When comes such another?" Never.

CONCLUSION

At the start of every boxing match, the referee calls both pugilists to the center of the ring and recites the rules of the conflict about to commence. The boxers come face-to-face knowing that in seconds they will be "throwing leather" at each other. Both are likely to be hurt in the encounter, and one may fall. Ali confronted his opponents in that manner through his sixty-one professional fights, winning all but five. Ali and the United States had the same sort of face-to-face encounter for most of the fighter's adult life. America threw a punch at its most unconventional hero, and Ali took that punch but kept fighting. He recognized the consequences of his actions and his words: "[R]egardless of what it costs me, I speak out for what I believe in." In the process, the gladiator left a legacy in both sports and politics. As Harry Belafonte said of Ali: "[O]ut of the womb of oppression, he was our phoenix. He was the spirit of all our young. He was our manhood."

It is also traditional at the last scheduled round of a fight for the referee to once again call both fighters to the center of the ring, where they touch gloves. At the last round of the U.S.-Ali battle, the combatants touched gloves, but the fight was over before another punch was thrown. On December 10, 1974, President Gerald Ford welcomed Muhammad Ali to the White House, seven years after he had been convicted of draft evasion and only three years after he had been victorious in court. The *New York Times* commented on the meeting: "No one there seemed to recall that the champion was stripped of his world heavyweight title" for refusing induction. America forgave Ali his transgressions and then, in a most remarkable turn of events, it showed the world that it treasured him. It was a complicated relationship.

On July 19, 1996, the games of the Twenty-Sixth Olympiad opened at Atlanta's Olympic Stadium. It was the centennial of the first modern Olympics, and 11,000 athletes from 197 countries paraded in. For the first time, all invited nations accepted the invitation to attend. A television viewing audience of 3.5 billion watched as the Olympic flame was passed from one athlete to another and finally to Janet Evans, America's premier swimmer, a four-time gold medal winner. The stadium crowd of 85,000 was delirious when Muhammad Ali, slowed and trembling from his Parkinson's disease, appeared to take the flame from Evans and lit the Olympic torch. Ali, the symbol of defiance and simple dignity, had been welcomed home to genuine love and affection.

In a 1972 interview with David Frost, Ali was asked how he wished to be remembered. Spontaneously, he wrote his own epitaph:

He took a few cups of love.
He took one tablespoon of patience.
One teaspoon of generosity.
One pint of kindness.
He took one quart of laughter.
One pinch of concern.
And then he mixed willingness with happiness.
He added lots of faith.
And he stirred it up well.
Then he spread it over a span of a lifetime.
And he served it to each and every deserving person he met.

On December 27, 1979, Soviet troops invaded Afghanistan, their southern neighbor, nominally at the behest of the puppet Communist regime in Kabul. American president Jimmy Carter vowed to stop this "expansionism" and punish the Soviets by boycotting the Olympic Games scheduled for Moscow. The Soviet Games proceeded nonetheless, attended by over 5,000 athletes from eighty nations, who enjoyed the festivities presided over by mascot Misha the Bear Cub. *AP Images*

Everything in our lives is governed by political decisions.
We have varying degrees of freedom, but that freedom is obtained
by political decisions. What we in sport and the Olympic movement
need is the interest and support of politicians, not their interference.
—*Lord Killanin, president of the International Olympic Committee*

History holds its breath—for what is at stake is no less than the future
security of the civilized world. —*Vice President Walter Mondale*

[6]
OLYMPIC BOYCOTTS AND INTERNATIONAL RELATIONS

In 1945, after the close of the Great Patriotic War, as the Russians called their life-and-death struggle with the Nazis, the Union of Soviet Socialist Republics faced the United States in the "Great Radio Chess Match." Conducted over the international radio links from New York and Moscow over a five-day period, ten leading masters from each country, seated 5,000 miles apart, faced off for chess supremacy. The Soviets trounced the Americans, and they would rule international team chess for the remainder of the century. Move for move, the Soviets outflanked and outthought the previously dominant American team.

The exercise of international politics in the cold war era was also a chess match on a global scale, with many moves, feints, and tactics. Armed with conflicting ideologies, the military forces of the United States and Soviet Union faced off in Berlin and Cuba, but never exchanged fire. The Korean conflict and the Vietnam War served as proxy hot wars between Communist and Capitalist forces, but throughout the decades of the cold war, the former allies' political confrontation never erupted into a direct military engagement. The cold war was fought in the meeting halls of the United Nations, in the competition for influence in the developing world, and on various economic fronts. After the advent of atomic weapons, with their potential for ending all human existence, the protagonists moderated their political and economic conflict to stand back from Armageddon. Although no one kept score, as they did in the Great Radio Chess Match, the rivals parried each other until the endgame came in 1991, when, for a variety of political and economic reasons, the Communists left the field of play, replaced by oligarchs masquerading as democrats in Moscow. Throughout the cold war, sports provided a critical venue for the rivalry between the great powers. Although no shots were fired, athletic success became the proxy for political supremacy, and the Olympics would serve as the premier setting for the sports struggle.

The quadrennial sports festival offered the world an actual scoreboard by which to measure national achievement. The press proclaimed nations as winners and losers by counting the number of medals awarded. Countries invested in their athletes as the equivalent of developing a national infrastructure. Some, like the East German government, would, in the quest for Olympic gold, even poison their youngsters with steroids, drugs that would cripple them after the contests were over. America increased its attention to women's sports in order to "beat the Russians." A gold medal counted just as much in the standings when it was won by a woman as by a man. For the major world powers, sports had become a patriotic duty.

Bob Mathias, the great American decathlete, explained what it felt like to arrive at the Helsinki Olympics in 1952, the first the Union of Soviet Socialist Republics would attend. "The Soviets were the real enemy. You just love to beat 'em. You just had to beat 'em. It wasn't like beating some friendly country like Australia." The Soviets later boasted that they had won seventy-one medals in Helsinki, second only to the United States, despite the fact, it claimed, that the CIA had enticed Soviet athletes to enjoy the delights of young women in Finland in order to distract them from their sporting goals.

Teams of athletes that gathered behind their countries' banners represented not only national physical and sporting prowess but also ideological primacy. Although admittedly an absurd premise, countries credited success on the playing field to their superior political, social, and economic systems. Without question, success at the Olympic Games fostered international prestige that enhanced political influence.

The Olympic movement had always claimed that it sought the universal participation of the world's finest athletes. All nations would be invited to attend, and each would send its best athletes to participate in the Olympics. According to Baron de Coubertin, the father of the modern Olympics, once the world's athletes arrived at the games, peace would break out all over the globe. Premier athletes competing on playing fields in peaceful sporting competition without regard to race or class was the fantasy, an ideal vision always blemished in reality.

When the modern Olympic Games began in 1896 in Athens, the contests were the preserve of the privileged. Baron de Coubertin and his founding colleagues insisted that only "amateurs" could participate. As he wrote later in an article about the Olympics in *Century Illustrated* magazine: "It is impossible to conceive the Olympic Games with money prizes." The typical Victorian definition of the term "amateur"—for example, from the 1878 rules for the Henley Regatta—excluded from participation any person who had *ever* been employed "for wages, a mechanic, artisan or laborer." Thus, the "lower orders" were not eligible to participate. It was not surprising, therefore, that the core of the American team at the first modern Olympics consisted of four juniors from Princeton, who had been excused from their classes, and five Harvard graduates associated with the Boston Athletic Club.

The International Olympic Committee later softened its blatantly exclusionary premise and only banned athletes who had received any material benefit, directly or indirectly, from participating in sports. It did not matter whether the athlete sought to participate in that sport in the Olympics. For example, a remarkable athlete like Jim Thorpe was stripped of the gold medals he won in the 1912 Stockholm Olympics in the pentathlon and decathlon because he had earlier played two seasons of semiprofessional baseball in the Eastern Carolina League for Rocky Mount, North Carolina, for two dollars a game. (Thirty years after Thorpe's death, the International Olympic Committee recognized the absurdity of its actions and restored his Olympic medals.) Until the 1980s, the Olympic Games were limited to those athletes who participated in their sport only as an avocation, not as a vocation, thus excluding all except those who were independently wealthy or had sources of income outside sports that would support their part-time athletic pursuits.

Although universality was its stated goal, many Olympic Games experienced boycotts of some sort. Although invited previously, the Soviet Union did not participate in the Olympics until 1952. For decades, it had denounced the Olympic movement as the instrument of bourgeois politics. The Soviets also used the sports boycott in other circumstances to indicate its displeasure with a country or its policies. For example, it refused to play Chile in World Cup soccer in 1973 because of the overthrow and death of Chile's leftist president earlier that year.

Western democracies had considered a boycott of the 1936 Olympic Games held under the Nazis, but it failed to materialize. At the Melbourne Olympics in 1956, the Netherlands, Spain, Sweden, and Liechtenstein boycotted in protest of the Soviet invasion of Hungary. Egypt, Lebanon, and Iraq also boycotted those same Olympics as a result of the Suez crisis. The People's Republic of China also refused to participate because of the inclusion of a team from the Republic of China (Taiwan). In 1976, after the International Olympic Committee refused to bar athletes from New Zealand, twenty-two African nations boycotted in protest because the New Zealand rugby union team had toured apartheid South Africa.

In addition to these boycotts, on other occasions the International Olympic Committee barred nations from participating. Austria, Bulgaria, Germany, Hungary, and Turkey were not invited to the 1920 Olympics, because they were the Central Powers in the recently concluded Great War. (Germany was also not invited in 1924.) Germany and Japan were not invited to the 1948 Olympic Games, once again because they had been the enemies of the triumphant Allies in the recently concluded Second World War. In 1964, South Africa was formally expelled from the Olympic movement as a result of its policy of apartheid. It would not be invited to participate again until 1992.

Sometimes partial boycotts arose spontaneously at or shortly before the Olympics, based more on petulance than on principle. At the 1912 Olympics in Stockholm, the French and Italians did not agree with the rules established for the fencing competitions. Therefore, the French did not send a fencing team. The Italians came to Stockholm, but because they did not agree with the rules for épée, the team simply withdrew from that competition. (The épée team stormed out singing a Fascist song.)

Although it always claimed to soar above pedestrian political squabbles, in fact the Olympic movement has always mirrored day-to-day world affairs. The political realities of the post–World War II world posed almost intractable problems for the International Olympic Committee. Propaganda and ideology made the intricate geopolitical puzzle difficult to solve, and any successful resolution of representational disputes often involved a significant dose of face-saving. Once the Soviets agreed to participate in the Olympics, it demanded structural changes in the governance of the Olympic movement that would reflect its superpower status. While some effort was made to place Communists on the IOC and its executive board, they were there to represent international sports and not their home countries, a concept the Soviets never fully accepted.

The postwar east-west division of conquered Germany generated numerous Olympic disputes. West Germany returned to the Olympics in 1952, but East Germany's National Olympic Committee was not recognized by the International Olympic Committee until 1955. East and West Germany competed as a joint team in 1956, 1960, and 1964, but then entered as separate teams starting in 1968 until the two nations reunified in 1990. A similar pattern was followed with regard to the two Chinas, always reflecting the current state of world politics. For example, in 1954 both Chinas were invited to send teams to the 1956 Melbourne Olympics. The Communists, who controlled the mainland, accepted, and, as a result, the Nationalists, who controlled only the island of Formosa, declined. The Nationalists then changed their mind, and the Communists withdrew. Each action was accompanied by accusations couched in gaseous ideological terms. In 1959, the IOC allowed the Nationalists to participate only as "Formosa." If they attended the Rome Olympics, they would be required to walk into the Olympic stadium behind a sign that read "Formosa." When the Nationalists protested, IOC president Avery Brundage retorted that the IOC "does not deal with governments and does not propose to become involved in political controversies," an absurd response after a decade of political controversy. The Nationalists arrived in Rome with the required sign, but then added an addendum to their banner: "Under Protest."

These were not the first Olympic controversies involving representation. In 1912, Austria and Hungary objected to participation in the Olympics by Bohemia, a Central European state that was then part of the Austro-Hungarian Empire. (Bohemia had participated as an independent nation in 1900 and

1908.) The dispute in 1912 was solved when the Bohemian team marched at a distance behind the Austrian team but carried its own flag.

One obvious solution to many of these representational disputes would have been to allow world-class athletes to participate as individuals, not as members of national teams. IOC head Avery Brundage even offered that principle in 1956. After Russian tanks had crushed the Hungarian freedom fighters, Brundage rejected the thought that this should have any international sports repercussions: "Every civilized person recoils at the savage slaughter in Hungary, but that is no reason for destroying the nucleus of international cooperation and goodwill we have in the Olympic movement. The Olympic Games are contests between individuals and not between nations." Of course, Brundage and the IOC offered the concept simply as a way to address (and then ignore) the Soviet repression in Budapest. In fact, they stayed firmly committed to the national organizing committee structure. Athletes would *not* be allowed to attend the Olympics as "individuals" and participate as citizens of the world.

IDEOLOGY, POLITICS, AND SPORTS

Life can be ambiguous and complex, so how can people explain the confusion all around us? Humans sense empirical patterns that repeat and assume that others see the same combinations of stimuli. Limited by personal experience, an actor in society must postulate hypotheses that explain the whole. Informed by family and others, they enlarge their bank of knowledge and inferences, but without the comfort of an all-encompassing catechism.

To fill in the inevitable gaps in personal experiences, all societies follow a set of principles and beliefs that offer a glossary for understanding. These ideologies emerged in prehistory as clans and families faced the labyrinthine challenges of human existence. The informal teachings of ancient tribes were passed down through the generations by oral traditions under the guidance of shamans. Religious dogma was all-encompassing, covering all aspects of secular and spiritual life. Complex modern ideologies—the successor to more primitive value systems—come equipped with guiding texts and cadres of en-forcers charged with ensuring adherence to established norms.

Ideology helped define individual and group identities and gave purpose to daily toils. People became part of something greater than the monologue that went on within their minds. When combined with political power, ideology provided a policy road map, even if it had to be readjusted from time to time to meet changing needs and altered circumstances. Ideological principles set out a path with no dead-ends.

Ideology and religion often aligned. Both offered value systems to guide individual and collective decision making. Both welcomed individual participation in achieving greater societal goals within the constraints imposed by the guiding principles and texts.

How then did ideology inform the world of sports? As we have seen, for the ancient Greek games athletes traveled to the sanctuary of Zeus, the *Altis*, where the pantheon of gods anointed their performances. In modern times, capitalist ideology fostered the commercialization of sports—whether through gambling on a championship horse race in the 1820s or the organization of team sport enterprises, such as baseball in the 1870s.

With the advent of twentieth-century ideologies, sports took on a vital representative role. Success in athletic competition was attributed to the ideological superiority of the sponsor. Nazism's political cult regaled in the 1936 success of heavyweight boxer Max Schmeling as the triumph of National Socialism and then quickly disowned him after his ultimate defeat in the Yankee Stadium ring in 1938. Americanism, as a brand of ideology that combined capitalism, the Christian religion, and a spectrum of values closely associated with a continental nation where economic success was an assumed birthright, also saw sports as validation. Triumphant in war and peace through its economic predominance, American exceptionalism rejoiced in all its victories throughout much of the twentieth century. Communism, an urban worker ideology devised in the British Library by a German of Jewish heritage, captured power first in an agrarian society and then expanded its influence by military means to attract adherents worldwide. It was an inspiration to the oppressed who felt that the dictatorship of the proletariat was preferable to the oppression of the masses. The Soviet Union was a continental power that could exert its influence through sports as well as military might. For every ideology, every triumph—whether social, political, or athletic—was attributed to its prevailing political, religious, and economic system.

THE MOSCOW OLYMPIC GAMES

The quadrennial modern Olympic festival would be a forum where the ideological contest could be translated into temporal supremacy through sports competitions. In October 1974, at the height of an era of east-west détente, the International Olympic Committee awarded the 1980 Summer Olympic Games to Moscow, selecting the Soviet capital over Los Angeles. The Nixon administration had done a dreadful job of promoting the candidacy of the California metropolis, although it did bribe numerous committee members in an effort to buy votes. The IOC would later award the United States the 1980 Winter Olympic Games and the 1984 Summer Olympics because Lake Placid and Los Angeles were the only bidders for those events.

Lord Michael Killanin, a journalist, film producer, author, business executive, and chief deputy to Avery Brundage, succeeded Brundage as president of the International Olympic Committee after the Munich Olympic Games of 1972. He saw the award of the Olympics to the capital of the Soviet empire as part of the Olympic movement's effort to foster world peace. The country that had previously spurned the Olympics as the product of bourgeois thinking would now be offered the opportunity to host the premier international sporting event. Killanin explained: "Today, thanks to the Olympic movement, countries which have very different political, religious and social views are able to come together in peace to compete in sport." The results would prove anything but collaborative.

Despite lingering distrust and ideological animosity, the economic and non-economic relationship between the United States and the Soviet Union had grown closer during the years of détente from the late 1960s until December 1979. Direct competition between the superpowers would continue in a variety of forums—in the exploration of space, in weapons development, and in the competition for political influence in the third world. Antagonism was generally modulated, however, as the superpowers sought accommodation and not confrontation. Trade between the countries increased. American farm products poured into the Soviet Union to compensate for their poor harvests, and these sales profited American farmers in the Midwest.

The competition between the global superpowers was always couched in ideological terms. Each side sought to define the terms of the dialogue. The United States labeled the Soviet Union a godless dictatorship, while the Americans saw themselves as the democratic defenders of the true faith. The Soviets decried the United States as the epitome of imperialist capitalism, run by bourgeois entrepreneurs for private profit at the expense of the proletariat. The Soviet Union, on the other hand, was the land where the masses would rule and each person receive what he needed to flourish. Both visions were caricatures, of course, painted in broad strokes. In fact, the ongoing political competition between the superpowers was motivated by nonideological concerns about national security and the capture of economic markets. Both countries needed to provide safety for their populations, purchase raw materials, and sell their products. Although wrapped in ideological propaganda, the decades-long contraposition was realpolitik on a grand scale.

The rival ideologies effectively explained the jumble of world facts. The Soviets knew why the United States kept thousands of troops in Europe long after the end of World War II. It did so in order to threaten the Soviets with extinction, as had the Nazis. America knew why the Soviet Union oppressed its satellites. It sought to promote its collectivist agenda by force. Both nations sought dominance over the other and maintained offensive capabilities in order to deter aggression. The two nations were fundamentally different, and their opposite number could not be trusted because of inherent conflicts in beliefs and worldviews.

During the 1960s and 1970s, the United States was a country mired in foreign and domestic turmoil. After the Cuban missile crisis and the assassination of President Kennedy, America began the arduous process of cleansing itself of the shackles of racism and sexism. In response to the military adventure in Vietnam and the political disgrace of the lawless Nixon presidency, Americans lost faith in their own ideals and righteousness, as their community changed rapidly. The nation's earlier unerring and unbeatable self-image had been tarnished. The election of James Earl Carter as president in 1976 offered the nation a respite. It would enjoy this opportunity to redefine itself, untainted by the scourge of Watergate and Vietnam and the violence in the streets of America's cities.

Jimmy Carter, governor of Georgia, was an unlikely choice for president of the United States. Virtually unknown to the American public before the start of the Democratic Party's 1976 nominating process, Carter seemed to many to be a comfortable change from the traumatic leadership of the prior decade. He triumphed over President Gerald Ford, who had been tainted by his pardon of Richard Nixon.

Carter was relatively unschooled in the ways of politics and totally naive when it came to international relations. Although armed with an understanding of American ideology, Carter's exercise of foreign policy stumbled along under the conflicting advice of key figures in his administration. Carter was wedded to detail, a characteristic that befitted an engineer who was a former captain of a navy submarine. While Carter learned the ways of the presidency, he unsettled the Soviets, who thought he was an untrustworthy hawk whose aim was to dismantle the USSR.

Despite some significant cooperative moves on international relations, such as the SALT II nuclear treaty and an agreement between Israel and Egypt, Carter's exercise of diplomacy was uncertain and erratic, a critical deficiency. Carter's commitment to human rights on a global scale offered a leitmotif but not a strategic policy that could be applied consistently. His occasional bumbling virtually destroyed détente and almost wrecked the one arena where global cooperation had generally flourished, within the international Olympic movement.

AFGHANISTAN

On December 27, 1979, Soviet troops invaded Afghanistan, their southern neighbor, nominally at the behest of the puppet Communist regime in Kabul, which had requested military assistance. Although the Kremlin thought the incursion would last only a few months, their troops would remain inside Afghanistan for more than a decade. Although the Soviet Union had previously sent its troops into many Communist countries in the post–World War II era, including Czechoslovakia and Hungary, this single action triggered a dramatic political response by the U.S. government, one that would change the course of world politics and sports. After the U.S.-led boycott of the 1980 Moscow Olympic Games, no one could doubt the synergy between sports and politics.

In the late 1970s, the Soviet Politburo was in turmoil because of the lingering illness of Leonid Brezhnev, general secretary of the ruling Communist Party. In 1978, local Communists in Afghanistan, the People's Democratic Party, took control of the Afghan government in a coup. The new regime was quickly opposed by rural mujahedeen resistance forces that threatened to topple the brutal, but for the most part inept, regime. The Democratic Republic of Afghanistan signed a friendship treaty with the Soviet Union in December 1978. The Soviets recognized that instability along its southern border constituted a threat to its own security, especially in those Islamic republics that made up the southern tier of the USSR. As Alexsey Kosygin, one of the most liberal members of the Communist leadership, wrote to fellow members of the Soviet Politburo: "We must put up a struggle for Afghanistan; after all we have lived side by side for 60 years." There was good evidence that a failure of the Soviets to intervene would lead to a toppling of the friendly regime in Kabul.

President Carter saw the Soviet action quite differently. To him, this was simply a repetition of the Nazi expansionism into the Rhineland, Czechoslovakia, and Austria in the 1930s. He was convinced the Soviet Union was intent on conquering its neighbors using whatever ruse was necessary. That, in turn, would lead the Soviets to undermine the West's oil lifeline from the Mideast. As Zbigniew Brzezinski revealed twenty years later in an interview with a French magazine, *Le Nouvel Observatur*, six months *before* the Soviet invasion, on July 3, 1979, Carter had signed a directive for secret military aid to opponents of the pro-Soviet regime. On that day, Brzezinski wrote a note to the U.S. president explaining that this secret aid to the mujahedeen "was going to induce a Soviet military intervention." He was correct.

Carter was convinced that by controlling Afghanistan the Soviets would have an easy entrée into Iran and the oil-rich Mideast. If the Soviets blocked the Straits of Hormuz, they could choke off oil shipments to the West. Carter was determined that the Russians should not be allowed such leverage. It would have to be punished for the invasion and deterred from ever engaging in such lawless behavior again.

Carter demanded that the Soviets immediately withdraw from Afghanistan. A few weeks later, on January 23, 1980, in his State of the Union address to Congress, the president emphasized: "The Soviet Union must pay a concrete price for their aggression. . . . The Soviet Union must realize that its decision to use military force in Afghanistan will be costly to every political and economic relationship it values." Carter had fundamentally misjudged the political and military situation in Afghanistan, but so had the Soviets. Brzezinski later recalled writing to Carter on the December day the Soviets invaded that "we now have the opportunity of giving the USSR its Vietnam war." Indeed, the Soviets would learn that their incursion into Afghanistan would prove costly in men and materiel. A decade in the mountains of their southern neighbor would bleed the Soviet military dry. The Soviet adventure would lead to the eventual demise of Communist rule in Mother Russia. Carter, in effect, wanted to punish an enemy that had decided to commit political and military suicide.

Afghanistan had a long history of bloody internal wars and external invasions. Landlocked but located along east-west trade routes, Afghanistan was critically situated and almost impervious to outside enemies. It was the one territory Alexander the Great could not conquer. The British fought two wars in the nineteenth century against the Afghans, but they never fully controlled the country. A land of mountains and deserts, divided into tribes, clans, and warlords, Afghanistan's physical, social, and political terrain resisted effective control.

The Carter administration claimed that the Soviet action had been unexpected and unforeseen, although security documents later made public indicate that the CIA had been monitoring the buildup of Soviet troops on its border for weeks and the Soviets had thousands of elite troops already strategically placed within Afghanistan. President Carter, however, publicly expressed his shock and surprise. The U.S. administration's response to the Soviet invasion of its neighbor was harsh on rhetoric but muted in action. As the president would later explain in a news conference: "When the Soviets invaded Afghanistan, I had the option of military action, economic action and political action. I decided not to take military action, to go to war with the Soviet Union—a wise decision, I think—but I did decide to exert a maximum amount of appropriate political pressure and economic pressure. . . . [The Olympic boycott] was a psychological blow to the Soviet Union."

In the coming months, administration officials, including the president and the vice president, would characterize the Soviet invasion as the greatest threat to world peace and stability since the close of the Second World War. American officials claimed this was the first time that the Soviet Union had used its military forces to expand its power, ignoring the fact that the Soviets were invited into Afghanistan, much the same ruse it had used for its military adventures in Eastern Europe. America demanded that the Soviets immediately withdraw, but it seemed incapable of doing anything that would coerce Soviet compliance. The United States did not cut diplomatic relations with the Soviets, nor did it mount any open military riposte. It did not increase its military presence in the Persian Gulf. In fact, words aside, nothing happened that signaled to the world that Carter's hyperbole was anything other than puffing.

In February 1980, the athletes of the world who competed on snow and ice, including those from the "invading" Soviet Union, as the administration repeatedly called its adversary, were scheduled to meet in Lake Placid, New York, for the Thirteenth Olympic Winter Games. There is no record that the Carter administration even considered barring the Russians from participating. World sports remained basically unaffected—at least for the moment. In fact, the U.S. boxing team was allowed to compete in an exhibition in Moscow within weeks of the Soviet invasion. Shortly thereafter, Soviet athletes participated in the Oregon Indoor Track and Field Meet in Portland.

Although wedded to its antagonism toward the Communist menace, America's credo also included a commitment to improving international relations through peaceful competition in sports. That perhaps explains why it rarely "punished" other rogue nations. Although it debated the issue at length, U.S. Olympians did not boycott the 1936 Berlin Olympics hosted by the century's most despicable regime. American athletes were allowed to compete against teams from apartheid South Africa, which maintained a malevolent police state that oppressed the vast majority of its citizens. Even when the Soviets subjugated political dissidents, America stood by.

A Presidential Commission on Olympic Sports, created by Carter's predecessor, Gerald Ford, had, among other things, studied the issue of sports boycotts. In a report issued in 1977, it strongly urged that governments not deny their athletes the opportunity to participate in international sports competitions. Other political and sports leaders were on record in support of participation as a peaceful method for engaging the enemy. Nonetheless, within days of the Soviet invasion, Carter publicly raised for the first time the possibility that America and its allies would have to respond to the incursion by boycotting the Moscow Olympic Games. (Walter Mondale later claimed that he had first raised the idea with the president.) America would withhold its athletes and pressure other nations to join suit.

Carter vowed that his administration would not look weak in the face of Soviet aggression. Already suffering from a crisis in Tehran, where students and militants held fifty-two U.S. diplomats hostage in the United States embassy, Carter knew he was seen by the public as an enfeebled leader. He would not compound the injury already done to his reputation. The administration understood that its options were limited. It was not going to invade Afghanistan or the Soviet Union. America had only recently begun to heal from a military adventure on the opposite side of the world in Southeast Asia. Instead, Carter decided that he would sacrifice the hopes, dreams, and careers of its Olympic athletes in order to embarrass the Soviets. From the beginning, the Olympic athletes opposed any boycott. Instead of using the Moscow Olympics as an international stage on which to demonstrate the superiority of the American system through athletic excellence, Carter decided to boycott the games.

On January 25, 1980, even before Carter's State of the Union address, fifty Olympic athletes training at the USOC facilities in Colorado held a news conference and issued a written statement that denounced "the use of athletes as a 'political lever,'" recommending instead a total economic boycott of the Soviet Union: "We must use actions which will achieve results, not symbolic gestures which only vent emotions." The athletes would later buckle under political pressure from the White House.

In its internal discussions, and later in its public pronouncements, Carter administration figures compared the situation it faced with the call in 1936 for a boycott of the Berlin Olympics. Many suggested to the president that if the Western democracies had refused to attend the Berlin Olympic Games, it would have altered history. While the debates about boycotting the Berlin Olympics focused on the prestige the Nazis would gain from hosting the world's athletes, no one had ever suggested at the time that a boycott would topple Hitler's regime or deter any of its subsequent aggression. In fact, that would not have happened. Had the British and French resisted the Nazi land grabs in the late 1930s and confronted the regime before it had fully remilitarized, then the course of history might have been altered. An Olympic boycott would have been a slap in the face, but not a blow to the solar plexus.

President Carter was unwilling to confront the Soviets with any action commensurate with the nature of the threat he claimed the Soviet incursion presented. Carter needed to do something dramatic, and he decided to sacrifice the aspirations and careers of a few hundred athletes. For once, the media was in his corner. Almost uniformly, the American press urged Carter to take that step even if it meant the destruction of the Olympic movement.

BLOCKING THE ROAD TO MOSCOW

In his State of the Union message on January 23, 1980, President Jimmy Carter formally announced the boycott: "I have notified the Olympic Committee that with Soviet invading forces in Afghanistan, neither the American people nor I will support sending an Olympic team to Moscow." He set a thirty-day deadline for the Soviets to begin removing their forces and thereby save their Olympic Games. The next day, the U.S. House of Representatives voted 386–12 to support Carter's call for a boycott. The *New York Times* agreed in an editorial the following morning: "It would be best, then, to ratify the President's judgment and to abandon plans to compete in Moscow. "

Other than its ill-fated refusal to participate in the League of Nations after World War I, the United States had never previously declined to participate in international events, sporting or otherwise. This time would be different. As David Kanin, a former CIA officer, wrote in the *Journal of Sport and Social Issues*, after the invasion of Afghanistan Carter found that "sport, that most peripheral and most publicized form of international relations, provided the perfect answer." The scheme proved as successful as most other actions of the Carter administration in altering the policies of the Soviet Union. It would have absolutely no impact on the Soviets' military actions in Afghanistan.

Although at first the American people supported the boycott of the Moscow Olympics, President Carter knew that his controversial stance would not be met with applause by the American sports establishment. He wrote to the president of the United States Olympic Committee, Robert Kane, urging him to advise the International Olympic Committee that unless Soviet troops fully withdrew from Afghanistan "within the next month, Moscow will become an unsuitable site for a festival meant to celebrate peace and good will." Kane rejected the president's attempt to influence or control determinations that were the exclusive province of a national Olympic committee, let alone to mandate a boycott: "If we started to make political judgments, it would be the end of the games." The guiding charter of the United States Olympic Committee fully supported Kane's position. It stated: "No member of the USOC may deny, or threaten to deny, any amateur athlete the opportunity to compete in the Olympic Games." Carter, however, was adamant. The administration genuinely thought the International Olympic Committee would cancel the Moscow Olympics if the United States applied enough political pressure. It was a significant misjudgment.

Carter continued to make adamant public pronouncements. On February 13, 1980, at a news conference, he said:

We have no desire to use the Olympics to punish, except the Soviets attach a major degree of importance to holding of the Olympics in the Soviet Union. In their own propaganda material they claim that the willingness of the International Olympic Committee to let the Olympics be held in Moscow is an endorsement of the foreign policy and the peace-loving nature of the Soviet Union.

To me, it's unconscionable for any nation to send athletes to the capital of [another] nation under the aegis of the Olympics when that host nation is actively involved in the invasion of and the subjugation of innocent people. And so, for that reason, I don't believe that we are obligated to send athletes to Moscow.

Carter wrote to Lord Killanin, the head of the International Olympic Committee, demanding that the Olympics be moved. Killanin responded through an intermediary: "It's Moscow or nothing." In March, Carter reiterated his commitment at a gathering of past and prospective Olympic athletes who had been invited to the White House: "I cannot say what other nations will not go. Ours will not go." As late as April 1980, apparently Carter still did not understand that the decision to send a team to the Olympics was made by a nation's Olympic committee and not by a nation's government. He said at a news conference that a "decision made by a nation's government . . . is a final decision."

Curiously, it was the success of the young U.S. hockey squad in Lake Placid that began to undermine the public's support for a U.S.-led boycott of the Moscow Summer Olympic Games. American television viewers were enthralled by the David-and-Goliath story played out on ice, especially because it was one of the rare times that America played the role of David. The Soviets were a professional team, the best in the world by far. The upset by college-aged athletes, broadcast worldwide, made Americans proud of their young men. Carter immediately invited the young hockey "heroes" and, as an afterthought, the entire U.S. Winter Olympic team to the White House, a move that further antagonized the international sports movement. This unprecedented politicization further enhanced the public perception that the Olympic movement as a whole was a valuable asset to democracy in general and to America in particular. Bringing all these athletes to Washington, however, created another significant risk for the administration. Eric Heiden, the great speed skater who had just won five gold medals at Lake Placid, solicited signatures on a petition denouncing the Moscow boycott. It was signed by dozens of his teammates.

Over the next few months, the Carter administration would use both "carrots" and "sticks" in its campaign to punish the Soviets with a boycott. It promised the United States Olympic Committee it would receive funding if it would turn its back on the IOC and Moscow. At the same time, it indirectly (and, at times, directly) threatened to destroy the USOC and, if necessary, the entire Olympic movement if it would not cooperate. Athletes were threatened that their passports would be confiscated if they tried to go to Moscow. The administration threatened to remove the USOC's tax-exempt status, a devastating blow, if it did not cooperate.

The administration did consider asking Congress for legislation to enforce the boycott, and the measures would have easily won approval. Although the statutes were never actually proposed, the administration drafted laws that would have allowed the government to withdraw the passports not only of athletes but also those of the broadcast media and the press who defied the boycott. Constitutional rights to travel and the freedom of the press would take second place to the administration's hubris. White House Counsel Lloyd Cutler repeatedly proposed in Oval Office meetings that the government sue the IOC and the USOC in U.S. federal courts for violating the antitrust laws, litigation that likely would have come up far short.

Despite the many months of deliberations, threats, promises, and bloviation, no one in the Carter administration actually thought that a boycott of the Moscow Olympic Games would force the Soviets to abate their military adventure. However, it was critical as a political matter that President Carter's pledge to respond to Soviet aggression not be abandoned. He must be seen by the American voting public as a strong and principled leader. He must not be allowed to suffer another international fiasco, especially during a reelection year when he faced a significant primary challenge from Senator Ted Kennedy. As a result, Carter was rigid and unyielding in supporting a strategy that he knew had no chance for success.

The internecine struggle over the boycott within America was mirrored in every non-Communist country in the world. American diplomats assiduously sought the support of other nations. Some Islamic countries joined the effort, not because of U.S. pressure but rather in brotherhood with its co-religionists under attack in Afghanistan. While Margaret Thatcher's government in Britain joined with its ally, the British national Olympic association voted overwhelmingly to attend the Moscow Olympics, a significant rebuke to the Iron Lady. The French, Italians, and most of the rest of Europe joined the Brits in participating.

Canada responded to the call of its southern neighbor to boycott, and Carter was able to pressure West Germany, Israel, and Japan—all of whom relied on extensive American military support—to join in the boycott effort. In total, sixty-two countries boycotted, eighty-one participated.

Britain had set the pattern, with a stalwart governmental commitment to boycott matched by an equally strong dedication by the national Olympic committee to participate in the world games. It was the national Olympic committee that had the final say under the Olympic structure. In some cases, such as Canada and West Germany, politics bested sports. In others, such as France, Italy, and Australia, athletics prevailed over politics. Sometimes the United States was directly involved in these country-by-country determinations, but in all cases American leadership of the "Free World" was at play.

Countries around the globe simply did not find the issue as clear-cut as the U.S. administration. There were costs and benefits on both sides of the equation. Practicality, tradition, and the role of symbols meshed into a jumble of conflicting influences. Ultimately, a significant number of countries did not send teams to Moscow, some simply because they did not have the financial resources to participate. For others, participation was too costly politically.

In May 1980, at the direction of the International Olympic Committee, president Killanin engaged in a last-ditch effort of personal diplomacy to try to bridge the gap between the superpowers. Armed only with the prestige of the Olympic movement, Killanin met first in the Kremlin with Leonid Brezhnev, who had trouble believing that the United States would use a sports boycott as its weapon of choice to counter the geopolitical and military policy of the USSR. For once in its dealings with the West, the Soviets could claim they were the victim. Killanin then traveled to Washington and met with Jimmy Carter, who reiterated the U.S. position. Carter then asked what he could do to strengthen the Olympic movement. Killanin responded that he should allow American athletes to participate in Moscow. Carter replied that "this was not possible." In his memoirs, Killanin wrote: "The more I look back, the more it is extraordinary that a vast country like the United States could not produce a greater leader or statesman than Carter."

The administration's anti-Moscow Olympics project considered as a whole showed a remarkable lack of knowledge by a range of American government officials about the nature of international sports organizations. At first, Carter and others thought that governments could simply order their national Olympic committees to follow their political directives. Carter would learn that was not the case, especially after Prime Minister Thatcher's government could not force the British Olympic Association to join the boycott. In a classic line, Denis Howell, a British MP (Member of Parliament), remarked: "This country is governed by the Magna Carta, not Jimmy Carter."

No one in the administration thought to consult with either the United States Olympic Committee or the International Olympic Committee *before* announcing its unilateral boycott policy. Instead, the president attempted subsequently to bully both bodies into compliance. The IOC would not be moved but, eventually, the USOC reluctantly voted to comply, especially after fifteen companies that had pledged financial support threatened to withdraw their monetary contributions if American athletes participated in the Moscow Olympics. (They had been "urged" to do so by the Carter administration.)

Finally, emissaries from President Carter met with Lord Killanin and told him that under Olympic rules the games could only be held with an international truce in effect. Of course, there was no such rule. The administration was referring to the false claim that in ancient Greece wars were stopped during the quadrennial Olympic festivals. Participants in those ancient games were given freedom to travel to Olympus while the wars proceeded. The war in Afghanistan kept no athletes off the road to Moscow.

The Carter administration's major response, however, was to use the nation's athletes as its pawns. On March 21, 1980, American Summer Olympics athletes attended a meeting at the White House for a briefing on Afghanistan. Presidential adviser Zbigniew Brzezinski explained that from its launching pad in Afghanistan the Soviets could now cut off the world's oil supply by blocking the Straits of Hormuz. (It could have done so without the invasion by using long-range bombers, but Brzezinski did not explain that.) He accused the Soviets of recklessly using chemical weapons against Afghan fighters and of building permanent bases.

Brzezinski rejected the fundamental apolitical conception of Olympism: "To the USSR, sport is an extension of politics." That was precisely why an American politically based boycott of the Moscow Olympic Games was warranted: "We can't say of sport that 'this is somehow immune.' It's not logical, not possible. Worse, it is symbolically wrong, morally wrong to hold this festival of peace in the capital of an aggressor nation posing a threat of such strategic significance." The athletes seemed impressed. Unannounced, President Carter then walked into the room. No one stood or applauded for the only time during Carter's term in office.

Carter's remarks to the athletes drew the comparison of the current situation to the Berlin Olympics of 1936, suggesting that a boycott then would have meant there would never have been a Second World War, a totally preposterous claim. He plainly stated that no matter what other nations did, "ours will not go." "I am determined to keep that national interest paramount—even if people I admire and love, like you, are forced to sacrifice." Carter urged the athletes to stand with him for what was best for America. He also claimed this would be the best outcome for the Olympic movement: "In my judgment what we are doing is preserving the principles and the quality of the Olympics, not destroying it." The audience applauded. However, a later poll of the athletes taken at the nearby Hay-Adams Hotel tallied forty-four opposed to a boycott, twenty-nine in favor, and twenty-four abstentions.

The United States would use all its national and international political influence and economic power to construct a boycott of the Moscow Olympics of 1980. To make sure there would be no backsliding, Carter pressured American businesses that stood to earn money from the Moscow Olympics to void their contracts. As a result, Levi Strauss, for example, declined to deliver the uniforms ordered for the Moscow stadium workers. NBC canceled its plans to cover the Olympics after Carter threatened to use the Emergency Economic Powers Act to block network payments to the Soviets. The administration banned the delivery of American sporting goods, chewing gum, soccer balls, and landing pits for the pole vault. As a result of the administration's action, some U.S. companies that had contracted to provide supplies to the Olympic Games went bankrupt. The administration embargoed grain shipments and restricted sales of computer and oil-drilling technology to the Soviet Union, but its major threat was using its athletes to make a political statement and deliver a political insult.

Carter recruited Muhammad Ali as his ad hoc ambassador to African nations to present the U.S. position, seeking their participation in the boycott. A few months earlier, Ali had won the heavyweight crown for the third time, and he was approaching retirement. The idea of using Ali came from three black Foreign Service officers with experience on the African continent. Ali was in India performing charity work when the president's request reached him. He just happened to be meeting with the Soviet ambassador to India, who explained the Soviet position to the great fighter. No one from the U.S. State Department, however, took the same time to brief Ali.

Not unexpectedly, Ali's mission was a disaster. While he was greeted by huge crowds as he toured the continent, he could not adequately explain U.S. policy because it had not been explained to him. His hosts, moreover, were not inclined to confront the Soviets, who had financed their sports and commercial development. In fact, before the trip had ended, Ali announced that his African hosts had persuaded him that the boycott was misguided!

Despite the congressional and public support Carter had received, not all Americans agreed with the boycott. Ted Sorensen, who had been special counsel to President Kennedy, had written in the *New York Times* the prior September: "Effective control over the conduct of foreign affairs is slipping away from Jimmy Carter, and that is sad to see. The need is not for more belligerence in President Carter's policy or more bombast in his speeches, nor for a strong warning to Congress unmatched by action. What's needed is presidential leadership."

The International Olympic Committee resisted being bullied by the United States. Secretary of State Cyrus Vance, addressing the IOC at its meeting in Lake Placid at the Winter Olympic Games, ordered the committee to cancel or postpone the Moscow Olympics. He repeated the mantra that the Olympics could not be held "in the capital of an invading nation." The IOC, however, stood steadfast in support of the Moscow Olympics, although IOC president Killanin acknowledged the reality: "Sports and politics unfortunately are frequently interrelated." This was despite an IOC rule that political interference by a government could lead to its expulsion from the Olympic movement. Killanin had advised the IOC (with Vance in attendance): "Do not use the Olympic Games to divide the world, but to unite it—do not use athletes for the solution of political problems."

Had there been any real possibility that the IOC might punish Moscow—and there was none—Vance's speech sealed the case. IOC members were not going to be bullied. They had been particularly appalled at the partisan jingoism shown by American spectators after the U.S. squad won the ice hockey gold medal at Lake Placid. The chants of "USA! USA!" rang a sour note. Now Vance was dictating that the IOC simply fall in line behind U.S. foreign policy.

During the Lake Placid Olympic Games, other administration officials met with U.S. Olympic leaders and made an even starker threat. If the USOC did not go along with administration policy, the White House would destroy the Olympic movement and the USOC in the process. Bullying had turned from bluster to coercion and browbeating reminiscent of Vito and Michael Corleone, the fictional godfathers.

Ultimately, the United States Olympic Committee was scheduled to meet in early April in Colorado Springs to decide whether it would heed the administration's call and boycott the Moscow Olympics. A week earlier, the administration had invited representatives of the national governing bodies for the various Olympic sports to the White House. The athletes came with their own counterproposal that would protect the Olympics and their careers while saving face for the administration. They proposed a significant visible protest in Moscow that would demonstrate to the world and the Soviets that the invasion of Afghanistan was intolerable. Although the United States' athletes would participate in their sporting events, they would not participate in the opening, closing, or medal ceremonies. Athletes would only stay in Moscow for the days of their events, and they would stay either in the Olympic village or at competition and training facilities. The administration flatly rejected any compromise at all. By the time of the Colorado Springs vote, the athletes had been beaten into submission by government coercion and simple blackmail. A vote to participate in the Moscow Olympic Games would be futile.

The night before the vote, President Carter had sent a telegram to USOC president Kane reminding him of the brutality of the Soviet invaders and how the aggressor jeopardized the security of the Persian Gulf area and threatened world peace and stability. The *New York Times* explained in an editorial the simple question before the USOC meeting: "whether participation in Games justifies humiliation of the American Presidency and a windfall coup for Soviet policy and propaganda." Not all newspapers were as committed to the boycott as the *New York Times*. The *Boston Globe*, for example, offered its opinion: "For more than three months the argument has been a misbegotten mess—an idea dreamed up by a few American sports writers, seized on by an American President who gives the distressing impression of making up foreign policy as he goes along; an idea of extreme political naivety and dismal immediate impact; an idea precisely calculated (if anybody was actually calculating) to produce the maximum Western disarray at a time when maximum Western solidarity was needed."

On April 11, 1980, Vice President Walter Mondale addressed the most important meeting in the history of the USOC at its session at the Antlers Plaza Hotel in Colorado Springs. His speech epitomizes how American ideology and politics had contorted world sports. Mondale's emotional appeal was phrased in the most hyperbolic terms: "History holds its breath, for what is at stake here is no less than the future security of the civilized world. If one nation can be subjugated by Soviet aggression, is any sovereign nation truly safe from that fate?" Mondale reasoned that the Soviets would use the presence of American athletes in Moscow as a testament to American approval of its brutal actions in Afghanistan: "I am convinced that the American people do not want their athletes cast as pawns in that tawdry propaganda charade." No mention was made of the Carter administration using American athletes as chess pieces in its propaganda farce. In their view, any athlete anywhere who travels to Moscow is guilty of "complicity" with the Communist perfidy in Afghanistan, in effect suggesting that they had become "fellow travelers" with the Communist menace. For Mondale, the boycott constituted a national imperative: "Athletes and sports organizations and national bodies around the world await your lead to mobilize their commitment. They do so for good reason. Today, virtually every industrial nation on earth is dangerously dependent on Persian Gulf oil. How could we convince the Soviets not to threaten the Gulf, if a blow was dealt to our deterrent? How could our government send a message to Moscow, if tomorrow's Pravda brags that our policies have been repudiated?"

Mondale used the analogy of the aborted Berlin boycott, but facts had intervened since that argument was first conceived. The great Jesse Owens had died two weeks earlier. His triumphs in Berlin had exposed Nazi ideology as a false testament of Aryan supremacy. In retrospect, had the Berlin boycott succeeded, Owens would not have become an international hero for all marginalized nations and people.

Mondale concluded his remarks with a call for patriotic service by the athletes acting in the national interest. He recognized what he was asking the athletes to do, "but I also know, as you know, that some goals surpass even personal achievement." He asked for "an unambiguous statement of our national resolve." The USOC House of Delegates applauded politely and then surrendered by a vote of 1,604 to 797, the only time the national organizing committee ever voted not to participate in an international sporting event. USOC president Kane explained the vote to the public on the basis that President Carter had represented the boycott as a matter of national security. The resolution the USOC approved stated: "Since the President advised the USOC that in light of international events the national security of the country is threatened, the USOC has decided not to send a team." President Carter welcomed the vote. The administration had won an important victory, but at a significant moral cost.

The payoff to the United States Olympic Committee in its surrender was substantial. There was talk that the athletes would each receive the Congressional Medal of Honor. In fact, they received something called the Congressional Gold Medal, which was a gold-plated bronze medal. It was paid for by the USOC. Twenty-seven years later, Congress corrected the slight and designated the previously tendered medals as America's highest civilian award. The administration did advance the USOC $4 million of a $16-million federal grant for grass-roots amateur athletic development. The administration pledged financial support for the Los Angeles Olympic Organizing Committee preparing for the 1984 Summer Games. Finally, it urged both U.S. corporations and the American public to contribute to the USOC's fundraising campaign, an effort that had been crippled since Carter first proposed the boycott three months earlier.

The athletes fought back in the only way they could, by using the court system. As soon as the USOC voted not to participate in the Moscow Olympics, Anita DeFrantz, a world-class rower, graduate of Penn Law School, and later a major leader of the American and international sports establishments, filed suit in federal court on behalf of twenty-five athletes. The court denied the athletes' request for injunctive relief based on their claim that the USOC did not have the power to refuse to send a team to Moscow under the terms of the Amateur Sports Act of 1978 and the U.S. Constitution. The court recognized the impact of the USOC action on the athletes, but claimed it was powerless to grant them a remedy:

Ordinarily, talent alone has determined whether an American would have the privilege of participating in the Olympics. This year, unexpectedly, things are different. We express no view on the merits of the decision made. We do express our understanding of the deep disappointment and frustrations felt by thousands of American athletes. In doing so, we also recognize that the responsibilities of citizenship often fall more heavily on some than on others. Some are called to military duty. Others never serve. Some return from military service unscathed.

Others never return. These are the simple, although harsh, facts of life, and they are immutable.

The judge was correct about the unfairness inherent in life and sports. For nearly half of the 1980 U.S. Olympic team, this was the only time they would ever qualify for the Olympic Games. They would never return to international competition.

UNDERSTANDING THE BOYCOTT

How then can we explain Carter's boycott? Undoubtedly, America's regret at its failure to boycott the Nazi Olympics of 1936 played a role, although that issue may have been raised as a makeweight, simply to justify a decision to boycott Moscow that had already been made. This time, in the face of Russian aggression, America would stand strong for what it deemed its moral responsibility. Also, 1980 was an election year, and Carter seemed destined to serve but one term. Amid his failed presidency, Carter was suffering in the polls from the effects of an oil boycott, rampant inflation, and the interminable hostage crisis in Tehran. His advisers, most importantly Lloyd Cutler, pressed the president to use the boycott of the Moscow Olympic Games to punish the Soviets, normally a useful political ploy during the cold war.

But why would Carter boycott Moscow if he knew it would not affect the Olympics or the invasion of Afghanistan? Perhaps he thought it would degrade the Olympics or at least embarrass the Soviets. There is no question that the Soviets intended to make diplomatic hay out of hosting the world sporting festival. Carter was correct that Communist propaganda would be as ubiquitous as Misha, the bear mascot of the 1980 Summer Olympic Games. Instead, by stepping ahead of the Soviets in the propaganda game, the U.S. administration was able to effectively convert the aggressor into a victim.

Why was Carter willing to place détente at risk? Was he just naive? Perhaps he thought the Soviets needed détente more than they needed a stable Afghanistan next door. The Soviets had shown in the face of the Nazi onslaught less than three decades earlier that they could survive a winter in Stalingrad without food and lose two million people to starvation. Why would the cutoff of American wheat exports affect a people able to accept such extreme privation? Why would the United States—the self-styled beacon of hope for the world—risk being blamed for killing the Olympic movement? When viewed through ideological lenses, the Carter administration was certain that the Soviets would bear the blame because they were the aggressors in Afghanistan. That was quixotic myopia. Throughout most of the world, the United States was seen as a reckless grandstander, unwilling to do more than bluster and strut.

In 1980, the United States played another international chess match against the Soviets as it had in 1945 in the "Great Radio Chess Match." Once again, the Americans came up short of victory. Carter was willing to sacrifice the nation's athletes as pawns in the global game of politics. He was not willing to risk its more valuable pieces. While occasional reference was made by administration figures to the Russians' godlessness, no American "bishops" were exposed to danger. The potent American fighting machines—the chess knights, if you would—were held back. The United States never had "winning chances," as they say in chess, and it played a sloppy game.

Even if the administration's action could be justified, the U.S.-led boycott was handled quite poorly. It proved a political disaster. Athletes from most of America's closest allies, including the United Kingdom, chose to participate in the Moscow Olympic Games even if their national governments were allied with America. The Soviets scored political points for resisting what it quickly and loudly proclaimed were "the forces of reaction." The Americans, the Kremlin wrote in its "Handbook for Party Activists," were "trying to exploit the Olympic Movement and games in the interests of the exploiting classes, for the goals of business and commerce, as propaganda for the bourgeois way of life, capitalist construction and its ideology, and for the distraction of youth from the political and class struggle."

A THIRD FORCE

Perhaps the most interesting result of the Moscow boycott fiasco was the realization that in addition to Soviet ideology and American ideology, there was abroad on the globe a distinctive and noteworthy third ideology that supported international cooperation rather than partisan dualism and confrontation. Maybe this is what Baron de Coubertin was striving for when he talked about "Olympism," something neither the Carter administration nor the Politburo appreciated. In a world divided between two rival military superpowers, there was a power, albeit not one armed with military or even spiritual force, imbued with the mighty secular theology of the Olympic spirit.

Adherents of "Olympism" would be considered naive waifs in the war rooms of the cold war. How could international sports figures produce anything of lasting value in the search for world peace? The ancient Olympics never stopped any Hellenic wars, and the modern Olympics had to be stopped for the two world wars. For some fearful right-wingers, "Olympism" seemed just a way station on the road to world government, something to dread rather than applaud. For others, "Olympism" was simply a vehicle to produce television programming that could be used to sell beer, cars, and other commodities.

Indeed, the Olympic movement, like other international and domestic activities, had its flaws. Wedded to its national Olympic committee structure, the movement enhanced the nationalism that was the cause of the political disruptions. The movement, it seemed at times, thought itself to be more important than the athletes. As a general matter, the world's athletes seemed uninterested in global politics. They trained for years to prepare for the Olympic sports festival, which could mean riches for some and recognition for many. They did not care in what country or city the track or pool was located, as long as it was an oval 440 meters in diameter and a pool 50 meters long.

It was hard to ask young athletes to give up their life's goal in the absence of a convincing case of national security, a case the Carter administration never really made. The administration used every weapon at its disposal, except real weaponry, to win using a political strategy that had no chance of success and would forever tar it as an abject failure.

GAMES TO PLAY

Eighty nations came to Moscow in the summer of 1980 to participate in the games of the Twenty-Second Olympiad. Many Americans came as spectators. The Soviet Union paid the way for the teams of many countries that were strapped for cash. It even promised Jordan a visit by the Bolshoi Ballet if it would attend, and it did. A total of 5,179 athletes competed in Moscow, compared with 6,084 four years earlier in Montreal. The United States tried to disrupt the Olympic Games and embarrass the Communists, but it failed to destroy them. The Olympic movement showed it was stronger than cold war politics. Nonetheless, the Moscow Olympics were not complete without the athletes of the boycotting nations. As a result of the U.S. response to the Soviet invasion of Afghanistan, détente was left spiritless, if not defunct. The Communist Party of the Soviet Union explained in robust ideological terms what had occurred:

> Attempting to bend other states to their will, ruling circles in the USA took the road of economic "sanctions" and curtailment of scientific-technical, cultural and sports exchanges, refusing obligations that had been accepted, and violating treaties and agreements signed by them. Anti-Sovietism and anti-Communism have been transformed into instruments for pressing forward the arms race, and into weapons of struggle not only against the USSR and other lands of social-ist solidarity, not only against Communists, but against all adversaries of war, peace-loving forces, and into a means of undermining détente.

While the Soviet leadership could not comprehend why the U.S. government would spearhead such a strategy of international insult, they had suffered far worse in their sixty years in power. The Olympics would go on without the boycotting nations.

Some observers characterized the Moscow Olympic Games as "joyless," but that might also have accurately represented daily life in the gray USSR. The Soviets had sanitized Moscow for international visitors, removing "trou-blemakers" from the city and barring suburbanites from Olympic sites. Gone were the endless lines for food; sidewalk tables now adorned Moscow's main streets. For Muscovites, the Olympic fortnight was true delight.

There were some notable sports achievements at the Moscow Olympic Games, and thirty-six world records were set. In some sports, however, the athletes missed the presence of the strongest competition. The Russian people could only understand the boycott as another example of the commitment of some Western countries (meaning primarily the United States) to destroy the socialist alternative to capitalist life.

Lord Killanin rued the boycott, but was realistic in his appraisal: "Alas, sport is intertwined with politics but, and I do not mind being accused of being naïve, sport and the Olympic Games must not be used for political purposes, especially when other political, diplomatic and economic means have not been tried." The United States gained no international prestige as a result of its effort to manipulate international sports for political reasons.

A PRICE TO PAY

Newton's third law of motion predetermined the consequences of the U.S.-led boycott of the Moscow Olympics: to every action there is always an equal and opposite reaction. As Dave Zirin, a modern-day commentator on sports, has written, the Olympics are political "morality plays." There is always a second act. The 1984 Los Angeles Olympics offered the Soviets and their allies an opportunity to redress the American insult by mounting a counter-boycott. Carter had used the Olympics as an instrument of foreign policy, and the Soviet Union and its allies would respond in kind.

This would be the second time Los Angeles would host the Olympic Games. In 1932, travel to America's West Coast was not easy, and in the early 1930s the world was suffering from a global economic disaster. Relatively few athletes traveled to Southern California for the games of the Tenth Olympiad. Even President Herbert Hoover did not attend. As usual, however, the IOC leadership pronounced the Olympics a great success.

By 1984, transportation was much improved, but the political climate had decidedly deteriorated. Even as President Carter announced the boycott of the Moscow Olympic Games, he and his advisers appreciated that the Los Angeles Olympics would be affected. At first, the Soviets indicated that they would participate, but as political leadership changed in the Kremlin, the urge to retaliate took over. Commencing two years before the Los Angeles Olympic Games, the Soviets began to raise concerns about the security of its athletes if they were to attend the games in America. They expressed concern about the safety of the Olympic village. They requested special accommodation to allow Aeroflot flights to land at the airport and for a Soviet cruise ship to dock at Long Beach. The Los Angeles Olympic Organizing Committee arranged for the special flights and the cruise ship accommodations. Nonetheless, the Soviets ultimately issued a statement explaining they would be forced to refuse to appear due to the "chauvinistic sentiments and anti-Soviet hysteria . . . being whipped up in the United States."

Only 6,000 athletes from 140 nations made the trip to Los Angeles, slightly more than came to Moscow but still not a complete Olympics. The Soviet Union and sixteen of its allies declined to attend. Eastern European bloc nations, with the notable exceptions of Romania and Yugoslavia, declined their invitations. Some countries did not send teams to Los Angeles for reasons unrelated to the great East-West political standoff. Bolivia, for example, had difficulty funding a team. Tony Kornheiser of the *Washington Post* wrote a column about the Bolivians' financial plight. Quite offended, the Bolivians announced they now would certainly not attend.

The 1984 Olympics was the first truly private and fully commercialized international sporting festival, an event fully aligned with American economic ideology. Peter Ueberroth, a former airline executive, directed the business effort. He sought commercial sponsorships on a scale previously unseen in the Olympics. In addition to the television rights, which totaled over $250 million, the Los Angeles Olympic Organizing Committee pocketed another $130 million from corporate sponsors. The thirty official sponsors included U.S. and international corporate giants like American Express, Anheuser-Busch, Canon, and Coca-Cola. Other corporations offered in-kind contributions, such as General Motors Buick cars and Xerox copiers. Ueberroth's business executives licensed other companies to sell "official" Olympic products. McDonald's sold the official hamburger of the Los Angeles Olympics, and the Mars bar was the official snack. Refuse companies even bid for the right to pick up the Olympic garbage. The capitalist Olympics turned a tidy profit of over $200 million while absolving the city of Los Angeles of any financial liability for the costs of the games. In fact, the surplus was used to establish a foundation to promote children's athletics in America.

The contests of the Los Angeles Olympic Games were a decidedly one-sided affair. The chauvinistic American spectators chanted incessantly, and they had much to cheer about. The U.S. swimming and diving teams won most available medals, as did the country's track competitors. The U.S. boxing team won nine of twelve gold medals. The American athletes dominated, winning 83 gold medals and a total of 174 medals of all colors. Not all journalists, however, were moved by the triumphant Americans. Frank Deford wrote for *Sports Illustrated*:

> Oh, what we've done to the Olympics. The Soviets & Co. perverted them by not coming, but it seems we've done as much violence to them by our presence. God only knows what the 2.5 billion people around the globe who are watching the Games will think of a vain America, so bountiful and strong, with every advantage, including the home court, reveling in the role of Goliath, gracelessly trumpeting its own good fortune while rudely dismissing its guests. At best, we've

been dreadful hosts; at worst, we've revealed ourselves as bullies—of our friendly competition and of an ideal.

The Carter boycott of the 1980 Olympic Games changed nothing in the geopolitical universe except that it undermined détente. The Soviets would continue to fight the mujahedeen in Afghanistan until the end of the decade. A decade or so later, after 9/11 it would be America's turn to fight the same enemy. The Americans invaded Afghanistan only months before the United States would host the 2002 Winter Olympics in Salt Lake City, but no country would boycott those games to punish the Americans. The irony of that reality showed that while ideology may be essential to the conduct of politics, it is an uncertain compass when it comes to sports.

Nelson Mandela, one of the greatest revolutionaries in world history, eventually would use rugby, his opponent's own sport, as the platform on which to secure the country's new multiracial democracy. After twenty-seven years of imprisonment, Mandela emerged to lead his party and, four years later, his nation. He would use a brilliant political ploy—adopting the Afrikaners' beloved Springboks as a symbol of all South Africans—to bring a measure of stability to his nation. *AP Images*

Sport has the power to change the world. It has the power to
inspire, the power to unite people that little else can. Sport can
create hope. It is an instrument for peace. . . . It is more powerful
than governments in breaking down racial barriers.

—*Nelson Mandela*

[7]
SPORTS AND
SOUTH AFRICAN
LIBERATION

Nelson Mandela was the greatest revolutionary in the history of the African
continent. He catalyzed fundamental political change in his country of South
Africa essentially without firing a shot. He used not guns but politics, negotiation skills, and the South Africans' love of sports to transform his nation from
a land of racist tyranny into a multiracial democracy elected through universal
suffrage. Then, in a remarkable demonstration of forbearance, Mandela and
the black masses of South Africa forgave their oppressors. It was an impressive,
almost impossible, story.

Mandela's reconstruction of South Africa—a fundamental change in its government—must be considered a revolution. Whether brought about by mobs
storming the Bastille in Paris or the Winter Palace in Petrograd or through the
actions of organizations that muster military and political power, revolution is
a transcendent, political, social, and economic struggle. It would seem a most
unusual occasion for the use of sports.

Nelson Mandela understood that the people and politics of South Africa
were burdened with the oppressive policy of apartheid. The self-image, respect,
and pride of the ruling Afrikaner minority were closely tied to maintaining
their position of absolute authority in a country with an overwhelming black

majority. Out of fear of the consequences of moderation, Afrikaners remained vigilant and unyielding. Mandela knew that achieving political power through the barrel of a gun, assuming it could be accomplished, would fracture his country, eviscerate its economy, and sentence South Africa to decades of misery. He understood intuitively both the concepts and methods of participatory politics and the axiological assumptions of the ruling class. As a politician, Mandela knew he needed to unify those who would mobilize against their rulers. As a revolutionary, he needed to reach beyond periodic elections that provided temporary political power to promote a substratal reform of values and perceptions.

Recognized as a savior by most black South Africans but as an object of fear by many whites, Mandela eventually would use rugby, the Afrikaners' own sport, as the platform on which to secure the country's new multiracial democracy. In the process, he would win broad acceptance from white South Africans. It was a longshot, but no more than the odds of the nation's rugby club, the Springboks, winning the Rugby World Cup.

Throughout the revolutionary process, Mandela would sustain a commitment to societal cohesiveness across a multiracial constituency while diminishing, as much as possible, the risks to life and property. That did not mean Mandela was a pacifist. While he knew the methods of Gandhi, he did not practice them. Before his incarceration at the Robben Island prison, Mandela had formed the armed wing of the African National Congress (ANC). He himself trained in the use of arms. Lives were lost and blood was shed in the revolutionary transfiguration, but the Mandela revolution was overwhelmingly peaceful.

After twenty-seven years of imprisonment, Mandela emerged to lead his party and, four years later, his nation. Negotiating universal suffrage with the white-run government would consume his energies after his release. Once achieving power through the ballot box, Mandela would lead a campaign to win the trust of the white minority. By his actions and his words, Mandela would show white South Africans first that he was tolerable, then acceptable, and then finally that he was the true leader of the nation. It would take a brilliant political ploy—adopting the Afrikaners' beloved Springboks as a symbol of all South Africans—to bring a measure of stability to his nation. He would show the white minority that he loved exactly what they loved, this sport that pitted two groups of fifteen burly men on a hundred-meter-long pitch, a game played with brutal physicality for two forty-minute periods. Ultimately, the national team, the Springboks, would play for all South Africans, and the team's victory would signal the final step in the genuine transformation of the country from an international outcast to an empyrean land of abundant potential.

MANDELA

Rolihlahla Nelson Mandela was born into a prominent family in 1918 in the farming region of the Transkei in southern South Africa. His father was counselor to Thembu tribal royalty. Eight years earlier, the Colony of South Africa had become an independent country, although remaining part of the British Empire. (The government would break all its ties with the British Empire on May 31, 1961, becoming a totally independent republic.) Britain had fought two wars in its colony against *die Boer*, the Protestant descendants of Dutch and French settlers who had fled from Europe centuries earlier to avoid religious discrimination. Before the whites arrived, black tribes had occupied the bounteous land. "When the whites came," an old African saying went, "we had the land and they had the Bible. They asked us to pray and when we opened our eyes, they had the land—and we had the Bible." The white settlers pushed the black tribes up the coast from Cape Town.

A handsome youngster with a pleasant demeanor, Mandela pursued all the education that was available to black South Africans, eventually training as a lawyer and opening the first black law firm in the country in Johannesburg. At university, he learned about the African National Congress, which would be his platform to effect change through protest, negotiation, and, if necessary, through violence.

APARTHEID

South Africa had always been a segregated society, but it would become an oppressive police state under the policies of apartheid. Black South Africans would become prisoners in their own land. In the 1948 election, the ruling party, led by General Jan Smuts, was opposed by the National Party of former Nazi sympathizers who ran an openly racist campaign in favor of instituting a policy of apartness, or "apartheid" in Afrikaner. South African blacks never had the right to vote, and they watched as their white countrymen elected the Nationals to a parliamentary majority.

Once in power, the "Nats," as they were called, quickly instituted fanatical policies reminiscent of the Nazis' early years. The races were classified and separated into their own towns and cities. The "immorality laws" prohibited friendships across color lines. Public facilities, even park benches, were designated for white use only. Mandela later referred to the government bureaucracy needed to carry out this universal plan as "diabolical in detail, inescapable in its reach and overwhelming in its power."

To understand the remarkable transformation that was later brought about by the Mandela revolution, we must recall the outrageous indignities of life for blacks under apartheid. All blacks were required to carry identity papers in a "pass book," the *dompas*, in order to enter white areas. The passbook had to be displayed upon request to any white civil servant, police officer, or government official. Public and private facilities were segregated by race, with all assets on the white side. The status quo was separate and very unequal, with no effort made to achieve equity. At its core, apartheid was based on the appalling absence of ordinary human respect and dignity for persons of color in a country where they were the vast majority.

The governmental authorities used the justice system as a tool of separation. Law, like everything else in South Africa, was unequal. The same crime committed by blacks would result in multiples of the punishments received by whites. The default punishment for blacks for a broad spectrum of crimes was death by hanging. It did not take much for the bureaucratic judiciary to take the life of a person who was not recognized as fully human. The white judiciary, however, would prove its independence regarding political crimes, often acquitting opposition leaders on legal, as opposed to political, grounds.

The ANC and other activists fought back against these indignities and injustices starting in 1950 with a one-day, stay-at-home strike against the new laws. Police fired into the crowds and killed eighteen protesters. The bloodletting had begun. In 1951, Mandela received his first "banning" order. He could not leave Johannesburg, as police kept constant watch on his law practice. The ANC-led protests continued, but government spies who had infiltrated the organization alerted the authorities of events to come.

In the mid-1950s, the ANC called for a "Congress of the People" to lay the groundwork for the future of the country as a multiracial democracy where all the people would rule. The Freedom Charter began: "South Africa belongs to all who live in it." The document was considered treasonous by the ruling Nats, and 156 people who were involved in its creation, including Mandela, were arrested and tried. The trial would last for five years. All were eventually acquitted. That same year, 1960, in the Sharpeville township, a suburb of Johannesburg, unarmed black workers gathered to protest their passes. Police opened fire. More than 200 were shot down by South African police, and 69 died in the massacre. The event catalyzed an international reaction for the first time, as photographs of dead protesters appeared on the front pages of the world's newspapers. The United Nations condemned the attack, the first of many such statements by the international body of nations.

Armed resistance and revenge by the ANC for the Sharpeville massacre would have been easy, but futile. Instead, Mandela called for a national day of mourning and a stay-at-home strike. As a result, the government banned the ANC, arrested Mandela again, and declared martial law. Activists, both white and black, were put on trial. The defendants were once again acquitted, and Mandela went underground, returning to the struggle.

It was at this point in the campaign for human and civil rights for all South Africans that Mandela was given permission by the ANC to form an independent military organization, while the ANC remained publicly committed to nonviolence. He modeled the "Mkhonto we Sizwe," or "The Spear of the Nation," on the Jewish Irgun underground that fought the British mandate in Palestine. It would launch guerilla raids against strategic targets. Small detonations were set off in government offices and electric power stations on nonwork days. Pamphlets that were distributed included Mandela's words: "The time comes in the life of any nation when there remain only two choices—submit or fight. That time has now come to South Africa. We shall not submit and we have no choice but to hit back by all means in our power in defense of our people, our future, and our freedom."

In response, the government enacted new legislation, the Sabotage Act, which pronounced the death sentence for these actions, even if no one was hurt. It was 1962, and neither the protest movement nor the guerilla attacks had scored any significant successes. Mandela was smuggled out of the country to raise money for weapons and receive training as an underground fighter. Returning to South Africa, he was arrested and tried for inciting a three-day nationwide strike by black workers and leaving the country illegally to seek support to topple the white-minority government. Presenting no evidence at his trial, Mandela offered a final statement that summarized his political philosophy: "I have fought against white domination, and I have fought against black domination. I have cherished the ideal of a democratic and free society in which all persons live together in harmony and with equal opportunities. It is an ideal, which I hope to live for and to achieve. But if needs be, it is an ideal for which I am prepared to die."

Mandela was forty-six years old when he was convicted of violating the Sabotage Act. In 1964, the South African government sent Mandela and other participants in "the struggle" to prison on Robben Island off the coast of Cape Town. By the early 1970s, the apartheid police state had rounded up and convicted all of the hardcore activists. Mandela and the other leaders of the movement would remain isolated inside their small cells for almost two decades.

ON REVOLUTION

Before examining how Mandela was able to successfully transform South Africa, it would be useful to explore Crane Britton's groundbreaking work *The Anatomy of Revolution*, published in 1938. Britton examined the English, American, French, and Russian revolutions to identify their commonalities—what he called "approximations of uniformities"—in the circumstances that led to "sudden or striking" political change. Would Britton have considered Mandela's triumph a classical revolution?

Revolutions, Britton wrote, germinate in the soil of governmental incompetence and financial bankruptcy. The old regime proves itself "unhealthy" and "politically inept," even if the society as a whole is on the upgrade economically. In a period of "rising expectations," the ruling class invites societal disequilibrium.

Contrary to popular belief, revolutions are born not from misery or economic distress but from "a feeling on the part of some of the chief enterprising groups that their opportunities for getting on in this world are unduly limited by political arrangements." Britton says that "the more prosperous the peasants, the more discontented." Economic advancement is rarely espoused as the goal of a revolution. Goals are more likely phrased in terms of the "justice" unobtainable because of the disorganization and ineptitude of the existing government. Action against the status quo is firmly based on a sense of "moral indignation."

One critical phase in the revolutionary process, according to Britton, is the "transfer of the allegiance of the intellectuals" who turn to attack existing institutions, joining those who seek a fundamental alteration in society, business, and government. They portray the old regime as "foreign" in origin and worthy of contempt. That may, in fact, lead to "a loss of self-confidence among many members of the ruling class," who "come to distrust themselves, or lose faith in the traditions and habits of their class."

The early stages of a revolution involve group action and agitation, generally through organized, but at times spontaneous, protests. There are often "dramatic incidents" that catalyze opposition. However, revolutions are not plotted like lines on a graph. Britton is clear that "history cannot neglect the drama of personality and chance": " . . . revolutions do grow from seeds sown by men who want change, and that these men do a lot of skillful gardening; but that the gardeners are not working against nature, but rather in soil and in a climate propitious to their work; and that the final fruits represent a collaboration between men and nature."

Revolutions succeed, at least in part, because governments fail to deploy decisive power in an efficient and skillful manner. In the first stages of revolution, opposition forces coalesce into an effective unit with the strength to persevere as the equilibrium of the old regime crumbles. Revolutionary leaders are likely to be the abler, more ambitious, and more respectable and successful members of the opposition, but under the old regime they were not able to succeed at a level commensurate with their abilities. They may even be disputatious and "contrary-minded" idealists. On the other hand, they are certainly not "the mob, the rabble, the riffraff," or the dregs of society.

The revolutions Britton studied generally experienced a period when moderates ruled, only to be succeeded by extremists: "The moderates by definition are not great haters, are not endowed with the effective blindness" that keeps extremists undistracted. Moderates employed compromise, common sense, toleration, and empathy to maintain their revolution. Especially in the French and Russian revolutions, moderates could not prevail against the devotion of fanatic extremists who brought about a reign of terror to accompany their ideals. Ultimately, the revolution returns to less heroic times; for example, the Thermidorian reaction to the French Revolution. Once the equilibrium is restored, the revolution is over.

THE SOUTH AFRICAN TRANSFORMATION

Professor Britton emphasized that not all revolutions are identical, and there are many variables at work in each instance. Nonetheless, his insights are useful in understanding the political transformation in South Africa that ended the worst abuses of the apartheid regime and set the path toward a lasting constitutional democracy. Like other revolutions, South Africa's was made in the name of freedom. Life in South Africa changed dramatically, with a new set of "myths, folklore, symbols, stereotypes [and] rituals," to use Britton's language.

The South African transformation of the 1990s conforms with much of Britton's political architecture. The National Party's apartheid policy divided South Africa by racial category. Although some blacks, like Mandela, could cross some apartheid lines through education to become, in effect, "black Englishmen," they could not change the color of their skin or their official status. White intellectuals, mostly of English origin, increasingly recognized the injustices of the apartheid police state and the growing ineptitude of the old regime. Some joined the African National Congress, which welcomed their support. Although the ANC never had an effective military counter to Pretoria's police, it certainly could call upon the millions of Africans to join in any armed struggle and thus had the potential for using the force of arms. World economic sanctions crippled the financial base of the apartheid government and fostered internal dissent within the white community. There were many incidents of violence, but no lasting military victories for either side.

The leaders of the Mandela revolution were much in the tradition of a traditional revolutionary vanguard. They were middle-aged, educated, able, and ambitious. Except when it unleashed its police power, the government establishment proved to be totally inept. The Afrikaner leadership came to lose confidence in itself.

Until Mandela's twenty-seven-year prison term, the efforts of the African National Congress to remove the yoke of apartheid from South Africa and establish a democratic political system with universal suffrage had followed many of the tenets of a traditional revolution. The ANC was solidly organized, and its interaction with the government was mostly peaceful, except for the occasional vicious attacks by police on unarmed protesters and some sporadic sabotage by ANC forces. The ANC used the periodic show trials of its leaders and their repeated acquittals as part of its worldwide campaign to focus global attention on the injustices of the regime. This facilitated its effort to seek international financing and political support for the freedom movement.

When Mandela went to jail, the movement lost its public voice, but it did not lose its revolutionary ways. Mandela used his time away from direct action to learn more about the men who ruled his country. He learned their language and their culture, and he would use both to free his people and his nation from the yoke of apartheid. Slowly, his bitterness and commitment to revenge gave way to a dedication to reform and reconciliation, a commitment to end apartheid by peaceful means and create a democratic union of peoples. Mandela certainly was not a saint, but he was a skilled politician and revolutionary figure seemingly devoid of the temperament that could destroy his plans for reforming his country.

In prison, Mandela learned the lessons of nonviolence from the writings of his predecessors around the globe. Dr. Martin Luther King Jr.'s famous "Letter from a Birmingham Jail," written with a pen borrowed from a jailer, set forth a strategy for change:

> In any nonviolent campaign there are four basic steps: collection of the facts to determine whether injustices exist; negotiation; self-purification; and direct action. . . . We know through painful experience that freedom is never voluntarily given by the oppressor; it must be demanded by the oppressed. Frankly, I have yet to engage in a direct action campaign that was "well timed" in the view of those who have not suffered unduly from the disease of segregation. For years now I have heard the word "Wait!" It rings in the ear of every Negro with piercing familiarity. This "Wait" has almost always meant "Never." We must come to see, with one of our distinguished jurists, that "justice too long delayed is justice denied."

THE LONG ROAD TO FREEDOM

In October 1962, while Mandela was on trial for the actions of his trained saboteurs, the ANC launched a national and international campaign to pressure the South African government to "free Mandela." The United Nations General Assembly voted to apply sanctions against South Africa, and individual nations would follow suit over time. However, it would take almost three decades for the campaign of sanctions to succeed.

South Africa was afflicted by periodic outbursts of violence. Police and right-wing vigilante groups carried out military actions against the leaders of the ANC, including Steve Biko, who was beaten to death in 1977. When the people of the black townships, like Soweto, responded by taking to the streets, police shot into the crowds. International outrage spread, but the government in Pretoria remained unyielding.

As a result of the efforts of South African opposition politicians such as

Makhenkesi Arnold Stofile, the developed nations of the world committed to altering South Africa's system of apartheid. Political and economic sanctions would gradually cripple the apartheid regime. The government sought to co-opt the imprisoned Mandela in 1985 by offering to negotiate. While Mandela urged everyone to avoid violence, he rejected negotiations, saying that "only free men can negotiate." In response, the government imposed martial law. Real negotiations between Mandela and the authorities would finally begin in 1988, and they gained momentum after the intransigent president, P. W. Botha, suffered a stroke in 1989.

SPORTS BOYCOTTS

Denying white South Africans the ability to participate in international sports proved to be the unkindest cut of all. It hit close to the core of the Afrikaners' national identity and would be a most effective revolutionary strategy. The international Olympic movement banned South Africa from participating in the 1964 Summer Olympics in Tokyo, a ban that would not be lifted until 1992. Fédération Internationale de Football Association (FIFA), the international soccer federation, banned the all-white South African team from playing international soccer. In 1985, New Zealand canceled the planned visit of the South African Springboks to play a series of rugby matches against their champion All-Blacks. Throughout much of the apartheid era, New Zealand had been a staunch supporter of South African participation in international rugby and had regularly scheduled visits to South Africa. The pressure of world opinion and political change in its government, however, turned New Zealand away from its policy of accommodation with apartheid. Because of New Zealand's role as the premier world rugby power and South Africa's place as the chief rival to the All-Blacks, the decision to cancel the New Zealand tour was politically significant. Stofile had triggered that boycott by using the New Zealand media to make his case. (There was always a price to pay, however. When Stofile returned to South Africa, he was imprisoned.)

The world's sporting nations—and that included virtually all countries—had turned their back on apartheid South Africa. Large economic players had cut off streams of financial support. Developing countries that were former colonies showed particular disdain for the outlaw regime in Pretoria. India, for example, defaulted in the finals of the 1974 Davis Cup tennis tournament rather than play South Africa, the only time that the championship had ever been forfeited. Trade restrictions injured the South African economy, but banning South Africa from international sports competitions was the harshest sanction of all, hurting the nation's pride and self-esteem. Racist South Africa became an isolated pariah, a rogue nation effectively expelled from the world community of sporting nations.

A TIME TO CHANGE

Both Mandela and his political jailers recognized that the status quo was unsustainable. South Africa was a pariah in the family of nations. Boycotts had made the country as separate from the channels of commerce and social intercourse as apartheid had made blacks separate from the economic and social life of their country. It was not simply desirable to change; it was imperative. On the other hand, civil war was unthinkable. The politics of negotiation would have to catalyze change.

Ultimately, the continuous and unyielding international economic pressure combined with the effective sports boycott caused the Afrikaner political leadership to modify its course. The government was bankrupt, both financially and morally. Its cultural links to the rest of the world were effectively severed. In 1990, Pretoria "unbanned" the ANC, and on February 11, 1990, after fourteen months of negotiations, the regime finally released Mandela from jail. The ruling Afrikaners were certain that, although Mandela might win a popular election in which blacks were allowed to vote, the African National Congress could never govern effectively. Mandela, however, knew that the movement and its reformed government would succeed. Through the force of his own personality and the use of retail politics and symbols, he and the ANC would prevail. Alone among history's revolutionaries, Mandela appreciated the role that sports would play in political change, and that insight would bolster his movement and the prospects for his country.

Negotiations take time and patience. Depending on the situation, negotiations may be more successful than violence or even elections. Incrementalism works only if it moves forward in the right direction. Those in power must appreciate that their rule is time-limited and not perpetual, and they must reach interim arrangements with other centers of power in society. Mandela knew that intuitively, but he would need to teach that lesson both to his followers and to the Afrikaner leadership. It was here that personalities would play a major, if not determinative, role. Individuals matter in resolving conflict at the negotiating table rather than in the streets.

SPORTS IN SOUTH AFRICA

One would have thought the sport Mandela would use for political purposes would be soccer, the "world game," played in every country by both the oppressed and the oppressors. Mandela had played soccer growing up in the Transkei. His followers in the African National Congress and the adherents of rival political factions played soccer in the prison yard at Robben Island.

Sports in South Africa were coded by color and ethnicity. Soccer was the sport of black South Africa. (The national soccer team was all black, nicknamed "Bafana Bafana," Zulu for "The Boys.") Cricket was the sport of those of English origin. The national cricket team was called "The Proteas," named for a flowering plant native to South Africa. The Afrikaners claimed rugby, and the national team was called the Springboks, after the native South African gazelle.

Mandela's soccer-loving ANC already were solid members of his constituency. Mandela knew, however, that rugby could be the instrument of change that would ultimately bring stability to a new South Africa. Only sports could serve as a common language in a country so divided by race, culture, history, and ethnicity.

SOCCER ON ROBBEN ISLAND

Robben Island is South Africa's Alcatraz, a desolate piece of land seven miles across the strait from Cape Town. In the nineteenth century, the island was reserved for lepers, criminals, and the insane, who stayed uncared for until they died. The description in a magazine article in *Littell's Living Age* in 1889 fit what Mandela and his cohorts found when they arrived in 1964: ". . . the island of desolation, low and flat, sad and sandy, with scarcely a vestige of vegetation, save patches of course, unlovely grass. . . . The buildings comprise about twenty low down-looking tenements, plus the mean-looking government establishments."

The sharks and the strong currents ensured that no one would ever make it to the mainland even if they made it through the barbed-wire fences unseen from the guarded watchtowers.

Conditions for the political prisoners on South Africa's equivalent of Devil's Island were cruel and inhumane. Food was scarce, torture ubiquitous, and living conditions impossible. Afrikaner guards sadistically beat prisoners as a matter of whim. Yet the political captives used the Robben Island experience to bolster their sense of personal dignity. Incarceration bonded revolutionaries with different views and backgrounds. Although leaders like Mandela were segregated from the general population in solitary confinement, others took up the leadership role to oppose the worst of the torments. They found some salvation in the sport of soccer.

When the afflicted unite in solidarity, it is hard for the oppressors to maintain intolerable, inhuman conditions. That applies whether the freedom fighters are crossing the Pettis Bridge in Selma, Alabama, or are political prisoners on Robben Island. Using periodic fasting and other techniques of peaceful opposition, the Robben Island prisoners eventually won the right to play soccer and then organize a league of teams. Soccer saved the Robben Island prisoners and unified them into a force that, when the time came, could run their own country. While the quality of play did not rival the game performed on the manicured pitches of England, that was not its purpose. It was an athletic diversion and a training ground that would maintain prisoner morale and physical fitness. It was an opportunity for many prisoners to hone their organizing skills in creating and enforcing the rules of the Robben Island soccer organization. Some were even involved in writing constitutions—although these were of the individual soccer clubs rather than countries or provinces.

Future leaders of South Africa sharpened their political skills in Robben Island soccer. After their release and the coming of the new regime, the men of Robben Island would play a prominent role in the new government. Dikgang Moseneke was chairman of the Robben Island soccer league and now serves as deputy chief justice of the Republic of South Africa. The late Steve Tshwete, who sought to broaden athletic opportunities for all the Robben Island prisoners, later served as South Africa's minister of sport and recreation. Mosiuoa Gerard Patrick Lekota earned the nickname "Terror" based on his style of play on the soccer pitch. Imprisoned on Robben Island from 1974 until 1982, he became the South African minister of defense and later the president of the Congress of the People political party.

Soccer on the island was taken very seriously by the prisoners. It bred passions, unleashed tempers, and sometimes generated controversies. It is important to remember these were not model prisoners, let alone angels. They were revolutionaries who were abandoned on a desolate rock, where they did their best to resist the iron fist of apartheid. Driven to win at soccer, prisoners held interminable meetings to fairly administer the league and the clubs. When hundreds of new political prisoners poured onto Robben Island after the 1976 Soweto massacres and the uprisings that followed, there were culture clashes with the much older, longer-term prisoners. While the younger cohort gave new life to the aging soccer clubs, it took a period of time for mutual respect to grow between the two generations. Sports in general, and soccer in particular, would help this process of unification of the leaders of the opposition.

There is a risk when talking about the men of Robben Island, in particular about Mandela, of transforming them all into idyllic figures. Mandela's blemishes were evident, however. He was not perfect, although he was unusually temperate and forgiving. So were the men who led the prison soccer league. They helped keep the flame alive across decades of incarceration.

RUGBY

Although the soccer matches consumed most of the attention of those on Robben Island, there was a large cohort of political prisoners who preferred to play rugby, generally seen in South Africa as a white Afrikaner sport. Rugby had always been played by blacks in the eastern provinces. The white Afrikaner prison guards had trouble believing that blacks could master their game, but a rough version of the sport was played for years on Robben Island.

Although segregated in isolation and not able to participate in any of the prison's recreation, Mandela recognized how important rugby was to the leaders of the country. He used his time in solitary confinement to learn more about this sport, which was foreign to him. He would use that knowledge years later when he became president of the republic. The Springbok rugby club and the game it played were symbols of white oppression, but Mandela would use that symbolism to his advantage. He would charm and then recruit the men who took to the pitch wearing Springbok green as soldiers in his reconstruction of South African society and government. How he accomplished this miracle is a great story.

There was always a spiritual side to rugby, a secular religion not totally divorced from the Dutch Reformed Church. Upon his release from prison, Arnold Stofile explained to his fellow ANC loyalists that rugby was "much more powerful and primal" than mere ideology. Mandela's use of rugby as a symbol of inclusiveness would add a measure of stability to the freedom the revolution achieved in South Africa.

"NO EASY ROAD TO FREEDOM"

During his 1964 trial that resulted in decades of imprisonment, Nelson Mandela explained in his defense that there was "no easy road to freedom." He predicted that there would be counterviolence by black Africans if the apartheid government continued its repression. The tyranny continued, however, as Mandela and his fellow freedom fighters went to prison. Inside his cell at Robben Island, Mandela formulated his plans to lead his country to freedom, but without the violence he had predicted long ago.

After his release from prison, Mandela toured Europe, Asia, and America seeking political and financial support. He continued his negotiations with the Pretoria government while unifying the anti-apartheid forces in the country and around the world. The government stalled in an effort to keep power by using black allies, such as Zulu Chief Buthelezi of the InKatha Freedom Party. Violence continued as death tolls mounted, but Mandela urged patience: "Take your guns, your knives and your pangas (machetes) and throw them into the sea!" Finally, in 1993, a Record of Understanding was reached, proposing a coalition government as part of a transition to a democratic election. In one last blow against change, apartheid loyalists assassinated Chris Hani, seen as a future president of the country, in the driveway of his home. Mandela appealed again for peace, and a bloodbath was avoided. The world recognized that change was happening at the southern tip of the African continent. In 1993, Mandela and F. W. de Klerk, the president who had freed Mandela and negotiated the end of apartheid, received the Nobel Peace Prize.

On April 17, 1994, Nelson Mandela was elected president of South Africa in a democratic election with universal suffrage. The political campaign had been mostly peaceful. It resulted in proportional representation in parliament, a body that had always been all white but now was all South African. Mandela knew, however, that the revolution had only begun. He would use his five-year term to place the political change on firm footing so it would last. He preached patience from his followers and reconciliation. In 1996, the Truth and Reconciliation Commission, chaired by Bishop Desmond Tutu, would hear testimony from apartheid and ANC leaders about their actions over the prior decades. No retribution was taken. To the astonishment of many, the much anticipated bloodbath did not occur.

POLITICAL THEATER

Many politicians have recognized the importance of political theater, the skillful use of the media, and the manipulation of the masses by words. Few have been as impressive and powerful in using these tools as Nelson Mandela. After his release from prison and without governmental power, Mandela used appearances even more than facts to bring about change. The government, after all, held most of the guns and the money. The army and right-wing paramilitary groups would not be easily swept aside. They would be vigilant and armed. A smile and a friendly gesture can disarm an enemy, however, especially if done with accomplished style. Mandela's release offered him and the ANC the opportunity to assuage white fears while giving substance to black aspirations. Power would come by negotiations and, eventually, through the ballot box.

SPORTS, POLITICS, AND NATION BUILDING

Mandela fully appreciated the power of sports: "We must use sport for the purpose of nation-building and promoting all the ideas which we think will lead to peace and stability in the country." He would use the fortunate coincidence of two events—his ascension to political power through a democratic election and the Rugby World Cup in 1995—to bring about lasting and fundamental change in his country. The path to peace, however, would not be straight and unburdened. ANC leaders had been assassinated, and the renegade Zulu tribe offered only treachery. Each harrowing incident presented the opportunity for catastrophe, but Mandela steered the ship of state forward.

Ordinary people normally sit out the throes of political upheaval. They worry about peace and prosperity rather than ideology. Few take to the streets and storm the barricades. It is that group of independents that every politician seeks to win over. They are moved by symbols and fear. In South Africa, they were moved by rugby and the self-respect the sport represented.

The white militant resistance tried to incite a race war, although they focused their attention mostly on the treacherous whites in government who had freed

Mandela and offered him power. Eventually, the "dead-enders" would be won over by the power of Mandela's personal reconciliation. Mandela met personally with the militant leaders of the white right wing, treating them with respect. As he had within his own government, he won over the dead-enders to the reality that no one would win a race war. As he explained: "You don't address their brains. You address their hearts."

Mandela knew that something more than an election victory was needed to cement reconciliation. He would build this consensus using rugby. It was a brilliant ploy. The World Cup offered the opportunity. Under the motto "One Team, One Country," the Springboks would lure the rejectionists into the nationwide constituency. The symbols flourished, as Mandela met with the club's captain, Francois Pienaar, befriended the team, and wore a Springbok cap and ultimately its green jersey. The Boks learned the black anthem, which had become part of the nation's new national anthem.

Mandela made sure the Springboks understood their role in society's transformation: "You have the opportunity of serving South Africa and uniting our people. Just remember, all of us, black and white, are behind you." As Pienaar said: "There's one guy that now we understand we have to play for, and that's the president."

THE WORLD CUP

The World Cup was the first major sporting event to take place in South Africa following the end of apartheid. It was also the first in which the new South Africa was allowed to compete, ending the world's boycott of South African athletes. In 1992, the Rugby World Cup Limited awarded the event to South Africa in the hope that it would aid in the political transition, but that gesture was not yet based on accomplished fact. Plans were made to move the tournament to New Zealand if the South African situation deteriorated.

The Rugby World Cup had become big business, the fourth-largest sporting event in the world in terms of television viewing. The South African World Cup was seen by an estimated 2.5 million viewers in 125 nations. For most, it was the first time the global community had seen anything involving South Africa, and it made a most favorable impression. Because Afrikaners had spent a considerable amount of public funds on facilities for their favorite sport, South Africa was well equipped with first-rate rugby stadiums. The World Cup offered South Africa the possibility of breaking with its recent past, but it was not a sure thing by any means.

Mandela came to visit the Springboks before their first match, a victory over the Australians, who were the reigning World Cup champions. He embraced the team as "my sons." The Springboks, in turn, visited Robben Island to see where their president had been imprisoned. With more victories in the World Cup competition, more black South Africans took notice and began to care about rugby and "their" team. The Springboks went out to a small black village to learn and to share. They won spirited international contests one after another on the pitches of their homeland. They were building the nation along with Mandela.

The South African media began to focus on what Mandela was accomplishing. The *Cape Town Argus* wrote: "Rugby, the remarkable new nation-building phenomenon, has amazed analysts as all races eagerly seize on the event which has released a wave of latent patriotism through the sports traditionally associated in South Africa with white Afrikaner males."

The symbol of the green Springbok jersey would be the final piece of Mandela's exquisite puzzle. When his bodyguards suggested wearing the uniform, Mandela sprang into action like a "¾ back" running for a touch. And, unknown to Mandela, black leaders of the ANC across the country dressed in the "enemy's garb" for the day of the World Cup final, when the revolution would finally be made whole.

Victory was won after a hard-fought defensive battle against New Zealand. South Africans sensed that the political future of the new country was on the line. The tension in the game and of the history it would write was palpable. With overtime—an ending perfectly fitting Mandela's experiment in nation building—the outcome remained undecided. Long after the 1994 election was won, the revolution was made complete. The game symbolized a nation united in a single cause, an effort to make a divided, troubled, and injured country one, free and united. At that special moment when victory was had, the emotions of thirty years were unleashed with pride, dignity, and exultation. Liberation had come for all South Africans.

Mandela played the game of politics with kindness and grace, but with a single-minded focus on building a new multiracial society, all to be accomplished in a very short period of time. He inspired and motivated, communicated and empathized, thereby modeling the way the divided country could gain trust. Rugby ultimately had made a difference. Mandela knew that advising his followers to embrace rugby was a tough pill to swallow, as was draining the fear from the proponents of apartheid. Ultimately, it was Mandela who worked the miracle. By the force of his own self-confidence and the confidence he had in others, he freed a nation—blacks from virtual slavery and whites from their foreboding. Could anyone else have done this? At this place and that time, only Mandela and the magical impact of a white sport and a green jersey could have brought this about. One nation, one team, one remarkable piece of history.

Governments have always used sports as a tool of social control and public amusement. In recent decades, the sports establishment has returned the favor, extorting millions from state and local government treasuries to erect private sports facilities based on the false promise that such expenditures would create local jobs and spur economic redevelopment. Local officials, such as those in the District of Columbia, recognized that sports subsidies were valuable because they offered political currency to politicians. The presence or absence of a local professional sports franchise certainly had a significant political value. *AP Images*

We play the Star Spangled Banner before every game.
You want us to pay taxes too? —*Bill Veeck*

Hell yeah, we'll get our money back. Think about it. [T]hink
about how high rent is going to be in 50 years. We're getting paid back and
then some —*Mayor Dave Perez, Industry City, California*

[8]
HARDBALL IN CITY HALL
PUBLIC FINANCING
OF SPORTS STADIUMS

As your mother likely told you many years ago, playing games involving a bat and ball in public spaces presents risk of injury to persons and property. In fact, the city of Pittsfield, Massachusetts, enacted a local ordinance in 1791 stating that "no Person, an Inhabitant of said Town, shall be permitted to play at any Game called . . . Baseball . . . or any other Game or Games with Balls within the Distance of Eighty Yards from [a] Meeting House." There is a place for everything, and the games we have discussed throughout this book are best played on designated fields. When political "games" are played in governmental places—city halls, state legislatures, even in the halls of Congress—the participants risk causing injury to the public treasury and the public welfare.

The fundamental issue in American politics has always been identifying the proper role of government. That is what consumed the Founders cooped up in Independence Hall in Philadelphia in the summer of 1787. The Articles of Confederation, ratified by all thirteen states by 1781, proved insufficient in establishing enough centralized governmental power to regulate interstate commerce, conduct a vigorous foreign policy, and raise sufficient financial resources, all significant deficiencies in the new nation-state. The Constitution addressed those deficiencies while creating a system of checks and balances that, at times, still incapacitate the federal government. There was enough room within that document, however, that it could be read by generations of Americans to meet their changing needs or, if necessary, to amend it.

While the particulars of the proper role of government are often debated—whether governments should provide for the less fortunate or bail out corporations that have carelessly lost their way—the underlying question has remained the same. Should government be an actor? An enabler? A regulator? A partner? A provider? Should it simply stay out of the way? What should be the proper role of government when it comes to private matters, such as whom you may marry or whether women can choose to have an abortion? How about a governmental entity providing public resources to private enterprises so they can make more money?

The Founders set forth some of the foundational principles for this ongoing conversation in 1776 in the Declaration of Independence. "Governments," that document reads, "are instituted among Men" in order to secure the "inalienable rights" of "Life, Liberty and the pursuit of Happiness." The document then lists the offenses to those basic rights committed by the British crown, but ends with a clear statement that the governments of free and independent states have the "full power" to "establish commerce." Even at its creation, the U.S. government was recognized as having the power, influence, and obligation to address business issues.

Eleven years later, in the Constitution, the delegates from the thirteen states specified that the federal government would have the authority to collect taxes in order to provide for the "general welfare." It seemed apparent that there would be a role for government to act for the benefit of the people by using moneys raised for that purpose. For almost 250 years, we have tried to define through our political processes just how those collected funds should be spent. Can federal, state, and local governments in the United States take money from one person and give it to another? Even if they have the power to do so, is it good policy for governments to exercise that power, and under what circumstances?

It would not take long for the states and the new nation to use the authorized power to aid businesses, and not every venture would prove successful. In 1791, for example, the New Jersey Legislature granted a ten-year tax abatement to Alexander Hamilton's Society for Establishing Useful Manufactures to develop land surrounding the Passaic River. Hamilton had promised his venture would create 20,000 new jobs. Within five years, the Society was bankrupt. No actual jobs were created.

One real difference between rich and poor—and it is a significant one—is in access to private capital and governmental largess. The U.S. government has long subsidized private businesses and made wealthy men wealthier. Government transfer payments have generally helped the well off and the well connected much more than they have assisted the poor and unconnected. Even in the uneven provision of basic governmental services—police, fire, and sanitation—the rich have benefited more than the poor. Governments have even spent billions of dollars on public stadiums to provide venues for sports.

Mayor Dave Perez of Industry City, California, a suburb of Los Angeles, is only the latest to fall victim to wishful thinking when it comes to the use of public funds to foster private development—in his case the effort to attract a National Football League franchise back to the Los Angeles area. Voters in the tiny municipality voted in January 2009 to authorize the city to issue as much as $180 million in bonds to pay for stadium infrastructure, but it will take much more to bring the NFL to town. The bonds would be financed through a tax on tickets and on parking at the stadium. Neighboring municipalities vowed a court fight against the project on environmental grounds, but Perez is undeterred. There is no indication that the NFL is interested.

GOVERNMENTAL POWER AND SPORTS

As we have seen, governments have always used sports as a tool of social control and public amusement. To maintain political power, politicians have looked to these games as instruments to be manipulated for strategic advantage and prestige. Pausanias, a second-century traveler through the Greek lands, wrote that a town lacking a gymnasium would not really qualify as a city. Similarly, today a city without a major league franchise in one of the four major team sports is simply a crossroads on a map. Whether promoted by an ancient village, a city boss, or a German dictator, sports have proven a useful instrument of public authority. There is a price to be paid, however.

The symbiotic relationship between sports and politics has provided an opportunity for private entrepreneurs to dip into public resources for their private benefit. Every business is looking for the edge in the marketplace, even public businesses, which seek good political friends and business supporters. For the owner of a sports team, the public treasury stands open and available to aid in a self-professed time of need, and it always seems to be a time of need. Even athletes have entered into the mix on occasion. Mexican German Silva, who won the New York City Marathon in 1994 and 1995, was asked by the governor of Veracruz province what he would want in recognition of his great victory. Silva asked him to provide his impoverished Mexican hometown of Tecomate with electricity and television, and it was done.

Starting in the early 1920s with the construction of the Los Angeles Coliseum, public funds from American state and local sources have been used in whole or in part to construct most sports stadiums. In the early 1950s, Milwaukee built a new baseball stadium—the first publicly funded field for the national pastime—as part of a governmental strategy to attract an existing Major League team from another city. Milwaukee County Stadium would first be used by the minor league Brewers, the top club in the Boston Braves farm system. By the time the stadium was completed in 1953, however, the National League Braves, which had suffered from years of poor attendance, had decided to move from Boston to Milwaukee. In 1966, the Braves moved again, this time south to play in the publicly financed Atlanta–Fulton County Stadium. Atlanta Mayor Ivan Allen had aggressively recruited the Braves and built the stadium, as he said, "on ground we didn't own with money we didn't have for clubs we had not yet signed." Thirty years later, the Braves moved crosstown to the former Olympic Stadium built by public money for the games of the Twenty-Sixth Olympiad. Despite its willingness to move to greener pastures over the course of its 135 years in Major League Baseball—the "green" being the public largess—the Braves have only won three World Series, one each in Boston, Milwaukee, and Atlanta.

The Braves' move to Milwaukee in 1953 and the St. Louis Browns' move the following year to Baltimore (to become the Orioles) altered the public's perception of who really owns and controls Major League franchises. The American and National leagues had remained stable for fifty years, with sixteen clubs located in the same midwestern and eastern cities throughout that time. The public came to refer to the franchises as "our" Braves or "our" Browns. That all changed in the 1950s, when franchises exercised their "free agent" rights to relocate.

While the public patronized and rooted for the franchises located in their cities, they were (and are) privately owned like any business and could be relocated at the discretion of the owners with the leagues' approval. To some, this was a revelation equal to discovering that Santa did not make his annual run using flying reindeer and an overloaded sled. The local baseball or football team had been part of the fans' identity, and it was ripped away without anesthetic. Bill Veeck, the clever, if somewhat eccentric, owner of a number of baseball clubs, explained after the Dodgers moved west to Los Angeles, leaving Brooklynites deserted, crushed, and heartbroken: "They discovered that they were wrong. The Dodgers were only a piece of merchandise that passed from hand to hand." Bob Irsay's stealth move of the NFL's Colts under the cover of darkness from Baltimore to Indianapolis in March 1984 confirmed this reality. As Irsay said: "I know one thing. I have a stock certificate, and at the bottom it says that I own the team."

While the public's attention has focused on direct government financial support for the construction of stadiums and arenas, sports entrepreneurs and government officials have been creative in devising less-obvious schemes that have made many franchise owners even richer. Bill Veeck negotiated a deal with the Los Angeles Chamber of Commerce in 1941 to move his St. Louis Browns to the West Coast. The chamber guaranteed attendance of 500,000 a year, a substantial increase for the lowly Browns, and offered the use of the stadium of the minor league Angels. Because of the outbreak of World War II, the deal was never consummated, but Veeck continued his search for additional financial resources. He uncovered a federal tax ruling under which franchises could depreciate player contracts over a five-year period. These federal allocations through tax expenditures proved to be a remarkably generous subsidy. Later owners negotiated for new variations on the tax concessions. For example, local and state governments have offered tax abatements to owners of sports franchises who either agreed to stay put or have relocated to the jurisdiction from another state.

Governmental subsidies are just as critical, if less obvious, when the construction of a new stadium or arena is accomplished with private money. Sports franchises have generally been able to use tax-free bonds to fund their projects, thus reducing their borrowing costs by about two percentage points. New facilities contain additional luxury boxes and suites leased by corporations that are allowed, under the federal tax code, to deduct a portion of the rent as a business expense. As a result, stadium owners are able to charge them higher fees. Normally, even if a stadium is publicly constructed, the sports franchises control the naming rights for the new facility, a multimillion-dollar bonanza. Privately constructed stadiums are often the beneficiaries of government-funded access roads and services.

The constitutionality of public subsidies to private enterprise has been the subject of much litigation, and, generally, courts have upheld these expenditures as serving a public purpose. Equally abundant has been the commentary about whether such use of limited governmental resources is fitting and proper, although the implication of a government's failure to pay is clear. Those municipalities that refused to play along have lost their local professional sports teams to cities that were willing to ante up the cash. This was not just a game; it was hardball at city hall.

JOBS, REDEVELOPMENT, AND PUBLICLY FINANCED STADIUMS

The principal argument in support of public subsidies for private enterprise, including sports stadiums and arenas, is that such expenditures create local jobs and spur economic redevelopment. However, virtually all economists who have studied the issue in the sports context have concluded to the contrary. The construction jobs are temporary. Few permanent, year-round stadium jobs are created, and the seasonal, underpaid jobs that result do little to address issues of unemployment. If the new stadium replaces an older facility, it may create no new jobs at all since, most likely, the employees will be transferred to the new stadium. Even if the stadium is used to attract another city's franchise, the impact on jobs is no big thing. On average, excluding a club's management team, a new stadium employs fifty full-time workers. By comparison, a new Wal-Mart employs on average 360 full-time employees.

The broader construct claims that building a new sports facility will boost the local economy. Repeated studies have found, however, that there is no statistically significant positive correlation between sports facility construction and economic redevelopment. Bringing a new sports team to town does mean there will be some additional spending on local goods and services by the club, its players, and other employees, but most players and management live (and spend) elsewhere. Simply building a new stadium to keep an existing franchise, of course, may not add an additional penny to local expenditures.

There is a tendency for supporters of public subsidies to descend into hyperbole when extolling the virtues of bringing a new sports franchise to town. Gregg Loukenbill, the former owner of the Sacramento Kings, gushed: "The [Oakland] Raiders coming to Sacramento would be an event the magnitude of the Gold Rush." Undoubtedly, Raiders owner Al Davis would have been successful panning for gold, as his predecessors did, but the gold would have been government bullion, not nuggets from the stream running behind Sutter's mill.

Proponents of public subsidies claim quite correctly that in calculating the economic effect of increased local expenditures that result from acquiring a new sports franchise one must consider a "multiplier." A dollar spent locally on goods and services is then respent by local businesses in the community. The size of the multiplier, of course, determines the magnitude of the positive economic projection. While the multiplier is certainly greater than one, critics question the commonly used two-and-one-half construct as being without empirical basis. These calculations also typically ignore the substitution effects of exchanging one sports stadium for another or simply moving private resources from another entertainment option to the publicly financed sports venue. The only viable hypothesis to support the economic benefits of public subsidies would be to count only those expenditures that would not otherwise have been made while deducting any economic losses incurred in the neighborhood around the old stadium if the new construction simply substitutes for the old.

Despite the abundance of data and the absence of objective support for their claims, all public authorities have justified their subsidies at least in part based on the jobs the new facilities will produce and the positive financial impact of the new facilities on the local economy. Building sports stadiums, however, is a poor investment for cities. No one, apparently, had thought it might be useful to guarantee the claims made by proponents of subsidies by including a "clawback" provision in the contract with the club under which the government would receive a return of its investment if the number of actual jobs created and the gross increase in tax revenues did not meet the owner's projections.

Rick Horrow, a leading proponent of public subsidies to private sports entities and a consultant to the NFL and many cities, testified before Congress in 1999 concerning the experience in Jacksonville, Florida, where he served as the outside consultant:

The Jacksonville Sports Development Authority and Chamber of Commerce suggests that the Jacksonville Jaguars and Alltel Stadium enrich the local economy by an estimated $131 million a year from visitors buying tickets, eating at restaurants, and staying at hotels. Additionally, they believe that the new team and facility have been indirectly responsible for the creation of upwards of 50,000 new jobs by virtue of companies expanding or relocating to Jacksonville as a consequence of a successful marketing campaign.

Horrow has been involved in more than one hundred deals involving public support for private sports stadiums and arenas, and academic critics have raised significant concerns about his boosterism of public financing.

A comprehensive 1997 Brookings Institution study concluded to the contrary regarding the economics of public subsidies: "No recent facility has earned anything approaching a reasonable return on investment. No recent facility has been self-financing in terms of its impact on net tax revenues. . . . The economic benefits of sports facilities are *de minimus.*"

Of course, as we learned in *Field of Dreams*, if you build a stadium—whether downtown or in an Iowa cornfield—"they will come." Fans will purchase the best sports entertainment available for their dollars, and that normally means seats and suites in the most comfortable and up-to-date sports facility. Some public funders justify their expenditures based on the premise that the new facility will attract new spectators who will dine out and stay over, enhancing the local economy and increasing overall tax revenues as a result. There is some evidence that building a sports facility in a distressed area of a city might catalyze some local redevelopment with the stadium as the magnet. A stadium ensures pedestrian traffic, which helps retail stores and hotels. What these studies do not address, however, is whether the new stadium takes business away from the neighborhood of the old, and now replaced, stadium.

Some cities have based their public expenditures on the hope that a new stadium (and a winning team) will attract more out-of-state visitors. There is some evidence of increased sports tourism based on new facilities, at least in the short term. Most of the spectators, however, would have come to town in any case and are simply moving their expenditures from one city venue to another. The private expenditures simply flow to the owner of the franchise with the new facility instead of the owner of some other entertainment offering. The addition of a sports team to a city does provide households with a new entertainment option. Consumers choosing to attend sporting events will spend less on other entertainment options, such as movies and dining out, thereby shifting, but not increasing, existing tax revenues and spending. The entertainment and sports dollar has minimal elasticity.

There remains the issue of whether the public is well served by these public subsidies. Are they good investments? Was it worth tens of millions of public dollars for New Orleans to construct the Superdome? What about the more than $50 million in public money for the Miami Sports and Entertainment Authority to build the Miami Arena for the Heat and the Panthers, which would be replaced by new arenas in a decade? Did the voters of Arlington, Texas, get their money's worth when they increased the local sales tax by 0.5 percent to build "The Ballpark" for George W. Bush's Rangers? What alternative public expenditures suffered when money was poured into these edifices?

In their book *Field of Schemes*, Neil deMause and Joanna Cagan include a handbook of rules for sports franchise owners as to the steps to take to tap the public treasury. First, the club must denigrate its current stadium as obsolete while suggesting (gently) that it might have to consider relocating to another city unless something is done. (This step is simple if the city has already lost a major league franchise in another sport, like hockey's Minnesota North Stars leaving Minneapolis for Dallas. Baseball's Twins did not have to say much to accomplish this first step.) In explaining the demand for a new facility, the club must rely on concepts of "fairness." Without a new stadium, the team simply could not remain competitive within the league.

A supplicant club needs to create numbers to support its plea, hiring consultants to accumulate data that will work in favor of the project. In order to get the city, county, and/or state to act, the club owner must also create some sort of a deadline after which it will order the Mayflower moving vans, as Robert Irsay did when he moved the Colts from Baltimore to Indianapolis in the dead of night. Finally, once the construction begins, the club can increase its demands. The governmental authority will never leave a project half-completed. Virtually every sports team has followed the deMause and Cagan primer.

As public resistance to cash payouts to franchise owners has increased, clubs and cities have cleverly devised alternative forms of financial subsidies. Tax abatement became the first alternative, but it was rarely enough to convince the owner either to stay or to relocate from another city. Using government bonds to raise construction funds cuts the cost of borrowing. Add to that a very low (if any) stadium lease fee, the franchise's capture of revenue from concessions, parking and non-sports events at the facility, and a governmental guarantee of a full house of spectators (i.e., covering the cost of empty seats). More recently, contracts with cities have included a provision similar to a public sector union "me too" clause. The city promises that the stadium it provides will meet the "state of the art." If other stadiums are "better," the city promises it will update its facility for the franchise at the public's expense.

Sports franchise owners have also devised new ways to secure public funding; for example, by making the new sports facility part of a comprehensive redevelopment package or, in the case of football, obtaining a promise from the NFL to hold the prestigious Super Bowl in the new stadium at some time in the future.

Modern financing of sports facilities is profoundly complex. Even if the transaction is transparent, the public—and likely the politicians—will be bewildered by the details. One way public management can respond to criticism of its subsidy to an existing franchise seeking a new facility is to provide "tax-increment financing" to the club owner. The state calculates the amount of sales tax it currently receives from the sports operation; if the sales tax increases after the facility's construction, that increment is returned to the franchise owner or used to pay the owner's share of the stadium construction cost. In this way, the state's tax revenue remains level. This type of tax-increment financing has been used to support other real estate developments, like Minnesota's Mall of America, but it does not answer the question of whether the construction would have proceeded in any case without a governmental subsidy.

Opponents of public subsidies tend to characterize these public transfer payments as "corporate welfare" and the strategy of franchise owners as "blackmail," but the name-calling does not help much in understanding the issues involved. Corporations and other businesses have long been the beneficiaries of public largess, none more imaginative than the nineteenth-century railroads that were paid for in cash by the mile constructed and deeded public lands adjacent to the railways, which skyrocketed in value as a result of their construction. Calling such use of public funds "extortion" escalates the discussion to a higher decibel level without informing the conversation. Instead, we should try to understand what really motivates such subsidies in order to answer whether they serve a legitimate public purpose.

Each year, it is estimated that billions of dollars in public moneys are spent on private sports facilities. It is an important part of the business of government. Critics retort that alternative uses might be made of these funds. Might the public benefit more from better public schools, transportation, housing, roads, and infrastructure? The answer, of course, is that there are always other—and perhaps better—uses for limited public resources. The issue is whether public authorities would have actually allocated these financial resources for purposes other than sports, and that seems quite unlikely. As Carl Pohlad, billionaire owner of the Minnesota Twins, concluded regarding alternative uses for money better spent on his club: "The world does not work that way." As we shall see, public entities bestow subsidies on sports because they cannot afford not to.

AN ALTERNATE RATIONALE

Despite the protestations of supporters of public subsidies, the economic rationale for the use of limited government resources to construct facilities for private sports entrepreneurs has slowly waned in the overall public debate. Researchers have concluded with some confidence that the economic equation points against public subsidies. The subsidies provide huge public expenditures in exchange for few new jobs and little economic revitalization. While direct economic benefit often remains the first argument offered in support of such expenditures, it rarely survives rebuttal either by experts who have studied the empirical data or by political opponents of the proposed allocation. Supporters need an alternate rationale, one that is more difficult to rebut.

Much has been written lately about what might be termed the politics of public happiness. A new stadium may not make a city richer, but it might make its inhabitants happier by improving their quality of life and civic pride, much like clean air, good weather, and scenic views. Community self-esteem, status, and prestige as a public good may be harder to measure than gross local domestic receipts, but it is just as real. As Art Modell, the owner of the NFL's Baltimore Ravens, which he relocated from Cleveland, explained: "The pride and the presence of a professional football team is far more important than thirty libraries." The opposite effect, of course, follows from the loss of a sports franchise. Cleveland, for example, has suffered from a community-wide malaise for decades. The loss of its beloved football franchise impacted on the psyche of inhabitants across the Western Reserve. Much the same happened decades earlier when Brooklynites lost their treasured Dodgers.

While long-term public happiness may ultimately depend on the success of the franchise in league competition, there is a genuine public benefit in civic pride from national recognition as a major league city even if the local club is an also-ran. The opportunity for city residents to root for their "home team" provides them with a common interest, a cohesive force for any city. One person's consumption of this public good does not deplete the psychic nourishment available to others, and no citizen can be excluded from its enjoyment, although not all can afford the price of a ticket to attend a game in person.

While large metropolises may have franchises in all four major team sports, smaller cities, such as Green Bay, Oklahoma City, Sacramento, and Salt Lake City, may have only a single franchise in one sport, but even that single entry places them among the premier cities of the country. There is some evidence that other businesses—those that actually create real, long-term, well-paying jobs—seek to locate in a city that can boast that it has a major league franchise.

Proponents of public subsidies have posited that new construction provides social benefits to members of the community, enhancing self-esteem and social cohesiveness. Not only do people feel better about their city, outsiders do as well. Cities make investments in the "goodwill" of their communities all the time. Museums, libraries, schools, and clean streets enhance the public's perception and attract outsiders to come and visit or even relocate. Although it may be difficult to monetize these intangible social benefits, no one doubts that they are real. While Art Modell may have been exaggerating by suggesting that a football team is more important to a community than thirty libraries, it seems that having a home club is more significant to the public than reconstructing its schools or repaving its roads.

Studies of the non-economic impact of public expenditures on sports facilities have not reached convincing conclusions. It is not as easy as counting jobs, gross receipts, or taxes. Professor Andrew Zimbalist of Smith College, one of the nation's leading sports economists, in his review of the work on the "public good" that flows from public subsidies, concluded that the methodologies currently employed have not reached conclusive results. Some studies have attempted to measure how much respondents would be willing to spend to "buy" the public good in question. In the aggregate, the purchase price falls far short of the amounts actually allocated by public authorities for the purchase in question. These studies, however, may underestimate the true value to the public of the public subsidies in question.

Each year, national publications announce their list of "the best cities" in which to live. These rankings base their assessments on counting things. For example, *Business Week* ranks the one hundred largest cities based on sixteen criteria: " . . . the number of restaurants, bars, and museums per capita; the number of colleges, libraries, and professional sports teams; the income, poverty, unemployment, crime, and foreclosure rates; percent of population with bachelor's degrees, public school performance, park acres per 1,000 residents, and air quality. Greater weighting was placed on recreational amenities such as parks, bars, restaurants, and museums, and on educational attainment, school performance, poverty, and air quality."

These factors seem plausible, but, at best, they are indirect measures of public happiness. While professional sports make the list, why are "semiprofessional" teams— big-time college football, for example—omitted? The Oklahoma Sooners and the Alabama Crimson Tide certainly make those states better places to live. *U.S. News and World Report*, a publication that has ranked everything but the best religions, examines in its rankings "strong economies, low living costs, and plenty of fun things to do." This is not quite junk science, but it is close.

Those who want to prove that public subsidies of private sports stadiums and arenas provide public goods that improve the community's psychological well-being should do so directly by measuring changes in public attitudes and beliefs about where they live. Behavioral science provides well-accepted methods to guide this type of social research. Comparing the results of carefully crafted surveys using representative samples performed before the public expenditure issue arises with those conducted when the facility opens and again some years later may produce useful information, especially when compared with other cities in the region that do not host major league franchises. It is possible to identify cities without major sports franchises that would likely acquire such franchises were any to relocate or if the sports leagues decided to expand. Los Angeles, the nation's second-largest city, currently does not host an NFL franchise, but it will certainly be first on the list for possible relocation or expansion. We can anticipate that any future Los Angeles sports franchise would seek a public subsidy. Now is the time to measure public attitudes relating sports and public happiness, before the issue of subsidies arises.

The public good and happiness factors were often raised in Cincinnati while tax increases were debated to fund two new sports stadiums. Municipal leaders insisted that the city should not become another Dayton or Louisville. Similarly, in Cleveland the comparators were Akron, Toledo, and Youngstown. In Minneapolis, the worry was that without adequate sports facilities the town would become Omaha, although that city was 400 miles to the south. Municipal aspirations and aversions offer potent hypotheses that can be measured systematically, although perhaps proponents of public subsidies might not want to discover that people could be just as happy and proud of their city without a new $500 million publicly financed stadium. The ultimate issue, of course, is not whether sports facilities would make people happier but how much citizens would be willing to expend in public resources in order to obtain that enhanced level of happiness. Cleaner streets make citizens happier, but are they worth a local tax increase of a thousand dollars a year? How much is it worth to bring a pro football team to town?

FUNDING PUBLIC SUBSIDIES
OF PRIVATE SPORTS FACILITIES

How do public authorities fund these expenditures? Adding a budget line for "pro football stadium," while perhaps once an option, would not be politically viable in an era of budget cuts and austerity. Public management normally insists to the press that the sports subsidy would not require the expenditure of any existing tax money. That may be literally accurate, because it will be *new* taxes that will pay for the public subsidy. Normally these are targeted taxes, such as a "sin tax" on sales of tobacco and alcohol, a very regressive levy that disproportionately affects members of the lower economic classes, who are least likely to be able to afford to make use of the new sports facilities. At other times, governments will use a targeted allocation of lottery revenue. Governments also have the power of eminent domain. They can evict current residents and take the property needed for the stadium footprint in exchange for payment of the "fair market value." Most municipalities and states issue tax-free bonds that will take decades to pay off or they simply offer tax abatements to sports magnates, which may indirectly result in significant cutbacks in social services.

The package negotiated between the club and the governmental entity will determine which party receives the revenue from the expected activities of the new facility. Art Modell's decision to move his erstwhile Browns to Baltimore produced a bonanza for the owner, perhaps enough to have fully compensated him for the scorn he received from Cleveland fans. He kept all the revenue from

Baltimore ticket sales plus lease payments on 108 luxury boxes and parking fees. He received the revenue from naming the stadium (first called the PSI Net Stadium and then M&T Bank Stadium) and all profits from concessions. The State of Maryland also gave Modell a $25 million relocation fee.

It is hard to blame the sports franchise owners as the "villains" of this piece. They are businessmen (and a few businesswomen) who own assets that have genuine value in the marketplace. (Actually, banks indirectly own most franchises; owners borrow to purchase their franchises.) Although they like to market themselves to the citizenry as fiduciaries for the public good, franchises are businesses that seek profit, as they should.

FRANCHISE FREE AGENCY

For decades, the marketplace for sports franchises has offered the opportunity for public subsidies. As long as there are more cities that want franchises and do not have them, club owners have market power. Can we really expect the owners not to demand more public funding?

The contrived scarcity of sports franchises is a critical component of the market equation. If anyone could start a team and compete in any professional sport at the highest level, the leverage of existing teams would be significantly diminished. The leagues carefully control entry, artificially maintaining scarcity and enhancing bargaining power. It is critical, however, that teams have a viable alternative. A threat to leave is only credible if there is someplace to go. Over many years, a collection of Major League Baseball club owners bullied their home cities by threatening to move to Tampa Bay. Tampa Bay had a completed domed stadium off the interstate highway in St. Petersburg. Seven different Major League clubs successfully used the same stratagem as leverage. Finally, perhaps in recognition of the fine service Tampa Bay had provided to Major League owners, the region was awarded an expansion franchise of its own in 1998. The Devil Rays (later renamed the Rays) have proven to be a financial disaster, suggesting that the successful ploy was really just a bluff.

Without the Tampa Bay option, baseball was left without its foil. Commissioner Bud Selig needed to find some substitute for leverage, and Portland, Oregon, was not quite a Major League alternative. Instead, the commissioner threatened to contract two clubs out of baseball, leaving their cities as potential relocation sites. The contraction scare ended as a product of the successful

2002 collective bargaining negotiations. Instead, clubs such as the Oakland A's have used relocation within their geographic region as a bargaining chip, albeit with less market strength.

Franchises in the same sport do not compete with one another for the same pot of public financing. In 1876, with the creation of baseball's National League, the magnates agreed to territorial exclusivity. While public financing of facilities was not yet a reality, owners knew that a local monopoly afforded significant economic advantages. When the American League posed a viable threat to National League hegemony in the early 1900s, the senior circuit capitulated and joined its new rival in reinstating territorial exclusivity, with the exception of a few cities large enough to support two clubs from different leagues.

By the 1960s, all new Major League baseball stadiums were being built with a component of public money. However, the threat of the creation of a rival league—the Continental League—and the possible presence of new teams in cities that desired a club of their own, decreased the availability of public financing of stadiums. Cities could resist the pressure as long as there was a possibility that a new circuit would place a franchise in their town. To fight off this threat from a rival league, Major League Baseball expanded from sixteen to twenty-four clubs. This dramatic increase in the supply of teams and a decrease in the number of major cities available for relocation resulted in a further decrease in market power for each existing club. As a result, only about 60 percent of stadium construction was publicly funded. Over the next thirty years or so, stadium construction for baseball and all other major sports leagues has been publicly funded at a rate between 65 and 80 percent. Since 1990, over ninety-five stadiums and arenas have been constructed for clubs in the major team sports, at an estimated cost to public treasuries of $27 billion.

The impact of building a new stadium, reducing tax obligations, and underwriting the operation of sports franchises through, for example, allowing the depreciation of player contracts, can dramatically increase the value of the club owner's asset. Some owners seek public concessions in order to market their interests at a higher price later on. The package is decidedly more valuable with the public subsidy already attached to the franchise. While public subsidies may not accrue to the economic benefit of the public, there is no question they improve the financial condition of the franchise owners.

WHY SOME CITIES SAY NO

The explosion in public subsidies in the last few decades may hide the fact that some governments actually refuse the demands of franchise owners. While there are certainly other factors that impact franchise relocations, whenever a sports franchise relocates, we know with some certainty that government has declined to meet the owner's demands. Between 1958 and 2008, there were six franchise relocations in baseball, nine in football, seventeen in basketball, and eleven in hockey, each with its own story of demands for public subsidies that were rejected. The great westward move of baseball from Brooklyn to Los Angeles after the 1957 season was triggered by the borough's refusal to build a new facility for the Dodgers. The baseball Giants had sought their own new stadium in Manhattan but without success. The club relocated to San Francisco. The *New York Times* referred to the Dodgers' and Giants' relocations as the great "transcontinental grief." When asked whether he had any remorse, Giants owner Horace Stoneham replied that he felt "bad about the kids, but I haven't seen many of their fathers lately."

The move of the Seattle Supersonics to Oklahoma City more than a half-century later was the result of a similar set of circumstances. After unsuccessful efforts to persuade Washington State government officials to provide funding to update the Key Arena, the ownership group sold the team. The new owners failed in their effort to persuade local governments to fund a $500 million arena complex, and they relocated the franchise in 2008. In February 2012, NBA Commissioner David Stern told the media that the NBA would consider going back to Seattle, but only if the city built a new facility. Seattle mayor Mike McGinn quickly responded that it was seriously considering a proposal for a new arena. Perhaps the Emerald City has learned to appreciate the power of the professional sports market.

Some public entities have refused the demands of franchise owners because voters have said no in public referenda. In many jurisdictions, voters must approve increases in certain types of tax levies. San Franciscans turned down a levy to build a new stadium for the baseball Giants four different times before new franchise owners decided to build it themselves, with, of course, considerable ancillary financial help from various levels of government.

Public referenda offer franchise owners and their leagues an opportunity to inform the public of the benefits of subsidizing new facility construction.

Their financial resources substantially outweigh those that opponents of public financing can bring to the debate. Opponents are aided, however, by the public's reluctance to vote for another levy that might be characterized as a tax. Meanwhile, the sports team in question is playing: if it does well, that will help the vote in favor of the levy; if it is performing poorly on the field, that simply proves that what the owner said was true—without a new facility, the team cannot be competitive. Either way, the owner usually wins.

Unless state law requires a direct affirmative vote, the ballot results may not be the final word. In Pittsburgh, for example, the citizens voted 2–1 in November 1997 against a proposed sales tax increase to finance new stadiums for the Pirates and the Steelers. At the behest of the local business community and the franchise owners, however, local government devised an alternate strategy that did not require a popular vote. Within four years, both clubs were playing in new publicly financed stadiums.

In some cases, citizen groups goad public authorities to deny these private demands for subsidies. Some groups form to protect an old ballpark, as in Boston and Detroit; others seek to reserve public money for what they consider more important purposes. Groups may mobilize around a public referendum or simply lobby the governmental entities directly. Most opinion polls show that citizens overwhelmingly oppose government subsidies for sports teams, but sometimes public sentiment does not translate into public policy. In any case, public views change when business has an adequate period in which to generate their "educational" campaigns.

Advocates for public subsidies of private stadiums obviously include the club owners, who benefit directly from the largess, but in many cases owners play a quiet role out of the public spotlight. Advocates of new stadiums are what Kevin Delaney and Rick Eckstein, in *Public Dollars, Private Stadiums*, called "local growth coalitions." These self-appointed civic groups are led by prominent members of the local corporate community, with financial institutions normally in the lead. Owners of media outlets usually play a supportive role, in particular local newspapers. Lawyers who stand to gain profit from the issuance of public bonds often play an influential role as well. These groups seek to define a dominant local ideology in support of public expenditures to help purely private business interests.

Most campaigns for public subsidies generate some organized counterpressure. A citizens group in Hartford, Connecticut, tried to undercut the effort of the New England Patriots to cash in on a proposed move of the football franchise from Massachusetts. However, the offer made by Hartford and the State of Connecticut was quite generous. The city would pay for virtually everything, including the stadium, infrastructure, parking, insurance, a practice facility, capital replacement costs, and improvements over thirty years. The National Football League, in which Patriots' owner Bob Kraft is a player of considerable influence, was not happy with his proposed move, although normally (or at least since Al Davis won his relocation case in court) it supports its members' efforts to secure the most lucrative stadium offers. The NFL had allowed franchises in Los Angeles and Houston to relocate. Adding the Boston metropolitan market to the mix of abandoned territories would have diminished the league's national footprint.

The proposed Hartford deal was a remarkable giveaway. The Patriots would keep every single dollar of revenue and operate the stadium rent-free. Club owner Kraft, however, eventually took the lesser offer from Massachusetts and stayed in the commonwealth to build his own stadium at Foxboro with private money—plus $70 million in roads and sewers paid for by the state. A local reporter from the *Hartford Courant* called him a "total nutcake."

Kraft's ultimate rejection of the Hartford giveaway is an example of the personal idiosyncrasies involved in each of these relocation/subsidy situations. A consummate businessman, Kraft certainly appreciated the scope of Hartford's offer. He knew, however, that delays in construction of any stadium would be inevitable and that environmental concerns associated with building a waterfront ballpark in Hartford would be substantial. Nonetheless, even a sweetened deal from the Massachusetts legislature could not come close to the Hartford financial opportunity, which some had valued as worth a billion dollars in free money. Kraft later said: "It was a long journey that brought us back where we began. That was a record breaking deal, but it was never about money. And people who think that don't really understand us. For us, your legacy is what you do for your family and your community."

Ultimately, Kraft was loyal to his home state. Born and raised in Brookline, Massachusetts, he found it difficult to desert the commonwealth.

Activist antisubsidy citizen groups can sufficiently annoy a team owner to make him accelerate his departure to another city that would be delighted to build whatever he wants and pay him for the pleasure of his company. At other times, public pressure groups will simply delay construction but not stop it. Some franchise owners have responded in kind by creating their own seemingly independent civic groups in support of their public subsidy. They have even started their own newspapers to spread the gospel. Looking to deflect public criticism, club owners and government officials have created "community benefits agreements" that guarantee specific investments in those neighborhoods affected by facility construction in exchange, of course, for their endorsement of the facility project.

Public authorities that refuse demands and then lose a franchise are often chastened by the event. Baltimore lost the Colts, but then it built a new stadium for the Orioles. Cleveland lost the Browns, who went to Baltimore when the Maryland county built a new football stadium. Cleveland then built a new stadium for the Indians and later a new stadium for the expansion NFL football franchise that carried the venerable name the "Browns." (A plaque inside the new stadium reads: "We proved that the Browns belong in Cleveland, the home of the greatest fans in the world . . . OUR TEAM . . . OUR NAME . . . OUR COLORS.") St. Louis lost its football Cardinals to Phoenix in 1988 and lured the Rams from the Los Angeles suburbs in 1995 with a remarkably lucrative stadium deal. The Rams would pay a very modest $250,000 a year in rent at the new publicly funded stadium, where the club captured all the revenue from luxury boxes and concessions and 75 percent of the advertising and naming-rights fees. In addition, St. Louis paid the Rams' owner $46 million for relocating. Apparently, a city does not make the same mistake twice. It just makes new mistakes.

The battle between cities to obtain sports franchises can only benefit the owners. The competing local media often play a cheerleading role, following the business deals as if they were touchdowns and home runs. In 1980, the *Los Angeles Times* editorialized its feelings about Al Davis's proposed relocation of his Raiders: "Sports business is [a] rough-and-tumble competitive business. Self-interest rules. We hope the Oakland Raiders will come to Los Angeles even though the move would hurt Oakland. Both cities need the team for the same reasons—to provide a sense of identity and some economic benefit . . . sorry, Oakland, but we'd like to have your Raiders."

PUBLIC SUBSIDIES AS POLITICAL CURRENCY

While public happiness might be a defensible goal for public subsidies, the reality is that sports subsidies are valuable because they offer political currency to politicians. D. Bruce Poole, a member of the Maryland House of Delegates at the time Baltimore and Maryland subsidized the construction of M&T Bank Stadium for the Ravens, testified before Congress in 1999. Although he had fought against the subsidy, Delegate Poole asked: "Who can say no?" He added: "Where are the public officials who are willing to walk away from having professional sports teams in their city or state at any cost? By that I am not speaking of state legislators—I am speaking of mayors and governors who ultimately have to make a very tough decision, knowing that if they do not get or keep a team, their jurisdictions will be marred. Loss of a professional sports team has become synonymous with loss of status, loss of prestige, loss of favorable exposure, and loss of opportunity at many levels." Losing a sports franchise or failing to attract a replacement, he explained, would have direct repercussions at the polls.

The presence or absence of a local professional sports franchise certainly has a political value. Although rarely expressed in such stark terms, a mayor who is responsible for a city's loss of its football, baseball, or basketball franchise—hockey does not have the same weight, except in Canada—will suffer at the polls. On the other hand, the executive who saves the city's franchise by responding to its demands will likely benefit at the polls.

It is, of course, possible that politicians who stand up against the demands of sports franchises may reap at least short-term political benefits depending on the desires of the electorate. While most voters dislike the idea of subsidizing wealthy entrepreneurs, whether in sports or other businesses, when it comes to losing your football team, the downside risks may later convert political courage into a disaster at the polls. Good politicians can gauge the political exchange; poor politicians head for retirement.

Some politicians see little benefit in opposing the demands of club owners. In fact, they may lead the parade for the subsidy. Rudy Giuliani wore his allegiance to the Yankees on his sleeve—actually on his ubiquitous baseball cap. When both New York City baseball franchises demanded new stadiums in the late 1990s, Giuliani responded forcefully that "both the Yankees and the Mets are entitled to new baseball fields." (It was a curious choice of words. "Entitlements" in political parlance normally refers to transfer payments to the poor and the senior population in the form of Medicare and Medicaid.) Eventually, new stadiums were built for both clubs, but the actual bricks-and-mortar construction was paid for with private funds. The public subsidy for land, parking garages, and tax abatements, however, was considerable. The new Yankee Stadium cost the city and state $551 million and the Mets' stadium $353 million.

Normally more than the executive branch is involved in providing governmental subsidies. Either the city council or the legislature (or both) has a role to play. However, because these bodies are made up of many people, the political responsibility may be diffused. Members of a legislative body who agree to authorize an expenditure of public money for the benefit of a sports team are likely to receive some allotment of positive political currency, but rejecting the demand could mean all those who voted against saving "our team" would feel the weight of public disappointment in the same manner as a mayor or a governor. Thus, there can be gain from supporting a public subsidy and much to lose by voting no.

Losing a major league team because of the municipal failure to offer a competitive subsidy cannot be measured simply in dollars and cents. Economics is almost beside the point. In actuality, as we have seen, a sports franchise is a very small business with the economic impact of a large supermarket. The "jobs" factor is rebutted by the evidence, although it continues to be adopted by politicians as their rationale for acting. They need some reason to expend limited resources other than as a means of retaining political power, which is likely their motivating force.

Public subsidies can be measured and evaluated based on their political impact on the decision makers. Elections are normally won or lost based on votes at the margin. Those votes can be affected by decisions that result in gaining or losing a professional sports franchise. Presumably, they can also be affected in the long term by failing schools or potholes left unfilled, but the impact of a sports decision is more direct and immediate.

BASEBALL RETURNS TO WASHINGTON

We can see all of the variables involved in public subsidies for private sports facilities in the recent political turmoil they caused in our nation's capital. Politics in the District of Columbia is normally quite a boisterous affair, but the real possibility that Washington could once again host a Major League baseball franchise caused political chaos. As a result of an ownership shuffle in 2001—John Henry sold the Florida Marlins and purchased the Boston Red

Sox, and Jeffrey Loria bought the Marlins and sold the Montreal Expos to Major League Baseball—the commissioner of baseball controlled a franchise he could market and relocate. One thing for certain was that it would not stay in Montreal, which, despite its long association with baseball, proved not to be a sufficiently profitable setting for the American national pastime.

In January 2003, a delegation that included Mayor Anthony Williams and D.C. Council chairwoman Linda Cropp met with baseball's relocation committee to discuss bringing the Montreal baseball club to Washington, D.C. The following month, the mayor's office announced that it was preparing a financing proposal for a new stadium. Skirmishing began almost immediately in the city council about who would be taxed to pay for a new stadium, and talks with Major League Baseball's representatives broke down in July 2003. In April 2004, Mayor Williams unveiled a proposal in which the District would fully fund construction of a new ballpark located next to city-owned RFK Stadium, thus decreasing the cost of acquiring new land. The mayor, however, had not briefed council members before he showed the plan to the public. Major League Baseball remained safely out of the fray. It had not even committed to placing the franchise in the District, although it did say it was serious about D.C. Private buyers for the franchise were yet to be identified. Baseball first wanted a financing plan approved by the council before it would move forward.

Politics about the baseball subsidy became front-page news in the *Washington Post*. By mid-July, two council members, Adrian Fenty and David Catania, had declared their opposition to a stadium that would be "entirely, or even substantially" financed with public funds. Mayor Williams, they claimed, was wrong if he thought that the D.C. Council would adopt a stadium financing package "in a snap." The two members stressed that public funds should be committed instead to schools, health care, employment, and libraries, improvements the District critically needed. The mayor's office responded that public services would not be affected by any plan for a baseball stadium because the city's bonds would be paid for by new revenue streams and not from the general fund or from new taxes on residents. Opponents quickly pointed out that the mayor's response did not address the dire shape of the public schools in the District. Hospitals and libraries were closing, and essential city services, including trash collection, were lacking.

As the D.C. Council and the mayor bickered, politicians in Northern Virginia entered the fray in late June 2004 with a rival offer to provide a totally publicly financed stadium located near Dulles Airport. The baseball relocation committee seemed to prefer the urban setting, but the politics in D.C. was making that option exceedingly difficult. In late August, the Service Employees International Union, which opposed public financing of a stadium, released the results of a poll of D.C. residents taken in June 2004. Of 571 people surveyed, 70 percent opposed public funding and more than half strongly opposed any public subsidy.

Stadium financing would become an issue of debate in the city council election races in the fall of 2004, and the opponents of public subsidies prevailed. The mayor now had a real deadline. The council would have to act before the newly elected council members were sworn in on January 1. The day after the primary, city officials and baseball's relocation committee met for eighteen hours to try to reach a memorandum of understanding that would govern the relocation, the temporary use of RFK Stadium for the team, and the financing and construction of a new stadium. On September 15, 2004, the District finally unveiled its official plan for a new stadium. In a presentation made by the mayor's office to the D.C. Council, the District offered to construct a new stadium near the Anacostia River waterfront as part of a $440 million package. The proposal would be financed with thirty-year bonds. Annual debt payments would be covered by a combination of a gross receipts tax on larger D.C. businesses, stadium rent from the team's owners, and in-stadium taxes on tickets, concessions, and merchandise. The District would fully finance the new stadium, but the deal would include free tickets for low-income children and priority consideration for D.C. residents and minority contractors for available jobs. The District had caved, and Major League Baseball was thrilled. On September 29, 2004, Commissioner Bud Selig called Mayor Williams to inform him that the Expos would be relocating to the District of Columbia for the 2005 season.

It would not be smooth sailing for the District, however. Opponents on the city council immediately began to criticize the agreement and vowed to vote it down. Ninety economists signed a public letter to Mayor Williams denouncing the stadium plan as economically disastrous. Other critics noted that the deal could significantly underestimate the cost of the stadium's construction. The stadium agreement placed responsibility for all potential cost overruns on the

District. Opponents questioned the city's dollar estimate since it did not include funding for necessary infrastructure and road improvements.

On October 5, 2004, hundreds of D.C. residents held a rally to protest the use of taxpayer funds of any kind to build a baseball stadium instead of funding schools, hospitals, or affordable housing. A loose coalition of interest groups called "No D.C. Taxes for Baseball" participated in the rally, along with dissenting members of the city council. Neighborhood meetings and public hearings offered critics a public forum for their complaints about the project. To add fuel to the fire, shortly before the open meetings, the chief financial officer for the District released an analysis that suggested that construction and renovation could cost $91 million more than the original $440 million estimate. The additional funds would be needed for road, sewer, and subway improvements, more RFK Stadium renovations, and a contingency fund in case of cost overruns.

When the city council began to debate the mayor's bill, he strategically added to his package a $450 million community fund for schools, libraries, and recreation centers, which would be funded by a combination of bonds, a portion of the annual gross revenue business tax, some existing funds in city coffers, and the creation of a tax-increment financing district around the stadium. In committee, tempers flared between council members opposed to the public subsidy and those who supported the mayor. However, the mayor appeared to have the votes he needed to pass the legislation.

Two days later, however, Council Chairwoman Linda Cropp shocked the pro-stadium advocates by breaking with Mayor Williams and proposing that the publicly funded baseball stadium be built at the RFK Stadium site as an alternative to the mayor's Anacostia site. Cropp, who had been a staunch ally of Williams throughout the relocation process, cited the excessive costs of the Anacostia site as her reason for preferring the RFK site. Cropp had read the political winds, and a gale was rising against the deal negotiated with baseball's relocation committee. A *Washington Post* poll indicated that more than two-thirds of D.C. residents opposed using public funds to build a baseball stadium in the city. In effect, Cropp's proposal was meant to save the relocation by lowering the cost to the District. Proponents of the Anacostia site lashed out at Cropp, who was now being mentioned as a possible mayoral candidate in 2006 along with other opponents of the mayor's plan.

The council was split on the relocation site as the vote approached. The mayor was able to procure one wavering vote by pledging that the first $45 million from the community investment fund would go to improve neighborhood libraries. Williams wooed additional votes with a promise to build a $5 million recreation center, $2 million for a high school, and $50 million for assorted commercial development.

On the day of the scheduled vote, after two hours of closed-door council debate, Cropp pulled another about-face. Seeing that Williams's Anacostia proposal had the necessary votes to pass, she exercised her power as council chairwoman to remove the bill from consideration, delaying the vote until November 23. In addition, she pulled her RFK Stadium site proposal and instead announced a plan to raise $350 million in private financing for a stadium to be located at the Anacostia site. While she had no funding details at the time, she planned to use the two weeks before the vote to finalize her alternative. Two days later, Cropp softened her stance on the stadium. She said she would support the mayor's stadium plan if the plan stipulated the possibility of private funding in the future. The mayor's coalition quickly accepted her compromise, agreeing to amend the bill to include a six-month search for private funding for the ballpark. None of these private funding alternatives would pan out, and the cost estimates for the ballpark continued to rise.

Last-minute maneuvering by opponents for individual council votes came to naught, and after seven hours of debate the mayor's stadium bill passed 6–4, with three members abstaining. Half of the votes for the bill came from lame-duck councilmen who had been voted out of office two months earlier. The following week, Major League Baseball owners voted 29–1 in favor of relocating the Montreal franchise to Washington. Under city council rules, however, a second vote was required to finally approve the package.

Linda Cropp sprang another last-minute surprise at the December 14 council vote. Eleven hours into the debate, unsatisfied with baseball's concessions and driven to keep the public's stadium costs down, she proposed an amendment that would require that the stadium construction be at least 50 percent financed with private funds. While the city would still be responsible for infrastructure costs, the amendment would limit the city's investment in the stadium construction itself to $142 million. Cropp threatened to vote against the stadium bill if the amendment did not pass. Concerned that the bill would not pass without Cropp's vote, council members voted to pass her amendment, 10–3. Mayor Williams stormed out of the council chambers shortly after the amendment passed and refused to speak to reporters. The stadium deal then passed, 7–6.

Baseball responded without hesitation on December 15, calling the new council bill "wholly unacceptable" and halting all business and promotional activity for the Washington franchise, now officially named the "Nationals," including the scheduled unveiling of the uniforms later that day. By requiring more private funding for the stadium, the council undercut baseball's efforts to sell its franchise, since it would receive a much lower price for a team without the certainty of a publicly built stadium. Cropp received a storm of angry phonecalls and e-mails from stadium supporters, including racist and sexist comments and two death threats, for her actions.

Faced with the reality of losing the baseball franchise, Cropp blinked. The night before the council's next meeting on December 21, she announced in a news conference that she and the mayor had agreed on a proposal in which the city would continue pursuing private financing of up to 50 percent of the project, but the deal would not be contingent on finding such financing. After an excruciatingly difficult political process, the Washington Nationals were born.

The political fallout from the protracted and divisive negotiation and approval process hurt all the principals. There were few political winners in the baseball deal. Most blamed Mayor Williams for negotiating a bad deal with baseball owners and failing to effectively sell the deal to the public. Only a minority approved of the way Chairwoman Cropp handled the baseball situation. Stadium opponents who had lauded her as a heroine for her stiff resistance to the baseball oligarchs felt betrayed by her ultimate support for a deal relying mainly on public financing. A vast majority of District voters still opposed the use of public funds to build a baseball stadium. For all the debate and discussion about the potential of private financing for construction, eventually the entire financing for the new stadium would come from the District's coffers.

Mayor Williams decided not to run for reelection in a crowded 2006 mayoral race in which no fewer than 5 of the 13 council members considered running. Instead, he would endorse sometime stadium foe Linda Cropp in the Democratic primary race. Adrian Fenty, a consistent opponent of the mayor's plan, ran away with the vote. After her campaign fell short, Cropp retired from politics. In all, after numerous cost estimates, each more than the previous one, the final public price tag for Nationals Park was $693 million.

The economic development that was touted for the District's waterfront area surrounding the stadium had not occurred as of 2012. Less than one-third of the neighborhood had been revitalized as planned. Properties in the area remained empty, barred to the public by fences adorned with artist renderings of future condos and hotels. The principals blamed the slow rate of development on the recession, and they preached patience. There was no easy way for the District's government to deal with baseball, but the jumbled and erratic political process caused a morass of intrigue, maneuvers, and double-dealing.

PUT YOUR BEST OFFER ON THE TABLE

When professional team athletes finally recognized in the late 1960s that they pursued their trade only at the pleasure of club owners, with terms and conditions of employment set unilaterally by management, the athletes collectivized their bargaining power and formed unions. Within a few years, professional sports unions had revolutionized the business model that had endured for decades and, in the case of Major League Baseball, for a century. By the mid-1970s, the unions—sometimes with the assistance of courts and labor arbitrators—had revolutionized team sports. They pressured sports management into creating a market for players that better reflected their contribution to the sports commercial enterprise.

Major league teams in the four team sports treat cities in a fashion similar to the way they had always treated their ballplayers. Playing one city against another, franchises demanded and received transfer payments for their agreement to locate in one place or move to another. As the only game in town in any one sport, the clubs extracted impressive public subsidies.

Cities without clubs in the four team sports would remain willing to pay to capture a major league franchise, just as Washington, D.C., did to secure the former Expos. They would use their powers of eminent domain to obtain land for a project and offer tax abatements. They would raise the capital needed to construct an attractive sports facility. As long as cities compete for the limited number of franchises, political realities will generate public subsidies. Only when cities in effect "unionize" to resist club demands will the economic coercion abate. That will likely require congressional action to avoid potential antitrust liability, and that is unlikely considering the current reality of the national political process. Moreover, cities that lack franchises would want nothing that could impede their franchise acquisitions. Cities will remain victims of their own greed for glory, while clubs walk away with the public fisc.

Authors deMause and Cagan summarized the current scorecard on governmental subsidies as follows: "[A]t any given time one quarter of major league teams is playing in a new building, one quarter is awaiting the construction of one, another quarter is lobbying to get one built—and a final quarter is waiting in the wings for its turn at the plate."

Enacted by Congress in 1972, Title IX offered girls and women the opportunity to develop leadership skills, learn teamwork, build self-confidence, and perfect self-discipline on the playing field. Politics brought about an explosion in women's sports, which, in turn, invigorated an entire generation of woman leaders and legislators. Title IX ordained a revolution in American life that would forever alter the established order. *AP Images*

Politics is not a game. It is an earnest business. —*Winston Churchill*

One of the penalties for refusing to participate in politics is that you end up being governed by your inferiors. —*Plato*   ·

[CONCLUSION]

The connection between sports and politics runs deep in human existence. From ancient days, humans developed their athletic attributes in order to prepare for the hunt and for the inevitable conflicts between clans and families. Those who led these human groups recognized the importance of physical fitness. They knew, as the Duke of Wellington would say millennia later, that "the battle of Waterloo was won on the playing fields of Eton." Practicing sporting skills had definite political implications, and a physically unfit nation was doomed.

We have come a long way from the cinder tracks of ancient Olympia in terms of biological, political, social, and technological developments. Humans have doubled their life expectancy. They have expanded their political communities to a continental scope and beyond. At times, they have demonstrated that they cannot only pledge allegiance to freedom and democracy but actually practice systems of politics that will preserve, protect, and defend those verities. Yet, they have also shown a willingness to use the innovations of civilization to oppress their fellow countrymen and impose their will on others.

Sports themselves are not good or evil. They are just sports. Sports can be used by emerging democracies, like South Africa, to help unify a multiracial nation arising phoenix-like out of a brutal police state. Sports can be used by dictatorships to flaunt their power and intimidate their rivals. How could something so impressive as the Berlin Olympic Games of 1936 be followed in a few short years by a world war sacrificing more than sixty million people? In 2003, the *Times of London* described a parade honoring the World Cup champion English rugby team as "like a sweet-natured version of the Nuremburg rally." However, while rugby is a collision sport, it has never produced death camps.

Sports can tell us something about who we are, both good and bad. Mostly, sports has been a tool, like a hammer, which in the hands of people of good will can result in building peace and even serenity, while, in the kit of miscreants, it can cause havoc. Nation-states have been the most prominent offenders, but tribes of soccer ultras, for example, can easily mutate into warriors. Sports can serve as a spark igniting a war between two small Central American countries or a trans-Balkan conflagration fought in part between paramilitaries of former soccer hooligans.

Sports cannot reform politics, although those who run an athletic enterprise can stand at the public trough and feed. The incessant demand for public subsidies by private sports franchise owners is organized extortion. Can we select as our political leaders persons who will resist this shakedown? Can we, the people, resist the compulsion to make rich people richer?

For better or worse, we deserve those who govern us. We vote for them in democracies. We abide them in those nations where rule is imposed by force. Caught in the web of a dictatorship, we can resist, if we have sufficient courage, or we can accept our fate. When discretion mandates caution, sports may offer us the safety of a diversion.

Every so often, out of the tangle of our sporting culture, a figure arises who can jump the gap to political leadership. Simply because a person first comes to our attention through sports excellence does not mean the athlete would serve us equally well off the "playing fields of Eton." Yet Joe Louis and Muhammad Ali became important symbols for an oppressed minority, providing hope along with a full measure of pride and self-esteem. We benefit from those who can demonstrate leadership, character, and competitiveness, developed in sports or elsewhere, because our clan's survival depends on the fitness of our leaders.

Sports and politics intertwine in modern civilization. Both are essential. Like water and fresh air, we need physical and governmental activity. However, do we tend to pollute the colorless and odorless gaseous and liquid mixtures that sustain our lives? We often do so as we direct our political units and organize our play. Sports can also be perverted by our political goals. Nonetheless, they are what we are all about.

POLITICS, SPORTS, AND SOCIAL CHANGE

On occasion, politics and sports combine to effect fundamental social change. In the 1960s, the United States underwent a transformation of rights as a result of peaceful, albeit direct, political action. The civil rights movement sought to redeem promises that were made a century earlier but were never fulfilled. Similarly, the women's movement fought the gender wars for official recognition of equality. Ultimately, both successfully used the political process to achieve goals that changed America.

Persons of color were systematically excluded from mainstream opportunities even if they were exceptional athletes. Jack Johnson, Joe Louis, Jackie Robinson, and Muhammad Ali were the exception rather than the rule. American politics, however, responded to Dr. Martin Luther King Jr.'s crusade because it touched the two main strains of the American ethos—conscience and economics. The Civil Rights Act of 1964 and subsequent legislation ended official racial apartheid, although it would take years of further struggle to convert congressional intent into reality.

Women sought equal rights through the enactment of an amendment to the Constitution. Congress approved the Equal Rights Amendment in 1972, but it fell three states short of adoption. Undeterred, the effort of women to abolish gender discrimination would find its greatest success in a thirty-seven-word statute enacted by Congress the same year—Title IX of the Education Amendments. Designed to end gender discrimination in education programs receiving federal funds, the potential impact of the legislation on high school and college sports was barely mentioned during the debate in Congress. While Title IX certainly impacted the work life of women in secondary and higher education, its greatest effect has been felt in the opportunities made available for girls and women to participate in athletics.

TITLE IX

In the definitive court case involving the rights of woman athletes, Judge Bruce Selya of the United States Court of Appeals for the First Circuit explained the benefits of sports participation: "For college students, athletics offers an opportunity to exacuate leadership skills, learn teamwork, build self-confidence, and perfect self-discipline. In addition, for many student-athletes, physical skills are a passport to college admissions and scholarships, allowing them to attend otherwise inaccessible schools. These opportunities, and the lessons learned on the playing fields, are invaluable in attaining career and life successes in and out of professional sports." According to Judge Selya, without access to the opportunities to participate in sports, women would be further relegated to second-class citizenship and the nation would be deprived of the talented contributions of half its population. Studies have proven Judge Selya's analysis correct: participating in team sports has resulted in lifelong improvements to women's educational, work, and health prospects.

In the early 1970s, one in thirty-five girls and women participated in sports in high school and college. Today, more than one in three participate, and more could if they wanted to. Title IX made that change happen. Most schools complied voluntarily with Title IX without the need for extended litigation. Politics brought about an explosion in women's sports, which, in turn, invigorated an entire generation of woman leaders and legislators.

Unlike only a few decades ago, women participate fully in American life. They constitute a majority of students in higher education. While the glass ceiling still inhibits the movement of women to the highest reaches of American business, it is no longer acceptable to engage in despicable sexism of the kind sports columnist Furman Bisher spewed in the *Sporting News* in 1974: "What are we after, a race of Amazons? Do we want to bring home a companion or a broad chewing tobacco? What do we want for the darling daughter, a boudoir or a locker room full of cursing and bruises? A mother for your grandchildren or a hysterectomy?"

Bisher was not alone. There were many in the sports establishment that saw Title IX as a threat to the old-boys network that controlled sports and, even more importantly, that governed society. Title IX ordained social changes that would alter this established order.

There are many who still adhere to archaic stereotypes that enslave women. Religious fanatics would have women relegated to the kitchen under the thumb of their male spouses. While politics periodically reverberates with a counterrevolution against women's rights on questions of pay equity, health care, and reproductive freedom, it may be too late to reverse history. We all want to be able to have the choice of what we want to be, and, as a direct result of politics, sports have led the way.

THE FUTURE OF SPORTS AND POLITICS

These stories of the linkage between sports and politics have offered numerous examples about how these two fields of human endeavor inextricably intertwine. That has always been so and likely will always be so. Every four years, the Olympics and the World Cup will excite nationalism and infuse politics in the context of sports. Expansion of the global economy may offer further opportunities for political realignments, but tribalism will remain a potent force. Conflicts will continue to divide us, but sporting competition—if not peaceful, then at least not lethal—will present alternatives to all-out conflagration. Keep awarding gold medals and victory cups, and, perhaps in time, we will learn to get along.

[NOTES ON SOURCES]

[INTRODUCTION] SPORTS AND POLITICS

The examples of the intersection of sports and politics are drawn from a variety of sources. John Sayle Watterson's collection of stories about the sporting habits of U.S. presidents in *The Games Presidents Play: Sports and the Presidency* proved particularly helpful. Lissa Smith discussed female athletes in *Nike Is a Goddess: The History of Women in Sports*, as did Susan Chan in *Coming on Strong: Gender and Sexuality in Twentieth-Century Women's Sport*. For general reference, consider Elliott Gorn and Warren Goldstein's *A Brief History of American Sports*, Kathryn Jay's *More Than Just a Game: Sports in American Life since 1945*, and Robert Lipsyte's *Sportsworld: An American Dreamland*.

[1] EARLY BASEBALL AND THE URBAN POLITICAL MACHINE

The literature on the history of baseball is broad in scope and rich in detail. All studies of the origins of the game must begin with Harold Seymour's seminal work *Baseball: The Early Years*. Although most books about the national game begin with the founding of the National League in 1876, there are a few splendid studies of the early amateur game, including Peter Morris's *But Didn't We Have Fun? An Informal History of Baseball's Pioneer Era, 1843–1870*, Warren Goldstein's *Playing for Keeps: A History of Early Baseball*, and Tom Melville's *Early Baseball and the Rise of the National League*. Of particular interest to those studying baseball archeology is David Block's *Baseball Before We Knew It: A Search for the Roots of the Game*.

Two books on Boss Tweed and Tammany Hall stand out for mention: Alexander B. Callow Jr.'s *The Tweed Ring* and Kenneth D. Ackerman's *Boss Tweed: The Rise and Fall of the Corrupt Pol Who Conceived the Soul of Modern New York*. They place the nefarious work of the urban machine in a social context that includes the activities of social clubs, including those that played baseball.

Over the past decade, researchers online have found contemporary newspapers, truly the "first rough draft of history," a phrase coined by Katherine Graham of the *Washington Post* in a speech in 1963. For the most part, early reports of baseball matches were short and hyperbolic. The press would not create separate sports pages until later in the nineteenth century. By comparison, broad attacks on the Tweed Ring, in particular in the *New York Times*, would fill pages of the dailies. Tweed famously dismissed the early *Times* reports, but recognized the political damage inflicted by the Nast cartoons in *Harper's Weekly*: "I don't care so much what the papers write about—my constituents can't read—but damn it, they can see pictures."

[2] THE NAZI OLYMPIC TRIUMPH

As part of the extensive scholarship on the Nazi regime, historians have focused on the events of the 1936 Olympic Games to try to understand the underpinnings of that malignant regime. *Berlin Games: How the Nazis Stole the Olympic Dream* by Guy Walters, *Nazi Games: The Olympics of 1936* by David Clay Large, and *The Nazi Olympics* by Richard Mandell are very good starting points for research. Jeremy Schaap, among the premier popular scholars on sport, has written an impressive biography of the most memorable athlete of the Berlin Games in *Triumph: The Untold Story of Jesse Owens and Hitler's Olympics*.

[3] THE WAR OF THE WORLD: JOE LOUIS V. MAX SCHMELING

Joe Louis, the boxer and the man, has fascinated America since his emergence on the world sports stage in the 1930s. There are a number of splendid resources on the two Louis-Schmeling fights. David Margolick's *Beyond Glory: Joe Louis vs. Max Schmeling, and a World on the Brink* is a comprehensively researched, brilliantly executed book that not only documents the events and the historical context of the bouts but also debunks many myths about the fighters. Lewis Erenberg's *The Greatest Fight of Our Generation* is of similar quality and usefulness. A new biography by Randy Roberts, entitled *Joe Louis: Hard Times Man*, combines thoughtful research with splendid prose. It is a welcome addition to the Louis library. Accounts of Louis's fights also filled the world's newspapers and highlighted the importance of the bouts as a reflection of world politics.

[4] THE "FUTBOL WAR" OF CENTRAL AMERICA

The literature on the "futbol war" is not extensive, but there are two stellar studies worthy of attention. The definitive work is Ryszard Kapuscinski's *The Soccer War*, translated from the Polish. Thomas P. Anderson's *The War of the Dispossessed: Honduras and El Salvador 1969* is also quite valuable. After war broke out, world newspapers provided contemporary press accounts of the conflict, in particular in the *New York Times*.

[5] MUHAMMAD ALI AND THE SYMBOLS OF POLITICS

David Remnick's *King of the World: Muhammad Ali and the Rise of an American Hero* is the premier resource for research on the "Greatest of All Time." David West collected the best contemporary writing on Ali in *The Mammoth Book of Muhammad Ali*. National and local newspapers told Ali's remarkable story as it unfolded, as did national sports magazines, such as *Sports Illustrated*. "The Champ" offers his own take on his life in *The Soul of a Butterfly: Reflections on Life's Journey*, coauthored with his daughter Hana Yasmeen Ali. Ali's famous poetry can be found in many sources, including Remnick's *King of the World* and Carol Dwec's *Mindset: The New Psychology of Success*.

[6] OLYMPIC BOYCOTTS AND INTERNATIONAL RELATIONS

The U.S.-led boycott of the Moscow Games generated some interesting work. In *Dropping the Torch: Jimmy Carter, the Olympic Boycott and the Cold War*, Nicolas Evan Sarantakes pulls no punches. It is a scathing critique of the Carter White House, well justified by the facts of the unfortunate events of 1980. Tom Carraccioli and Jerry Carraccioli take a different approach, explaining in *Boycott: Stolen Dreams of the 1980 Moscow Olympic Games* how the actions of the U.S. government impacted individual athletes. It is a telling recital of the facts and implications of the boycott.

[7] SPORTS AND SOUTH AFRICAN LIBERATION

Nelson Mandela has been the subject of numerous biographies. Among the best is Christina Scott's *Nelson Mandela: A Force for Freedom*. John Carlin's definitive work on the revolutionary's use of sports, *Invictus: Nelson Mandela and the Game That Made a Nation*, was made into a major motion picture. Mandela's autobiography, *Long Walk to Freedom: The Autobiography of Nelson Mandela*, offers his personal account of the period. For a thoroughly researched account of a country in transition, see William Beinart's *Twentieth-Century South Africa* and Leonard Thompson's *A History of South Africa*.

[8] HARDBALL IN CITY HALL
PUBLIC FINANCING OF SPORTS STADIUMS

The foremost work on public subsidies of private sports franchises remains *Sports, Jobs and Taxes: The Economic Impact of Sports Teams and Stadiums*, by the two premier scholars in the field, Roger Noll and Andrew Zimbalist. *Field of Schemes: How the Great Stadium Swindle Turns Public Money into Private Profit* by Neil deMause and Joanna Cagan is more colloquial, but valuable for its insight. There is also an accompanying website that updates the latest developments. Robert Trumpbour's *The New Cathedrals: Politics and Media in the History of Stadium Construction* and Kevin Delany and Rick Eckstein's *Public Dollars, Private Stadiums: The Battle Over Building Sports Stadiums* are also quite useful.

[CONCLUSION]

Judge Selya's opinion for the First Circuit Court of Appeals is *Cohen v. Brown University*, 991 F.2d 888 (1993). The suit was brought by a class of woman athletes at Brown University after their college abolished the gymnastics team. Amy Cohen, the captain of the team, was the lead plaintiff, but she had long graduated by the time the case was resolved a decade later in the most significant case under Title IX. I discuss the case in depth in Chapter 6 of *Sports Justice: Law and the Business of Sports* (University Press of New England, 2010). Welch Suggs's *A Place on the Team: The Triumph and Tragedy of Title IX* remains the best study of the impact of the federal legislation.

[BIBLIOGRAPHY]

Abrams, Roger I. *Legal Bases: Baseball and the Law.* Philadelphia: Temple University Press, 1998.

———. *Sports Justice: Law and the Business of Sports.* Hanover, NH: University Press of New England, 2010.

———. *The Dark Side of the Diamond: Gambling, Violence, Drugs and Alcoholism in the National Pastime.* Burlington, MA: Rounder Books, 2007.

———. *The First World Series and the Baseball Fanatics of 1903.* Boston: Northeastern University Press, 2003.

———. *The Money Pitch: Baseball Free Agency and Salary Arbitration.* Philadelphia: Temple University Press, 2000.

Ackerman, Kenneth D. *Boss Tweed: The Rise and Fall of the Corrupt Pol Who Conceived the Soul of Modern New York.* New York: Carroll and Gray, 2005.

Agnew, Paddy. *Forza Italia: The Fall and Rise of Italian Football.* New York: Random House, 2007.

Alexander, Charles C. *John McGraw.* Lincoln: University of Nebraska Press, 1988.

———. *Rogers Hornsby: A Biography.* New York: Henry Holt and Co., 1995.

———. *Spoke: A Biography of Tris Speaker.* Dallas: Southern Methodist University Press, 2007.

———. *Ty Cobb.* New York: Oxford University Press, 1994.

Allen, Oliver E. *The Tiger: The Rise and Fall of Tammany Hall.* New York: Addison-Wesley Publishing Co., 1993.

Anderson, Thomas P. *The War of the Dispossessed: Honduras and El Salvador, 1969.* Lincoln: University of Nebraska Press, 1981.

Ashe, Arthur. *Day of Grace.* New York: Ballantine Books, 1993.

Bak, Richard. *Peach: Ty Cobb and His Time and Ours.* Ann Arbor, MI: Sports Media Group, 2005.

Bassford, Christopher. *Clausewitz in English: The Reception of Clausewitz in Britain and America.* New York: Oxford University Press, 1994.

Beatty, Jack. *Age of Betrayal: The Triumph of Money in America, 1865–1900.* New York: Alfred A. Knopf, 2007.

Beckles, Hilary McD. and Brian Stoddart. *Liberation Cricket: West Indies Cricket Culture.* New York: Manchester University Press, 1995.

Block, David. *Baseball Before We Knew It: A Search for the Roots of the Game.* Lincoln: University of Nebraska Press, 2005.

Brands, H. W. *Bound to Empire: The United States and the Philippines.* New York: Oxford University Press, 1992.

Breslin, Jimmy. *Branch Rickey.* New York: Penguin Group, 2011.

Britton, Crane. *The Anatomy of Revolution.* New York: Random House, 1938.

Bronson, Eric. *Baseball & Philosophy: Thinking Outside the Batter's Box.* Chicago: Open Court, 2004.

Callow, Alexander B., Jr. *The Tweed Ring.* New York: Oxford University Press, 1966.

Caraccioli, Tom and Jerry Caraccioli. *Boycott: Stolen Dreams of the 1980 Moscow Olympic Games.* New York: New Chapter Press, 2008.

Carlin, John. *Invictus: Nelson Mandela and the Game That Made a Nation.* New York: Penguin Books, 2008.

———. *Playing the Enemy: Nelson Mandela and the Game That Made a Nation.* New York: Penguin Books, 2009.

Carney, Gene. *Burying the Black Sox: How Baseball's Cover-up of the 1919 World Series Fix Almost Succeeded.* Washington: Potomac Books, Inc., 2006.

Casway, Jerrold. *Ed Delahanty in the Emerald Age of Baseball.* Notre Dame, IN: University of Notre Dame Press, 2004.

Chan, Susan K. *Coming on Strong: Gender and Sexuality in Twentieth-Century Women's Sport.* Cambridge, MA: Harvard University Press, 1994.

Clausewitz, Carl von. *On War.* Princeton, NJ: Princeton University Press, 1976.

Cook, William A. *The Louisville Grays Scandal of 1877.* Jefferson, NC: McFarland and Co., 2005.

Davidoff, Nicholas. *Baseball: A Literary Anthology.* New York: The Library of America, 2002.

Deford, Frank. *The Old Ball Game.* New York: Atlantic Monthly Press, 2005.

Delaney, Kevin I. and Rick Eckstein. *Public Dollars, Private Stadiums: The Battle Over Building Sports Stadiums.* New Brunswick, NJ: Rutgers University Press, 2006.

deMause, Neil and Joanna Cagan. *Field of Schemes: How the Great Stadium Swindle Turns Public Money into Private Profit.* Lincoln: University of Nebraska Press, 2008.

DeValeria, Dennis and Jeanne Burke DeValeria. *Honus Wagner: A Biography.* Pittsburgh: University of Pittsburgh Press, 1995.

Devine, Christopher. *Harry Wright: The Father of Professional Base Ball.* Jefferson, NC: McFarland and Co., 2003.

Dickson, Paul. *The Dickson Baseball Dictionary*. New York: Facts on File, 1989.

Dougan, Andy. *Dynamo: Triumph and Tragedy in Nazi-Occupied Kiev*. Guilford, NC: The Lyons Press, 2001.

Dwec, Carol. *Mindset: The New Psychology of Success*. New York: Ballantine Books, 2006.

Dyja, Thomas A. *Play for a Kingdom*. New York: Harcourt Brace, 1997.

Early, Gerald L. *A Level Playing Field: African American Athletes and the Republic of Sports*. Cambridge, MA: Harvard University Press, 2011.

Elias, Robert. *The Empire Strikes Out: How Baseball Sold U.S. Foreign Policy and Promoted the American Way Abroad*. New York: The New Press, 2010.

Erenberg, Lewis. *The Greatest Fight of Our Generation: Louis vs. Schmeling*. New York: Oxford University Press, 2006.

Foer, Franklin. *How Soccer Explains the World: An Unlikely Theory of Globalization*. New York: Harper Perennial, 2006.

Frankel, Glenn. *Rivonia's Children: Three Families and the Cost of Conscience in White South Africa*. New York: Farrar, Straus and Giroux, 1999.

Gay, Timothy M. *Tris Speaker: The Rough-and-Tumble Life of a Baseball Legend*. Lincoln: University of Nebraska Press, 2005.

Gems, Gerald R. *The Athletic Crusade: Sports and American Cultural Imperialism*. Lincoln: University of Nebraska Press, 2006.

Ginsborg, Paul. *Silvio Berlusconi: Television, Power and Patrimony*. New York: Verso, 2004.

Ginsburg, Daniel E. *The Fix Is In: A History of Baseball Gambling and Game Fixing Scandals*. Jefferson, NC: McFarland and Co., 1995.

Giulianotti, Richard and Roland Robertson. *Globalization and Sport*. Malden, MA: Blackwell Publishing, 2007.

Gmelch, George. *Baseball without Borders: The International Pastime*. Lincoln: University of Nebraska Press, 2006.

Goldstein, Warren. *Playing for Keeps: A History of Early Baseball*. Ithaca, NY: Cornell University Press, 1989.

Gorn, Elliott J. and Warren Goldstein. *A Brief History of American Sports*. New York: Hill and Wang, 1993.

Halberstam, David. *The Fifties*. New York: Random House, 1993.

Hardy, James D., Jr. *The New York Giants Base Ball Club: The Growth of a Team and a Sport, 1870–1900*. Jefferson, NC: McFarland and Co., 1996.

Harris, Robert. *Imperium*. New York: Pocket Books, 2006.

Helyar, John. *Lords of the Realm: The Real History of Baseball.* New York: Random House, 1994.

Herring, George C. *From Colony to Superpower: U.S. Foreign Relations Since 1776.* New York: Oxford University Press, 2006.

Hill, Christopher R. *Olympic Politics.* New York: Manchester University Press, 1992.

Hittner, Arthur D. *Honus Wagner: The Life of the "Flying Dutchman."* Jefferson, NC: McFarland and Co., 1996.

Hobbes, Thomas. *Leviathan Parts I and II.* Indianapolis, IN: The Library of Liberal Arts, 1958.

Holtzman, Jerome. *The Commissioners: Baseball's Midlife Crises.* New York: Total Sports, 1998.

Honig, Donald. *Baseball: When the Grass Was Real.* Lincoln: University of Nebraska Press, 1975.

Huey, Linda. *A Running Start: An Athlete, a Woman.* New York: Quadrangle Books, 1976.

Hunt, Thomas M. *Drug Games: The International Olympic Committee and the Politics of Doping, 1960–2008.* Austin: University of Texas Press, 2011.

James, C. L. R. *Beyond Boundary.* Durham, NC: Duke University Press, 1993.

Jay, Kathryn. *More than Just a Game: Sports in American Life Since 1945.* New York: Columbia University Press, 2004.

Josephson, Matthew. *The Robber Barons.* New York: Harcourt Brace Jovanovich, Inc., 1962.

Kapuscinski, Ryszard. *The Soccer War.* New York: Vintage Books, 1992.

Karnow, Stanley. *In Our Image: America's Empire in the Philippines.* New York: Ballantine Books, 1989.

Kimball, George and John Schulian. *At the Fights: American Writers on Boxing.* New York: The Library of America, 2011.

Kirsch, George B. *Baseball in Blue and Gray.* Princeton, NJ: Princeton University Press, 2003.

Klein, Alan M. *Growing the Game: The Globalization of Major League Baseball.* New Haven, CT: Yale University Press, 2006.

Klein, Maury. *The Life and Legend of Jay Gould.* Baltimore: The Johns Hopkins University Press, 1986.

Knight, Julian. *Cricket for Dummies.* Chichester: John Wiley and Sons, Ltd., 2006.

Kohout, Martin Donell. *Hal Chase: The Defiant Life and Turbulent Times of Baseball's Biggest Crook.* Jefferson, NC: McFarland and Co., 2001.

Koppett, Leonard. *Koppett's History of Major League Baseball*. Philadelphia: Temple University Press, 1998.

Korr, Chuck and Marvin Close. *More than Just a Game: Soccer v. Apartheid: The Most Important Soccer Story Ever Told*. New York: St. Martin's Press, 2008.

Kuper, Simon. *Soccer Against the Enemy*. New York: Nation Books, 2006.

Large, David Clay. *Nazi Games: The Olympics of 1936*. New York: W. W. Norton and Co., 2007.

Levine, Peter. *A.G. Spalding and the Rise of Baseball*. New York: Oxford University Press, 1985.

Lieb, Fred. *Baseball as I Have Known It*. Lincoln: University of Nebraska Press, 1977.

Lipsyte, Robert. *SportsWorld: An American Dreamland*. New York: Quadrangle Books, 1975.

Locke, John. *Second Treatise of Government*. Lexington, KY: Pacific Publishing Studio, 2010.

Machiavelli, Niccolo. *The Prince*. Chicago: University of Chicago Press, 1985.

Maeder, Jay. *Big Town, Big Time: A New York Epic, 1898–1998*. New York: Daily News Books, 1999.

Mandell, Richard D. *The Nazi Olympics*. Chicago: University of Illinois Press, 1971.

Margolick, David. *Beyond Glory: Joe Louis vs. Max Schmeling, and a World on the Brink*. New York: Vintage Books, 2005.

Markovits, Andrei S. and Lars Rensmann. *Gaming the World: How Sports Are Reshaping Global Politics and Culture*. Princeton, NJ: Princeton University Press, 2010.

Masur, Luis P. *Autumn Glory: Baseball's First World Series*. New York: Hill and Wang, 2003.

McCulloch, Ron. *From Cartwright to Shoeless Joe: The Warwick Compendium of Early Baseball*. Toronto: Warwick Publishing Inc., 1998.

Melville, Tom. *Early Baseball and the Rise of the National League*, Jefferson, NC: McFarland and Co., 2001.

Menand, Louis. *The Metaphysical Club: A Story of Ideas in America*. New York: Farrar, Straus and Giroux, 2001.

Morris, Peter. *A Game of Inches: The Stories Behind the Innovations That Shaped Baseball*. Chicago: Ivan R. Dee, 2006.

———. *But Didn't We Have Fun? An Informal History of Baseball's Pioneer Era, 1843–1870*. Chicago: Ivan R. Dee, 2008.

Murdock, Eugene C. *Ban Johnson: Czar of Baseball*. Westport, CT: Greenwood Press, 1982.

Myers, Gustavus. *The History of Tammany Hall*. Ithaca, NY: Cornell University Library, 2009.

Myler, Patrick. *Ring of Hate: Joe Louis v. Max Schmeling: The Fight of the Century*. New York: Arcade Publishing, 2005.

Nandy, Ashis. *The Tao of Cricket: On Games of Destiny and Destiny of Games*. New Delhi: Oxford University Press, 2000.

Nemex, David. *The Beer & Whiskey League*. Guilford, NC: The Lyons Press, 2004.

Pietrusza, David. *Judge and Jury: The Life and Times of Judge Kenesaw Mountain Landis*. South Bend, IN: Diamond Communications, Inc., 1998.

Postman, Andrew and Larry Stone. *The Ultimate Book of Sports Lists*. New York: Black Dog and Leventhal, 2003.

Rader, Benjamin. *Baseball: A History of America's Game*. Chicago: University of Illinois Press, 1992.

Reilly, Edward J. *Baseball: An Encyclopedia of Popular Culture*. Lincoln: University of Nebraska Press, 2000.

Reisler, Jim. *Ruth: Launching the Legend*. New York: McGraw-Hill, 2004.

Reiss, Steve A. *City Games: The Evolution of American Urban Society and the Rise of Sports*. Chicago: University of Illinois Press, 1989.

———. *Major Problems in American Sport History*. New York: Houghton Mifflin Co., 1997.

———. *Sports in Industrial America, 1850–1920*. Wheeling, IL: Harlan Davidson, Inc., 1995.

———. *Touching Base: Professional Baseball and American Culture in the Progressive Era*. Chicago: University of Illinois Press, 1999.

Remnick, David. *King of the World*. New York: Random House, 1998.

Rhoden, William C. *Forty Million Dollar Slaves: The Rise, Fall and Redemption of the Black Athlete*. New York: Three Rivers Press, 2006.

Ritter, Lawrence S. *The Glory of Their Times*. New York: William Morrow, 1966.

Roberts, Randy. *Joe Louis: Hard Times Man*. New Haven, CT: Yale University Press, 2010.

Roosevelt, Theodore. *Essays and Addresses*. Mineola, NY: Dover Publications, Inc., 1899.

Rosner, Scott R. and Kenneth L. Shropshire. *The Business of Sports*. Sudbury, MA: Jones and Bartlett, 2004.

Ross, Charles K. *Race and Sport: The Struggle for Equality on and off the Field*. Jackson: University of Mississippi Press, 2004.

Rossi, John P. *The National Game: Baseball and American Culture*. Chicago: Ivan R. Dee, 2000.

Ryan, Joan. *Little Girls in Pretty Boxes: The Making and Breaking of Elite Gymnasts and Figure Skaters*. New York: Warner Books, 1995.

Sarantakes, Nicholas Evans. *Dropping the Torch: Jimmy Carter, the Olympic Boycott, and the Cold War*. New York: Cambridge University Press, 2011.

Schaap. Jeremy. *Triumph: The Untold Story of Jesse Owens and Hitler's Olympics*. New York: Houghton Mifflin Co., 2007.

Scott, Christina. *Nelson Mandela: A Force for Freedom*. London: Andre Deutsch, 2010.

Seymour, Harold. *Baseball: The Early Years*. New York: Oxford University Press, 1960.

———. *Baseball: The Golden Age*. New York: Oxford University Press, 1971.

Shirer, William L. *The Rise and Fall of the Third Reich*. New York: Simon and Schuster, 1959.

Skolnik, Richard. *Baseball and the Pursuit of Innocence*. College Station: Texas A&M University Press, 1994.

Smith, Lissa. *Nike Is a Goddess: The History of Women in Sports*. New York: Atlantic Monthly Press, 1998.

Solomon, Burt. *Where They Ain't: The Fabled Life and Untimely Death of the Original Baltimore Orioles, the Team That Gave Birth to Modern Baseball*. New York: The Free Press, 1999.

Spalding, Albert G. *America's National Game*. Lincoln: University of Nebraska Press, 1992.

Speer, Albert. *Inside the Third Reich*. New York: The Macmillan Co., 1970.

Spink, Alfred H. *The National Game*. Carbondale: Southern Illinois University Press, 2000.

Spivey, Nigel. *The Ancient Olympics: A History*. New York: Oxford University Press, 2004.

Stevens, David. *Baseball's Radical for All Seasons: A Biography of John Montgomery Ward*. Lanham, MD: Scarecrow Press, Inc., 1998.

Stille, Alexander. *The Sack of Rome: How a Beautiful Country with a Fabled History and a Storied Culture Was Taken Over by a Man Named Silvio Berlusconi*. New York: Penguin Press, 2006.

Stradling, Jan. *More Than a Game: When Sports and History Collide.* London: Murdock Books Ltd., 2009.

Stump, Al. *Cobb.* Chapel Hill, NC: Algonquin Books of Chapel Hill, 1996.

Suggs, Welch. *A Place on the Team: The Triumph and Tragedy of Title IX.* Princeton, NJ: Princeton University Press, 2006.

Thompson, Leonard. *A History of South Africa.* New Haven, CT: Yale University Press, 2000.

Thorn, John. *Baseball in the Garden of Eden: The Secret History of the Early Game.* New York: Simon and Schuster, 2011.

Tomlinson, Alan and Christopher Young. *National Idenity and Global Sports Events: Culture, Politics, and Spectacle in the Olympics.* Albany: State University of New York Press, 2006.

Trifonas, Peter Pericles. *Umberto Eco and Football.* Cambridge: Totem Books, 2001.

Trumpbour, Robert C. *The New Cathedrals: Politics and Media in the History of Stadium Construction.* Syracuse, NY: Syracuse University Press, 2007.

Tygiel, Jules. *Past Time: Baseball as History.* New York: Oxford University Press, 2000.

Vincent, Ted. *Mudville's Revenge: The Rise and Fall of American Sport.* New York: Seaview Books, 1981.

Vogt, David Quentin. *American Baseball: From the Gentlemen's Sport to the Commissioner System.* University Park: The Pennsylvania State University Press, 1983.

Walters, Guy. *Berlin Games: How the Nazis Stole the Olympic Dream.* New York: Harper Perennial, 2006.

Walzer, Michael. *Just and Unjust Wars.* New York: Basic Books, 1977.

Ward, Andrew. *Football's Strangest Matches.* London: Portico, 1999.

Ward, Geoffrey C. and Ken Burns. *Baseball: An Illustrated History.* New York: Alfred A. Knopf, 1994.

Watterson, John Sayle. *The Games Presidents Play: Sports and the Presidency.* Baltimore: The Johns Hopkins University Press, 2006.

Weintraub, Stanley. *Silent Night: The Story of the World War I Christmas Truce.* New York: Penguin Books, 2002.

West, David. *The Mammoth Book of Muhammad Ali.* London: Constable and Robinson, 2012.

Westbrook, Deanne. *Ground Rules: Baseball & Myth.* Chicago: University of Illinois Press, 1996.

White, G. Edward. *Creating the National Pastime: Baseball Transforms Itself.* Princeton, NJ: Princeton University Press, 1996.

Wikipedia, *The New York Mutuals.* Memphis: Books LLC, 2010.

Wiggins, David K. and Patrick B. Miller. *The Unlevel Playing Field: A Documentary History of the African American Experience in Sport.* Chicago: University of Illinois Press, 2005.

Williams, Jack. *Cricket and Race.* New York: Berg, 2001.

Wolff, Leon. *Little Brown Brother: How the United States Purchased and Pacified the Philippine Islands at the Century's Turn.* New York: Bookspan, 1960.

Xu, Guoqi. *Olympic Dreams: China and Sports, 1895–2008.* Cambridge, MA: Harvard University Press, 2008.

Zimbalist, Andrew. *May the Best Team Win: Baseball Economics and Public Policy.* Washington: Brookings Institution Press, 2003.

Zirin, Dave. *A People's History of Sports in the United States.* New York: The New Press, 2008.

———. *What's My Name, Fool? Sports and Resistance in the United States.* Chicago: Haymarket Books, 2005.

Zoss, Joel and John Bowman. *Diamond in the Rough: The Untold History of Baseball.* Chicago: Contemporary Books, 1996.

[INDEX]

Balkan Wars (1990s), and soccer, 114–15

Ball, Rudi, 64

Baltimore Orioles, 198

Baltimore Ravens, 205, 208–9

Baltimore-to-Indianapolis Colts move, 199, 203

baseball: commercialization of, 28, 29–31, 33, 41–43; expansion of teams (1960s), 210; fame of Dominican Republic's players, 6; Flood's appeal to rights for players, 19; initial racial integration of, 124; and nationalism, 4; origins of, 24–31; and presidents, 2, 3, 40–41, 43; professionalization of, 29–31, 41–43; public subsidies for stadiums, 198–99, 209–10, 211, 212, 215–22; racial segregation in, 125; role of politics in, 18–19, 21–24, 31–41. *See also individual ball clubs*

basketball, 2, 4, 11, 125–26, 211

Bavarian Winter Olympics (1936), 46, 63–64

Beecher, Henry Ward, 26

Belafonte, Harry, 140

Berbick, Trevor, 140

Beria, Laverentiy, 12

Berlin Olympics (1936): and anti-Semitism, 62–63; boycott failure, 56–62; conduct of, 66–69; Nazi aggressions prior to, 64–65; Nazi preparation for, 47–49; overview, 44; propaganda value of, 44–47, 70–71; torch relay, 65–66; and U.S. boycott of Moscow Olympics, 156, 162, 165

Berlusconi, Silvio, 10–11

Biko, Steve, 183

Birchall, Frederick, 71

Bisher, Furman, 228

Black Muslims. *See* Nation of Islam

Black Panther movement, 119–20

blacks, American, in Berlin Olympics, 68, 69. *See also* Ali, Muhammad; Owens, Jesse; race and racism

Bolanos, Amelia, 111

Bonavena, Oscar, 137

Bond, Julian, 135

Bopanna, Rohan, 105

Borrow, George, 77

Botha, P. W., 184

boxing: commercialization of, 77–78, 79; Jack Johnson's impact, 81–83; and politics, 11–12, 73–76, 99; and race, 73–79, 81–83, 125; T. Roosevelt's participation in, 3. *See also* Ali, Muhammad; Louis, Joe; Schmeling, Max

boycotts and bans for sporting events: Berlin Olympics boycott failure, 56–62; historical overview, 143–48; Ireland (1904), 54; Los Angeles Olympics, 171–73; Moscow Olympics, 142, 150–70; politics of, 58–59; South Africa as pariah during apartheid, 155, 184–85; Soviet Union's early disapproval of Olympics, 146

Braddock, James J., 90

Bradley, Bill, 11

Brazil, and World Cup championships, 108

Brezhnev, Leonid, 152, 160

Britain: boxing in, 77; and colonial uses of sports, 16; English Premier League, 105, 116; FIFA World Cup influence on elections, 4; Heysel soccer disaster, 106; Moscow Olympic boycott debate, 159; and soccer's origins, 105–6; and South Africa, 177

Britton, Crane, 180–81

Brookes, William, 52

Brooklyn Eckfords, 30, 38

Brooklyn Excelsiors, 42

Brooklyn-to-Los Angeles Dodgers move, 199, 211

Broun, Heywood, 73

Brundage, Avery, 15, 57–59, 60–61, 68, 147, 148

Brzezinski, Zbigniew, 153, 161

Burke, James, 77

Burns, Tommy, 125

Bush, George H. W., 2

Bush, George W., 2, 11

Buthelezi, Chief, 189

Byrne, Simon, 77

Caesar, Julius, 10

Cagan, Joanna, 203, 223

Cahners, Norman, 60

Cammeyer, William H., 30

Campbell, Hugh, 32

Cannon, Jimmy, 99

Carlos, John, 4, 125

Carnera, Primo, 84

Carter, Jimmy, 151, 153–54, 155–59, 160–62, 164, 166, 167–68

Cartwright, Alexander, 24, 25, 26, 27

Castro, Fidel, 5

Catania, David, 217

Ceausescu, Nicolae, 107

Chadwick, Henry, 26

Champburger Corporation, 136–37

chess, U.S. vs. Soviet Union, 143

Chicago, baseball development in, 42

China, and origins of soccer, 106

Churchill, Winston, 225

Cincinnati, Ohio, 41, 42, 43, 207–8

Cincinnati Red Stockings, 42, 43

citizens group pressure against public financing of sports stadiums, 212–13, 219

civic groups as surrogate boosters for owners, 212, 213–14

civic pride and social-psychological value of sports, 42, 205–8

civil rights movement in U.S., 119–20, 128, 131, 227

Civil War, 21

Clausewitz, Carl Philipp Gottlieb von, 102–3

Clay, Cassius Marcellus. See Ali, Muhammad

Cleveland Browns (expansion team), 214

Cleveland Browns (original), 208–9

Clinton, Bill, 2, 3

Cold War politics, athletics as substitute for war, 144. See also Moscow Olympics (1980)

Collins, Bud, 138, 139

colonialism, sports as tool of, 16–17

commercialization of sports: baseball, 28, 29–31, 33, 41–43; boxing, 77–78,

New York City, and origins of baseball, 20, 21, 24–25, 27, 31–39

New York Eckfords, 32

New York Nine baseball team, 25–26

New York-to-San-Francisco Giants move, 211

New York Yankees and Mets stadiums (1990s), 215–16

New Zealand, 184, 192

Nigerian civil war, 104–5

Nixon, Richard M., xiv, 3, 150, 151

Nuremburg Laws (1935), 62–63

Oakland-to-Los Angeles Raiders move, 201, 214

Obama, Barack, 2

Oklahoma City Thunder, 211

Olsen, Jack, 134–35

Olympic Games: Ali at torch lighting (1996), 122–23, 141; Ali's performance in (1960), 121, 127; amateur vs. professional status of athletes, 43, 51, 57–58, 145–46, 166; ancient Greek, 50–52, 104, 129–30; banning of South Africa from, 184; Black Power protest (1968), 4, 125; cheating in, 9; commercialization of, 57–58, 172; creation of modern and vision of ancient, 50–55; and nationalism, 45–46, 54, 55, 144, 148; ostensible political neutrality of, 61; politics in, 46–47, 52–54; resistance to commercialization of sports, 57–58; Soviet bloc use of performance-enhancing drugs, 15–16; Soviet

Union's early disapproval of, 146; wartime suspensions, 104; and women's role in sports, 14–15. *See also specific Games by city name*

Olympic rings, origin of, 66

Olympism, 52–53, 57, 66, 161, 168–69

Organization of American States (OAS), 112, 113

Orwell, George, 104

Owens, Jesse, 45, 46, 66–68, 165

owners of sports franchises, and public subsidies for facilities, 202, 203–4, 208–9, 210–12, 213–14

Pacquiao, Manny, 12

Parkinson's disease, Ali's, 122, 123

Patterson, Floyd, 121, 128, 130

Pausanias, 51, 197

peace, world, Coubertin's vision of Olympics as agent of, 50, 52

Peacock, Eulace, 67–68

Pele, 5, 11

Perez, Dave, 195, 197

performance-enhancing drugs, Soviet bloc usage of, 15–16

Peru–Argentina soccer match riot (1964), 107, 114

Pheidippides, 53–54

Phoenix Cardinals, 214

Pienaar, Francois, 191

ping-pong diplomacy, 17–18

Pittsburgh, alternate financing for stadiums, 212

Plato, 225

play, origins of, 7–9

organization of international, 105–7;
Pele, 11; and political corruption,
12–14; Ukrainian mythical match
against Nazis, 5–6; violence among
spectators, 13, 106–7, 111, 113–16;
World Cup, 4, 107–9, 113, 184,
191–93

social clubs, baseball teams as outgrowth
of, 27–28

social good, sports' shifting reputation
as, 7–8, 19, 26, 42, 205–8

Sorensen, Ted, 163

South Africa: apartheid's structure and
effects, 177–80; boycotts and bans
in sports, 155, 184–85; Mandela, 174,
175–77, 178–80, 182–83, 184, 185–93;
and origins of revolutions, 180–81;
political transformations, 181–84;
pressure and negotiation for ending
apartheid, 185–86

Soviet Union: Afghanistan war, 152–56;
boycott of Los Angeles Olympics, 171;
chess, vs. U.S., 143; détente period
in U.S./Soviet relations, 150, 152, 167,
170; dissolution of, 144; doping of
athletes, 15–16; early denouncement
of Olympics, 146; Hungarian defeat
of in water polo, 6; ice hockey loss to
U.S., 6, 74–75, 158; ideological battles
through sports, 149, 150–52. *See also*
Moscow Olympics (1980)

Spalding, Albert, 21

Spanish Civil War, 65

Spinks, Leon, 139

sports and politics. *See* politics and
sports

Springboks rugby team, South Africa,
176–77, 184, 186, 188, 191

stadiums, sports. *See* public subsidies for
sports stadiums

Stalin, Joseph, 12

Starostin, Nikolai, 12

Stern, David, 211

St. Louis Browns, 198

St. Louis Rams, 214

St. Louis-to-Phoenix Cardinals move,
214

Stockholm Olympics (1912), 145, 146

Stofile, Makhenkesi Arnold, 184, 188–89

Stoller, Sam, 68

Stoneham, Horace, 211

Stupar, Miroslav, 108

Sullivan, John L., 77, 78, 82, 125

symbols and politics, overview, 123–24

table tennis and U.S.–China relations,
17–18

Taft, William Howard, 2

Tammany Hall, 20, 33–39, 35

Tampa Bay, Florida, as leverage for
public financing pressure, 209

Tampa Bay Rays, 209

taxation schemes for funding sports
facilities, 204, 208, 219

Tegucigalpa, Honduras, 111

tennis, 14, 105, 184–85

Terrell, Ernie, 121

Thatcher, Margaret, 159

Thorpe, Jim, 54–55, 145

Title IX and women's sports, 224, 227–28

torch relay for Olympics (1936), 65–66

Trikoupis, Charilaos, 53

truces set to allow sporting events
during wars, 104–5
Truth and Reconciliation Commission,
South Africa, 189–90
Tschammer und Osten, Hans von, 47
Tshwete, Steve, 187
Turner, Mary, 134
Tutu, Desmond, 189–90
Tweed, William Magear, 20, 21, 31, 33–39
Tweed Ring, 34–39, 38

Ueberroth, Peter, 172
unions, players', 222
United Kingdom. *See* Britain
United Nations, sanctions against South
Africa, 179, 183
United States: American vs. Soviet
ideologies, 149, 150–52; Berlin
Olympics boycott proposal,
58–59; chess, vs. Soviet Union,
143; colonialist use of sports by,
17; détente period in U.S./Soviet
relations, 150, 152, 167, 170; and
Escobar's own goal incident, 108;
general cooperative attitude on
Olympics, 155; ice hockey win over
Soviet Union, 6, 74–75, 158; influence
in Honduras, 110; Lake Placid Winter
Games, 150, 155, 158; Los Angeles
Olympics, 171–73; popularity of
soccer as arena not dominated by,
108; powers of central government,
195–96; pride in ice hockey victory
over Soviet Union, 6, 74–75, 158; rise
of boxing in, 77–78; Schmeling's
fondness for, 80; social attitudes
towards sports in history, 7–8; war
and sports alignment in, 103–4. *See
also* Moscow Olympics (1980); race
and racism
United States Olympic Committee
(USOC), 57, 157, 159, 160–61, 164–66
universal suffrage, 22–23
urbanization and rise of baseball, 21–22,
23–24
Uruguay–Brazil World Cup (1950), 108

Vance, Cyrus, 163
Veeck, Bill, 195, 199
Vietnam War, Ali's protest role in, 119,
121–22, 133–36, 138
violence, 13, 32, 33, 106–7, 111, 113–16
voluntary associations and American
politics, 23–25
voting rights, universalization process,
22–23
"V" symbol for victory or peace, 123

Wangenheim, Konrad Freiherr, 69
warfare and sports, historical alignment
of, 102–4
wartime interruptions to sporting
events, 104
Washington, George, 8
Washington Nationals, 42, 217–21
Webb, Violet, 71
Weimar Republic, 47, 55–56
West vs. East Germany in Olympic
politics, 147
Wheaton, William, 24
White, Byron "Whizzer," 11
Wildey, John, Jr., 31, 32, 39